Frontispiece **Portrait of Kate Chopin. Carte de visite photograph by J. J. Scholten, 1869. Missouri Historical Society, St Louis.**

Kate Chopin's
The Awakening

Kate Chopin's *The Awakening* (1899) was damned upon publication for engaging with the taboo issues of female sexuality and infidelity. It is now hailed as a key early feminist text and an important work of American literature.

Taking the form of a sourcebook, this guide to Chopin's widely debated novel offers:

- extensive introductory comment on the contexts and many interpretations of the text, from publication to the present
- annotated extracts from key contextual documents, reviews, critical works and the text itself
- cross-references between documents and sections of the guide, in order to suggest links between contexts and criticism
- suggestions for further reading.

Part of the *Routledge Guides to Literature* series, this volume is essential reading for all those beginning detailed study of *The Awakening* and seeking not only a guide to the novel, but a way through the wealth of contextual and critical material that surrounds Chopin's text.

Janet Beer is Professor of English, and Dean and Pro-Vice-Chancellor, at Manchester Metropolitan University. **Elizabeth Nolan** is Associate Lecturer in the Department of English at Manchester Metropolitan University.

Routledge Guides to Literature offer clear introductions to the most widely studied authors and literary texts. Each book engages with texts, contexts and criticism, highlighting the range of critical views and contextual factors that need to be taken into consideration in advanced studies of literature.

Routledge Guides to Literature*

Routledge Guides to Literature offer clear introductions to the most widely studied authors and literary texts.

Each book engages with texts, contexts and criticism, highlighting the range of critical views and contextual factors that need to be taken into consideration in advanced studies of literary works. The series encourages informed but independent readings of texts by ranging as widely as possible across the contextual and critical issues relevant to the works examined and highlighting areas of debate as well as those of critical consensus. Alongside general guides to texts and authors, the series includes 'sourcebooks', which allow access to reprinted contextual and critical materials as well as annotated extracts of primary text.

Available in this series

Kate Chopin's
The Awakening
A Sourcebook

*Edited by Janet Beer
and Elizabeth Nolan*

Routledge
Taylor & Francis Group

LONDON AND NEW YORK

First published 2004
by Routledge
11 New Fetter Lane, London EC4P 4EE

Simultaneously published in the USA and Canada
by Routledge
29 West 35th Street, New York, NY 10001

Routledge is an imprint of the Taylor & Francis Group

Editorial matter and selection © 2004 Janet Beer and Elizabeth Nolan

Typeset in Sabon and Gill Sans by RefineCatch Ltd, Bungay, Suffolk
Printed and bound in Great Britain by
TJ International Ltd, Padstow, Cornwall

British Library Cataloguing in Publication Data
A catalogue record for this book is available from the British Library

Library of Congress Cataloging in Publication Data
A catalog record for this book has been requested

ISBN 0–415–23820–X (hbk)
ISBN 0–415–23821–8 (pbk)

Contents

2: Interpretations

Critical History   53

Nineteenth-Century Responses   56

Contemporary Reviews   56

Modern Criticism   61

3: Key Passages

4: Further Reading

Illustrations

Annotation and Footnotes

Annotation is a key feature of this series. Both the original notes from reprinted texts and new annotations by the editor appear at the bottom of the relevant page. The reprinted notes are preface by the author's name in square brackets, e.g. [Robinson's note].

Acknowledgements

We would like to acknowledge the help of Dr Mary Reilly, Anthea Jarvis of the Gallery of English Costume, and Teresa Egan in the preparation of this volume. We would also like to acknowledge the supportive and silent contribution of Eamonn, Lucy and Andrew Nolan.

The following publishers, institutions and individuals have kindly given permission to reprint materials:

DUKE UNIVERSITY PRESS for 'The Teeth of Desire: *The Awakening* and *The Descent of Man*' by Bert Bender in *American Literature* Vol. 63 (1991), and 'Alien Hands: Kate Chopin and the Colonization of Race' by Michelle A. Birnbaum in *American Literature* Vol. 66 (1994). All rights reserved. Used by permission of the publisher.

DUKE UNIVERSITY PRESS for 'Maternal Discourse and the Romance of Self-Possession in Kate Chopin's *The Awakening*' by Ivy Schweitzer in Boundary 2, Volume 17, No. 12/31/1899. Copyright 1990, Duke University Press. All rights reserved. Used by permission of the publisher.

MISSOURI HISTORICAL SOCIETY for extracts from Kate Chopin's Commonplace Book in *Kate Chopin Papers*, and the portrait of Kate Chopin.

MODERN LANGUAGE ASSOCIATION OF AMERICA for '*The Awakening* in the Context of the Experience, Culture and Values of Southern Women' by Elizabeth Fox-Genovese from *Approaches to Teaching Chopin's The Awakening*. Reprinted by permission of the Modern Language Association of America.

STUDIES IN AMERICAN FICTION for 'Un-Utterable Longing: The Discourse of Feminine Sexuality in *The Awakening*' by Cynthia Griffin Wolff in *Studies in American Fiction* 24:1 (1996).

SYMBIOSIS: A JOURNAL OF ANGLO-AMERICAN LITERARY RELATIONS, 1.1 (April 1997) for 'Walking Through New Orleans: Kate Chopin and the Female Flâneur' by Helen Taylor. Reprinted by permission of the editors.

Every effort has been made to trace and contact copyright holders. The publishers would be pleased to hear from any copyright holders not acknowledged here so that this acknowledgements page may be amended at the earliest opportunity.

Introduction

First published in 1899, Kate Chopin's *The Awakening* provoked significant controversy because of its engagement with the taboo issues of female sexuality and infidelity. Chopin depicts Edna Pontellier as repeatedly flouting convention in the search for autonomy and self-fulfilment outside of her role as middle-class wife and mother. She creates a heroine who boldly claims, 'I don't want anything but my own way', and thus offers a direct challenge to the expectations of Victorian society in America. The censure and moral indignation prompted by the novel was expressed in a rash of outraged reviews; the text quickly went out of print and remained so for almost fifty years, during which time it was essentially unremarked, ignored by critics.

The effects of this early reception and publication history belie the level of popularity which the novel enjoys today; it now has a reputation as an important early feminist text. The recovery and re-evaluation of Chopin's writing is due, in large part, to the efforts of the Norwegian scholar, Per Seyersted, who published her collected works in 1969. During the 1970s, Chopin's questioning of the limited roles available to women in her writing struck a chord with the second wave feminist movement, generating much scholarship and critical debate. In recent times Kate Chopin's literary reputation has grown. Once considered a fair practitioner of 'local colour' fiction whose dalliance with risqué material ensured a passage into literary obscurity, she is now widely regarded as a major figure in American letters. Her work has broad appeal to a modern readership and *The Awakening* is regularly included on undergraduate courses.

This Sourcebook is designed as a guide for the undergraduate student of *The Awakening*; it will situate the text in its historical and social context, highlight major thematic strains in the novel, and aid negotiation of the wide-ranging and sometimes complex theoretical debates surrounding the work. The bringing together of documents from the period of the novel's composition, a selection of modern critical work and key passages annotated to illustrate their significance serves to enrich the student readership's understanding of the text. This volume offers the reader a tool with which to approach *The Awakening*, and through which to formulate responses to the various readings the work invites. It is intended to facilitate the development of independent critical thought and to enable an informed analysis of the novel and its major themes.

The first section of the Sourcebook, 'Contexts', provides biographical information on Kate Chopin herself, together with a selection of contemporary material which is included to give a sense of the historical and cultural backgrounds against which she lived and worked. The 'Contextual Overview' which follows this introduction discusses the influences of Chopin's Louisiana Creole heritage, a cultural legacy which is, of course, of central importance in the novel. This section also provides a wider picture of society in the America of the 1890s to serve as a framework in which *The Awakening* can be better understood. For example, the extracts from popular journals and magazines of the day which appear here give an indication of the expectations placed particularly on women in this era and provide a measure against which Edna Pontellier's unconventionality can be judged. The 'Chronology' provides details of the author's relatively short life – she died at the age of 54 – and a professional writing career which spanned just over ten years. For a life so recently lived there is relatively little that is known for certain about Chopin; as Emily Toth, her biographer notes, 'she remains [. . .] a woman of "mysterious fascination"'.

In 'Interpretations', the second section of this volume, the focus is placed on the critical reception of the novel including both early reviews and a sample of the diverse critical debate which the work has engendered in recent years. The former contains a review from Willa Cather, amongst others, and the latter has contributions from some of the leading scholars in the field of Chopin studies. Amongst these are extracts from Cynthia Griffin Wolff's, 'Un-utterable Longing: The Discourse of Feminine Sexuality in *The Awakening*' (1996), an examination of Chopin's engagement with female sexuality, and from Bert Bender's influential essay 'The Teeth of Desire: *The Awakening* and *The Descent of Man*' (1991) which discusses the influence of Darwinism on Chopin's work. In addition, the 'Critical History' provided undertakes a survey of significant essays and book-length studies in Chopin criticism, tracing all important developments. The extracts included here, together with the critical history, are supplemented by the material in the 'Further Reading' section at the end of the volume which provides the student reader with a comprehensive listing of all major criticism on Chopin's work in general and *The Awakening* in particular.

An important feature of this Sourcebook's content is to be found in the 'Key Passages' section. Here, selected chapters of the original text are reproduced and extensive commentary and notes provide the reader with the tools to explore issues raised in the novel and to make connections between these and the materials and debates presented elsewhere in this volume. However, whilst a significant number of the novel's chapters are reproduced here, the Sourcebook is not intended as a replacement for the complete text but rather as a complementary reference work to be read alongside the whole. Recommended editions of the novel can be found at the end of the volume.

1

Contexts

Contextual Overview

Kate Chopin's *The Awakening* appeared at a particularly multiform moment in American literary history but has, as its setting, a distinct culture and locale amongst the French-Creoles of Louisiana. The following section contains documents, contemporary with the novel, which will give a historical, cultural and social context, enabling the modern reader to appreciate fully the exceptional qualities of the artist and her work in its time. The selection of material will give a sense of the prevailing ideologies, social mores and expectations – particularly those relating to the role of women in late nineteenth-century America, as well as a picture of the society into which the text was received and which roundly condemned it as immoral. The contemporary material substantiates the context in which the multiple transgressions of the heroine were received by the novel's readership, some of the reasons for its chequered publication history and the extent to which this text can be said to be ahead of its time, the latter evidenced by its appeal to a modern audience.

The Awakening was published in 1899, on the eve of a new century, and into a period of social adjustment which would see women's roles change remarkably. As mass immigration, urbanisation and industrialisation radically altered the social map of America, women, angered by their exclusion from much opportunity in this vibrant, progressive nation, stepped up their efforts to win full and equal citizenship. In 1890 the two main suffrage organisations joined forces, gaining momentum in their final push for the vote. In the year before Chopin's text appeared, social reformer and activist, Charlotte Perkins Gilman, one of the many voices raised in protest, published her treatise, *Women and Economics*, in which she addressed the inequalities between the sexes which resulted from women's financial dependence on men. This was the era of the 'New Woman': she rejected traditional stereotypes of woman as delicate, passive and domestic; she demanded, and began to move towards obtaining, education, careers, dress reform and suffrage. As is true of any period of significant social change, however, there was, at this time, an accompanying measure of resistance, tension and anxiety.

Such a mood of uncertainty makes itself evident in a variety of sources, from the gentle lampooning of the 'New Woman' figure in satirical magazines of the day, to the alarmist righteous indignation expressed by conservative, moralist commentators like Mrs Amelia Barr, airing her views on 'proper' femininity in the *North American Review*. One of Mrs Barr's chief concerns is the appearance of the bold, free-thinking, self-opinionated woman in the fiction of this period; one might say, exactly the kind of character Kate Chopin has a penchant for creating. The modern novel is, to her, a serious danger to impressionable young, female minds, threatening irreparable damage to family values, womanly duty and morality as promoted by its 'safer' counterpart, the domestic novel. If standards of morality and the risqué content of modern literature are issues for the traditionalist Mrs Barr, then she is not alone. Many reformers drew the line at greater sexual freedom for women, a topic definitely not to be found on the agenda of most women's rights organisations. Even Charlotte Perkins Gilman's theories, radical as they were, have an overarching moral code in which fidelity within monogamous marriage is posited as the only acceptable framework for a sexual relationship. That Kate Chopin, then, in addition to creating a character who rejects all of the traditional expectations of womanhood also explores female sexual desire outside of marriage, and outside even of a loving relationship, accounts for the moral condemnation of her work.

It is clear that Chopin, as a woman and as a writer, and *The Awakening*, as a literary work, are far ahead of their time, that turn of the century America, despite its advancement and progression, was not ready to accept transgression as practised by Edna Pontellier. On her first reading of the text in 1970, Chopin's most recent biographer, Emily Toth, claims to have been, 'astonished that a woman in 1899 had asked the same questions that we, in the newly revived women's movement, were asking seventy years later'.[1] That Chopin was so forward thinking, independent and radical in thought is even more remarkable considering that she was a product of America's Southern states. Here progress was markedly slower than in other regions of the United States: the women's rights movements, as Evelyn Ordway's article (pp. 43–5) demonstrates, took longer to become established, and traditional perceptions and expectations of womanhood, as promulgated in prescriptive etiquette manuals, prevailed longer than they did in the North. But Kate Chopin herself conforms to none of the stereotypical notions of Southern womanhood, all of which she so ably invokes in her creation of Madame Ratignolle. Toth's biography claims that in a photograph at the age of five, Katherine O'Flaherty already has 'rebellion in her eye'. Such 'rebellion' endured. In her life, and in her work, Chopin, although uninterested in organised women's rights movements, continued, on an individual basis, to test the boundaries of acceptable behaviour for women, to question the limited options of marriage and motherhood, and to make the issue of women's independence her life-long concern in her fiction. On other matters she similarly resisted conformity to the mores and values of her contemporaries. In a post-Civil War South riven by racial tension, Kate Chopin's attitudes appear surprisingly open-minded.

---

1   Toth, Emily, *Kate Chopin: A Life of the Author of The Awakening* (London: Random Century, 1990), 9.

Although her husband, Oscar, was an active member of a white supremacist league, in her writing Chopin presents both positive and negative qualities in black and white characters. One might imagine that the seeds of such unconventionality must surely lie in the particularities of Chopin's life – her home, her family, the people, places and events which influenced and formed her thinking, her attitudes and values. It follows then, that a full appreciation of such a unique and remarkable literary work as *The Awakening*, necessitates a consideration of the life of its author.

Born on 8 February 1850, Katherine O'Flaherty spent her early years in an impressive family home on Eighth Street, St Louis. Her father, Thomas O'Flaherty, an Irish immigrant, having established himself as a successful businessman and trader, secured his social standing through successive marriages to the daughters of two of St Louis' old French families: Catherine Reilhe, with whom he had a son, George, but who later died in childbirth, and Kate's mother, Eliza Faris, whom he married in 1844. To all intents and purposes, the O'Flahertys appeared to be a traditional southern family. Supporters of the Confederacy during the Civil War, they owned several slaves. A religious man, Thomas O'Flaherty attended Catholic mass each morning and in 1855 enrolled the five-year-old Katie at the Academy of the Sacred Heart. It was during her time at the convent that her tastes in reading and her desire to write began to be formed, one of the nuns encouraging her to keep the commonplace book, extracts from which are provided here. For Chopin the commonplace book served as a diary, a confidante, and a space for noting observations and fledgling literary compositions. For us it provides an invaluable document in tracing her developing independence of thought. The academy though, was primarily an institution which promoted duty and submissiveness as true feminine qualities, the sisters there preparing their charges for a life of marriage and motherhood. That despite such tuition, Kate Chopin clearly developed and retained such a keenly questioning mind, and refused merely to follow tradition and expectation, is perhaps grounded in her dual heritage and particularly in a strong matriarchal influence. This influence was strengthened when her father died in a railway accident in the same year that she began to attend the academy; as a result she was raised in a female-dominated home with her mother, grandmother and great-grandmother, all of them independent, single women by virtue of widowhood.

Chopin's great-grandmother, Victorie Verdon Charleville, was, according to Toth, a forward-thinking woman who regaled the young Katie O'Flaherty with tales of the sexual exploits of scandalous women from old St Louis, and instilled in her the notion of a distinct women's culture, and a sense of their shared heritage of 'a long line of determined maternal ancestors'.[2] It was the independent and unconventional Victorie Charleville who immersed her great-granddaughter in a French culture and language which would later lead to a great appreciation of French literature, particularly the work of Guy de Maupassant, some of whose works Chopin would later translate, and who she credited as her literary

---

2   Ibid., 35.

inspiration and model. As Toth notes, although the mature Chopin read the works of American writers such as Ruth McEnery Stuart, Mary E. Wilkins and Sarah Orne Jewett, she also 'persisted in reading authors who were considered improper [. . . and] her model remained Guy de Maupassant'.[3] This identification with French literature – a connection often made by critics, including Willa Cather (see **Contemporary Reviews, pp.** 56–60), who consider *The Awakening* to be an American *Madame Bovary* – places Kate Chopin outside of the New England Protestant intellectual elite and tradition dominant at the time. It also aligns her work more closely with the kind of risqué 'foreign' literature, which, as the *Harper's Bazaar* article, 'French Novels for Public Libraries' reveals, was deemed possibly unsuitable for the shelves of public libraries.

The duality fostered by the diverse cultural influences in Kate Chopin's early life remained ever present, her later life characterised by the treading of a conventional path coupled with fierce independence of thought. It is true that she went on to fulfil the expectation of her convent training, becoming a society debutante at the age of eighteen. But thoughts recorded in her commonplace book from this time reveal her lack of enthusiasm for the round of social engagements, her questioning of the obligations they placed upon her, 'What a nuisance all this is – I wish it were over [. . .] parties, operas, concerts, skating and amusements ad infinitum have so taken up all my time'.[4] In 1870, by the age of twenty she made a sociably acceptable match with Oscar Chopin, son of a plantation owner and a successful cotton trader, a marriage which would last twelve years until Oscar's early death, and produce six children. Yet again, a 'traditional' lifestyle choice was accompanied by a measure of individuality and difference. The apparent happiness of the Chopins' marriage was possibly based on Oscar's ability to accommodate his wife's desire for much greater freedoms than would normally have been afforded a woman of her standing in this era, freedoms that her contemporaries would have undoubtedly regarded as eccentric. Nearly three decades before her fictional creation, Edna Pontellier, would do the same, Emily Toth notes that Kate Chopin herself explored the city streets of New Orleans, where she had made her marital home, unaccompanied; she also openly smoked cigarettes. As the *Daily Picayune* article reveals, even at the end of the century ladies were not supposed to smoke at all, let alone some thirty years earlier, and in public. Throughout her life there is evidence that Chopin was attracted by such flouting of convention. The extracts from her honeymoon diary, included here, demonstrate how she was interested by and drawn to the boldness displayed by a Miss Clafflin that she encountered on a train. This would have been either Victoria or Tennessee Clafflin, sisters who were both activists on the extreme fringes of the women's rights movement. Publishers of the newspaper, *Woodhull and Clafflin's Weekly* they were often surrounded by scandal, particularly in their advocacy of 'free love'. Victoria Clafflin, under her married name of Woodhull ran for president

---

3 Ibid., 272.
4 Kate O'Flaherty, Commonplace Book, entry for New Year's Eve 1868, reprinted in, Toth, Emily and Per Seyersted, eds, *Kate Chopin's Private Papers* (Bloomington and Indianapolis: Indiana University Press, 1998), 64.

in 1872. Chopin was also attracted to the difference and the daring she recognised in the customs and cultures of the European countries she visited – at one point tempted to take a turn at the gambling table but, at this stage, not having the courage to do so.

In 1879 the failure of Oscar's business resulted in the family's move to rural Cloutierville, Louisiana. Whilst her husband ran his new venture, a general store, Kate, again according to Toth, established herself as a figure of note, this time parading the streets of the small town in her fashionable city attire and taking long, lone, 'unladylike' rides on horseback. It was during this time that she began to gather material for a writing career which would not begin in earnest for some time. Several of the stories penned later were drawn from and informed by her life among this small town community of mainly Creoles and Acadians, or 'Cajuns', French-speaking migrants from Canada, including her first collection, *Bayou Folk*, published in 1894. In 1882, just three years after the move to Cloutierville, Oscar Chopin died of swamp fever. His widow, at only thirty-two years of age, was left to manage Oscar's business and his debts, and to raise her children alone. But widowhood, as with many other phases of life was, for Kate Chopin, anything but conventional. In her fictions, bereaved women are seen to experience a kind of euphoria as they are liberated from marriage to pursue new opportunities. In life Chopin herself apparently explored wholeheartedly the possibilities that her new found 'freedom' afforded, her experiences finding expression as perhaps the most controversial feature of her writing – female sexual abandon, desire and adultery. Although no documentary evidence exists, Emily Toth makes a strong case for the young widow having embarked upon a scandalous and passionate affair with Albert Sampite, a married planter whose property bordered her own in Cloutierville. Sampite, Toth suggests, provides a model for a number of men in Chopin's fiction, all of whom are named Alcée, and all of whom, 'kindle desire, and [. . .] devote themselves to sexual pleasure'.[5] The short story, 'The Storm', which she made no attempt to publish, contains the most explicit sexual encounter known to have been written by Kate Chopin, and involves a character named Alcée Laballiere. And, of course, there is *The Awakening*'s Alcée Arobin.

In 1884, following her affair with Albert Sampite, Kate Chopin sold the business, paid off the debts and returned to St Louis with her six children, where, as Emily Toth notes, she supported herself and her family with income earned from real estate. It was here, in more familiar surroundings and encouraged by her friends, that she began to write seriously. By the end of 1889 she had published her first literary work, a poem entitled, 'If it Might Be', and had seen her first story 'A Point at Issue!' printed in the *St Louis Post-Dispatch*. In the following years several of her stories appeared in some of the most prestigious journals of the day, including *Century*, *Vogue*, *Harper's*, and *Youth's Companion*. She was less successful with her novels: *At Fault*, a Louisiana tale dealing with alcoholism and divorce was published privately in 1890, at her own expense; another novel,

5   Toth, 169.

Young Dr Gosse, remained unpublished, and the manuscript was later destroyed. The publication of two collections of short stories, *Bayou Folk* in 1894, and *A Night in Acadie* in 1897, however, earned Kate Chopin a reputation as a practitioner of 'local colour' fiction, a literary form which focuses on the regional and the rural, giving a flavour of the language, the customs and culture of a particular area of America. Those identifying her as such, including her first biographer, Father Daniel Rankin, whose text, *Kate Chopin and her Creole Stories* was published in 1932, clearly do not take heed of the range of complex issues, particularly those affecting women, embedded in her texts. Indeed the controversial content of many of her stories, so evident today, often went unremarked because of the 'local colour' tag.

This was not to be the case for long, however. A consequence of Chopin's growth and development as an artist was an ever increasing lack of inhibition in her work, as she began to overtly engage with taboo issues, particularly female sexuality. The reasons for *The Awakening*'s great appeal to modern feminist scholars and critics are precisely the same reasons for its condemnation at the time of its publication. The strong, independent-minded and sensual Edna Pontellier, no respecter of the cult of femininity and the restrictive bounds of marriage and motherhood, is today a feminist icon, but was, in Victorian America, viewed as an aberration and a threat to moral values. Through the figure of Edna, Chopin managed to undermine the entire social fabric of middle-class America, with a consistent rejection of each and every one of the traditional expectations of womanhood. The setting for the novel is amongst the elite Creole society of New Orleans, both in the city and at their Grand Isle summer retreat. Kate Chopin herself had spent summers here when her children were young. 'The Summer Problem' article, included here, describes vacationing arrangements in which husbands remain at home during the week, joining families at the weekend – a model favoured by many Creole families of the day. In the text, the resort of Grand Isle serves as a space outside of the norm, essentially an 'other' place, exotic and languid, where, in the frequent absences of her husband, Edna's original 'awakening' takes place. The setting facilitates her awakening to dissatisfaction and a sense of limitation, which in turn leads to the extremes of transgressive behaviour which are contextualised here.

Contrary to advice given in etiquette manuals of the day, Edna is seen to walk the city streets alone, to neglect her social obligations and to receive male visitors in her husband's absence. In addition, traditional religion is critiqued as Edna finds the atmosphere in church stifling and oppressive and seems to find no comfort in her own or her husband's faith. Chopin was knowledgeable and widely read in the major intellectual movements of her time, and there is substantial evidence of the influence of Darwinism in her work. Although Léonce Pontellier is far from a tyrant, marriage is another institution under intense scrutiny in the novel. At a time when, as Jessie J. Cassidy's document (**pp. 41–2**) demonstrates, the legal status of women in Louisiana is subordinate, property and parental rights largely the jurisdiction of the husband, Edna asserts her autonomy, absolutely rejecting the notion of herself as a piece of property, 'I am no longer one of Mr Pontellier's possessions [. . .] I give myself where I choose'. Ultimately, marriage itself is rejected, the marital home abandoned and maternal responsibility abnegated in favour of personal fulfilment.

The fashion plates included in this section indicate the accepted dress codes of the day, and the range of attire deemed appropriate for various social functions and obligatory duties. Edna's rebellion against convention is often articulated through dress, the replacement of her 'usual Tuesday reception gown' with an 'ordinary house dress' signifying her permanent, and somewhat scandalous, withdrawal from the expected round of polite visiting. The article on, and images of, nineteenth-century swimming costumes demonstrate the extreme modesty with which this activity was approached, and place into stark relief Edna's naked entry into the sea. Note that many female bathers of this period insisted on the incorporation of a corset into their swimming attire.

The publication of *The Awakening* on 22 April 1899 was greeted by a number of outraged reviews, a commentator for *The St Louis Republic* declaring the text 'too strong drink for moral babes', which 'should be labelled "poison" '. Stung by the criticism, Chopin issued a response in the form of an 'apology', deeply laced with irony, which appeared in *Book News* in July of that year:

> Having a group of people at my disposal, I thought it might be entertaining (to myself) to throw them together and see what would happen. I never dreamed of Mrs Pontellier making such a mess of things and working out her own damnations as she did. If I had had the slightest intimation of such a thing I would have excluded her from the company. But when I found out what she was up to, the play was half over and it was then too late.

As Emily Toth establishes, despite its tumultuous reception, *The Awakening* was never, as has been claimed, banned or removed from library shelves. Neither did it silence Chopin's literary voice completely, she did continue to write and publish her stories. But the novel did prove to be her last major publication, a later collection of stories, *A Vocation and a Voice* being declined by her publisher Herbert S. Stone. The last of Kate Chopin's stories to be printed was 'Polly' which appeared in *Youth's Companion* in 1902. Two years later, and just six years on from the commotion caused by what is now widely regarded as a literary classic and her greatest work, Kate Chopin died from a cerebral haemorrhage. She was fifty-four years of age.

After Chopin's death, the novel was forgotten, remaining largely ignored until French academic Cyrille Arnavon recovered and reappraised it, publishing a French translation. Arnavon also encouraged a young graduate student, Per Seyersted, to consider Chopin's life and work as a research topic. Seyersted went on to devote much of his academic career to Kate Chopin, publishing both *A Critical Biography* and *The Complete Works* in 1969. His efforts coincided with the second-wave feminist movement who adopted the text, rediscovering its powerful theme of a woman's search for self and quest for autonomy. From the 1970s onwards, critical interest in the timeless questions posed by *The Awakening* has gathered pace. The many connections and identifications made between the modern reader and the rebellious, nineteenth-century Edna Pontellier ensure that, more than a century later, this text remains central to feminist literary studies.

Further Reading

Flexner, Eleanor, *Century of Struggle: The Woman's Rights Movement in the United States*, Cambridge, Mass.: Harvard University Press, 1996.

Goldsmith, Barbara, *Other Powers: The Age of Suffrage, Spiritualism, and the Scandalous Victoria Woodhull*, New York: A.A Knopf, 1998.

Marks, Patricia, *Bicycles, Bangs and Bloomers: The New Woman in the Popular Press*, Kentucky: The University Press of Kentucky, 1990.

Chronology

Bullet points are used to denote events in Chopin's life, and asterisks to denote historical and literary events.

1850
- Born Katherine O'Flaherty, 8 February, in St Louis, Missouri, to Thomas O'Flaherty, an Irish immigrant, and Eliza Faris, a French-Creole

1852
* Harriet Beecher Stowe, *Uncle Tom's Cabin*

1855
- Enrols in Academy of the Sacred Heart; death of father, Thomas O'Flaherty, in railway accident

1857
* Gustave Flaubert, *Madame Bovary*

1861
- Despite living in the Unionist state of Missouri the O'Flahertys are supporters of the Confederacy
* Abraham Lincoln elected President; outbreak of American Civil War

1863
- Death of great-grandmother, Victorie Verdon Charleville; death of half-brother George, a Confederate soldier
* Emancipation proclamation

1865
* End of Civil War; assassination of Lincoln

1868
- Graduates from Sacred Heart Academy; enters into St Louis society during debutante season of this year
- * Louisa May Alcott, *Little Women*

1869
- Writes short story, 'Emancipation: A Life Fable' (unpublished)

1870
- Marriage to Oscar Chopin, cotton trader and son of plantation owner; Chopins embark on three-month honeymoon tour of Europe, incorporating visits to Germany, Switzerland and France; returns to set up home in New Orleans
- * Franco-Prussian War

1871–8
- Five sons born: Jean Baptiste (1871), Oscar Charles (1873), George Francis (1874), Frederick (1876), Felix Andrew (1878)

1871
- * Charles Darwin, *The Descent of Man and Selection in Relation to Sex*
- * George Eliot, *Middlemarch*

1872
- * Herbert Spencer, *The Study of Sociology*

1873
- Death of brother, Thomas, in buggy accident

1879
- Following the failure of Oscar's cotton business, the family moves to Cloutierville, a rural area of Louisiana; daughter Lélia born
- * Ibsen, *A Doll's House*

1881
- * Henry James, *Portrait of a Lady*

1882
- Death of Oscar Chopin

1883–4
- Alleged affair with Albert Sampite

1884
- Kate Chopin returns to St Louis

1885
- Death of mother, Eliza O'Flaherty
* Women's rights activist, Susan B. Antony, visits New Orleans and addresses large audiences
* Mark Twain, *The Adventures of Huckleberry Finn*
* Guy de Maupassant, *Bel-Ami*

1889
- First published literary work, 'If It Might Be' (poem); publishes first short story, 'A Point at Issue!', in *St Louis Post-Dispatch*; begins work on first novel *At Fault*

1890
- Publication of *At Fault*, at Chopin's own expense.

1895
- Collection of Guy de Maupassant translations rejected by publisher, Houghton, Mifflin
* Elizabeth Cady Stanton, *The Woman's Bible*

1894
- Publication of *Bayou Folk*, a collection of short stories; *Vogue* publishes 'Dream of an Hour' ('Story of an Hour')

1897
- Publication of second collection of stories, *A Night in Acadie*; death of grandmother, Athénaise Charleville Faris

1898
* Charlotte Perkins Gilman, *Women and Economics*

1899
- *The Awakening* is published to largely hostile reviews
* Edith Wharton, *The Greater Inclination*

1900
- Publisher Herbert S. Stone declines to publish the collection of stories, *A Vocation and a Voice*

1902
- Last publication, 'Polly' (story) appears in *Youth's Companion*

1904
- Kate Chopin dies in St Louis on 22 August.

Contemporary Documents

Albert Rhodes, 'The Louisiana Creoles', *The Galaxy*, Vol. 16, August 1873, pp. 252–60

During the 1870s, Albert Rhodes wrote for a variety of periodicals, including *The Galaxy, Scribner's Monthly* and *Harper's New Monthly Magazine*. Subjects he addressed included social and political issues and commentary on foreign cultures, particularly those of Europe. In this article he provides a comprehensive contemporary interpretation of nineteenth-century Louisiana Creole culture, the world which Chopin chooses as the setting for *The Awakening*. His article paints a picture of the particular characteristics of the 'artistic', 'exotic' Creole and a life of social gatherings, musical soirées, and convivial dining which has many resonances with the lifestyles depicted in Chopin's novel. One Creole proverb cited here finds a direct echo in the text, when, in Chapter Twenty-Two, Léonce Pontellier tells Doctor Mandelet that he is 'of that old Creole race of Pontelliers that dry up and finally blow away'. What Rhodes also does here is to juxtapose, often favourably, the values and customs of the Creole against those of their American neighbour, for example, the Creole's warmth and vivacity against the American's hard, sombre, utilitarian nature. Rhodes comments that the two cultures, placed in such close proximity in the city of New Orleans, with its French and American quarters, 'do not understand each other'. One of the central tensions of Chopin's novel is, of course, dependent upon just such a lack of understanding – the series of events and consequences which result from the 'American' Edna, from a Kentuckian Presbyterian background being introduced into the languid, flirtatious, and very different world of the Louisiana Creole.

The Paris of Louisiana Creoles is New Orleans [. . .]

Canal Street is the dividing line between France and America. That portion of the city on the upper side is the domain of Columbia's sons; that below, of the children of the Gaul. In America there is thrift and cleanliness; detached frame houses surrounded with green gardens, orange trees with their golden fruit relieving on sombre foliage. White is the prevailing color of the dwellings, and they usually stand behind four great columns which give the tenement the appearance of something incidentally attached. The spacious portal promises much, which is not made good by what lies behind it. Doric grandeur without and mean proportions within are characteristic [. . .] In the interiors of these columned dwellings, the civilization has much the same character as that found in other cities of the Southwest. Morally, there is church-going and a healthy religious faith; mentally, a roughness and self-assertion usually found in partially educated Anglo-Saxons; materially, an absence of art in the kitchen and the drawing-room. [. . .]

In the lower part of the town Sunday is a day of recreation. During the forepart there is much going to and fro to mass. The old cathedral on Jackson square is filled to overflowing [. . .] Mass over, the women linger [. . .] to discuss the questions of finery and social cancan. Old negro women in yellow turbans, at the corners of the edifice outside, are seated behind little stands bearing candies, oranges, and bananas. By one o'clock the churches are emptied; then there is general visiting during the afternoon, at which there is lively chat of a local character. Toward evening there is convivial dining, to which family connections gather in groups at the house of the senior, generally a father or grandfather [. . .] They are enjoyable feasts, and the time spent on them probably furnishes the happiest hours of the week. At night, among the higher classes, musical and dancing soirées frequently take place. I was present at one of these, as a spectator. The front of the house was closed, but the back looked out on a broad veranda and spacious garden of Southern flowers and trees, and through the open doors and windows the perfume of the magnolia was wafted by a soft south wind, gentle as a maiden's whisper. Without, a group or two sat in the midst of the moon-tinted shrubbery; within, there was the badinage of the French *salon* doubled with American flirtation, and the *entrainant* music of Offenbach. To the Creole, in all this there was no guile.

But the centre of Creolian delights of a Sunday evening is to be found at the French theatre, usually filled to its capacity [. . .] This is the occasion for representing the kind of comedy usually seen at the Palais Royal of Paris, and the mirth is Homeric. The eating of bon-bons and ices and drinking of light beverages between the acts, is part of the entertainment, as in the minor theaters of the French capital. No fixed, taciturn face meets the eyes, and no English word reaches the ear. The enclosure is as much in France as if the scene transpired at Bordeaux.

It is a relief to turn from the hard, dry, pushing, utilitarian American, to this milder and more artistic type. It is like getting out of the blare of trumpets into the sound of the gentle flute – out of the whizz and whirr of steam and wheels into the bosom of pastoral nature.

Creoles are described as the descendants of European ancestors, Spanish and French. In Louisiana the number of Spanish descent is small compared to those of French, and the Creole may generally be regarded as a Frenchman a few generations removed. He is proud of his origin, and considers himself in some sense a Gaul. Some uninformed persons of Europe, and even of the United States, have a vague idea that there is negro blood in the veins of this race. This furnishes amusement to the good-natured Creole, and annoyance to the sensitive one. The influence of caste has kept the races apart here as elsewhere in the United States, as far as marriage is concerned; but union not recognized by law has always been tolerated, which accounts for the numbers of mixed race, classed as negroes.

The American criticizes his Creole neighbor with severity. He avers that he is neither practical, energetic, nor able; that he is a stumbling-block in the way of progress. These words may rest on some foundation, but they require modification. If the deficiencies exist which are charged to his account, the Creole has compensating qualities for which his critical neighbor does not give him credit. If happiness is to be taken as a guide and test of excellence in man, the Creole is nearer the right path than the American, for the latter compared with him is a sombre, perturbed soul. The probabilities are that steam and telegraph have lessened the sum of joy on earth; in the slower times of turnpikes and mail-coaches, life was deeper and mellower. The Creole still lingers in the past, dallying with the flowers of love and sentiment, while the American hurries forward with unhappy haste to pluck the thorns of ambition and pelf. One is like a steam-tug, wheezing, tugging, and tossing; the other like a Nile-boat loitering along the shores of lotus-land.

The American is only satisfied when all foreign elements are thrown into the national turning shop and come out turned to his own exact proportions. The Creoles for generations have steadily refused to be planed, and this irritates the American. He of Anglo-Saxon stock regards American civilization as the highest in the world, and insists that this Creole native shall square himself to it but he persistently refuses – he prefers his own. Elsewhere the turning shop works successfully. The Indians are shaved down almost to annihilation; Mexicans of California and Texas assume the national shape; Alaskans even are being cut down to the required model; and as for the Irish, they are hardly landed on the Battery before declarations are filed and they are turned out after the approved pattern. The Creole alone resists, and to the urgent demands of the Anglo-Saxon neighbor his 'Non, monsieur', comes back as unerringly as the refrain of Poe's raven.

The Creole is wedded to Louisiana soil as the American has never been. Often, when the latter has made his fortune, he hies him to other lands to enjoy it. The descendant of the Gaul clings to the land of sugar until the end. He may once or twice make excursions to the country of his fathers, to dip himself anew into that civilization which he affects, but he generally returns to find truer happiness in the place of his birth. He has a proverb to the effect that he who is accustomed to Mississippi water can never relish any other.

[. . .] There is general integrity of character in the Creole. In the city of his heart – New Orleans – he may go to the theater and dance on Sundays, for which he is continually reproved by his neighbors; but, as a rule, he may be depended on for the fulfilment of mundane obligations. He lives long. Fair food and wine, easy digestion, and a pleasant life, generally carry him, with but little incidental sickness, past the line of fourscore. Thus his death follows with the natural sequence of night to day. A Creole proverb puts it that at last he dries up and blows away. He is hospitable according to his means, which are usually limited, compared to those of the American. He is not cosmopolitan, taking little interest in anything outside of his local affairs; but whenever his mind moves out of the home groove, it travels Franceward to the cradle of his race [. . .]

He is habitually polite, and in this he is strikingly superior to his American neighbors [. . .] A man cedes his place to a woman with polite word and smile, and she remembers the donor for weeks; another surrenders the place roughly: she reluctantly accepts, and he who confers the favor passes out of her mind as soon as he is out of sight.

A young Creole woman enters a full car on Rampart Street, and a rough Anglo-Saxon at the other end rises to his feet. 'Pray keep your seat – I can just as well stand', observes the young woman, to which he has the heart to respond: 'I don't care whether you stand or not – I'm going to get out.' One can imagine the chagrin of this young person, and how unhappy this man made himself as well as others. Peace is the root, happiness the growth, and politeness the fruit of life. Only a pacific soul may be happy, and only a happy man may be polite. Vindictive natures are occasionally polite through effort, but they may not be consistently and untiringly so.

The Creoles have conserved their language, many of them speaking but imperfect English. Considering the generations they have been American citizens, their French is quite pure [. . .]

In Louisiana the French race is an exotic which has never thrived as in their parent land. Indeed, this holds good of this people everywhere out of the mother country – in Algeria, Martinique, Cochin China, and Canada. In this respect they are in striking contrast to the Englishman, who imposes his civilization and his roast beef wherever he goes, becomes rooted to the place of his adoption, and gets the upper hand in the direction of affairs [. . .]

As to the Americans and Creoles, they do not seem to understand each other, although they think they do. The harsh, hard ways of these Americanized Englishmen are naturally repugnant to the more artistic nature of the Creoles, who do not go to the core, the better part of their rough neighbors, but stop at an unprepossessing exterior. On the other hand, the pretty form with which the Creoles try to invest life is regarded by the men of angles as a sort of Miss Nancyism, indicating weakness of character, when it is really a sentiment of art which is creditable wherever found. A cosmopolitan would find the Creole civilization more pleasing than the American, as it exists in this quarter. In the latter are to be found strong prejudices of race and locality, with an unpleasant way of showing them. The expansive cordiality and courteous manners – albeit there is but little strength behind them – of the Creoles, produce an impression on the mind of the stranger not easily effaced. In one race there is swagger, boasting, tobacco-chewing, carelessness of costume, and strength and wide-awakeness; in the other, evenness of manner, moderation of speech, clean linen, softness of tone, inactivity, and weakness. One is rugged and ugly, the other pretty and feeble [. . .]

The Creole woman [. . .] has an eye for form and color which few American women of Louisiana possess, and has always kept up her communications with the Rue de la Paix in the art of dressing. Her resources are slender, she being generally in modest circumstances, but she does much with what she has. In an assembly or soirée composed of the two races, one can generally distinguish the aesthetic Creole from her neighbor in the make and color of a robe, the arrangement of the hair, the disposition of a flower, or in some such mark.

The Creole woman is prettier than the French woman. There is a climatic influence in America which refines features and gives delicacy to the complexion. This is especially the case in Louisiana [. . .] She inherits from her mother over the sea the physical characteristics of round limbs and delicate extremities, with a figure something slighter – another effect of climate; also that sense of art with which people are born, but can never entirely acquire. From the same source come her coquetry and her grace of speech and action, but modified. She does not wear crude colors or awry shapes; nor does she expresses herself with unseemly gesture or discordant tones. Her dress is rather sombre than gay, and her carriage simple and conventional – for they all walk alike. Smoothness and graceful propriety are hers; in a word, there is an absence of angles in her general conduct.

Most of the young women are educated at the Ursuline convent, whence, after being finished, they are returned to their respective families with the modest demeanor and downcast eyes of young nuns, or something approaching thereto. However much they may think about the young men whom they meet on the street, they hardly look at them. Their feminine eyes pass over the masculine flesh and blood as if they were mortar and bricks. This is in accordance with their training; they may not look at the Creole cocks who gallantly parade before them. For the young woman to walk with one of them would be to defy public opinion; and to go out at night to the theater or concert with him would be to fly in the face of Providence. Entertaining such ideas touching the deportment of young women, the Creoles are naturally scandalized at the conduct of their American neighbors, who in this respect allow themselves a wide latitude [. . .]

Amelia E. Barr, 'The Modern Novel', *The North American Review*, Vol. 159, Issue 456, November 1894, pp. 592–600

The nineteenth-century *North American Review* was a journal of literature and culture whose contributors included Walt Whitman and Henry James. During the 1890s, social commentator Mrs Barr contributed a series of articles to the magazine in which she voiced her fears concerning the changing nature of society and women's role within it. Note her particular anxiety about modern literary trends and what she saw as their negative effect on standards of morality, family values and the 'proper' duties of motherhood. Kate Chopin's *The Awakening* must surely have qualified for the category which Mrs Barr defines as the 'erotic-sensational' novel.

It is the erotic-sensational novel which deserves unqualified anger and disgust, for it is the representation, by genius, of a society that lives for the gratification of its five senses, and that only. These novels, with their demi-nude and demi-monde experiences, sap all moral perceptions, and teach only one vile lesson – that we may sin, if we only sin neatly and take care not to be found out. A good writer stooping to work of this kind is like a fine lapidary wasting his skill in cutting pastes instead of diamonds. And the worst of the position is that he knows it and makes money by it. [. . .] Both in the criminal and the erotic-sensational novel, the most dangerous element is the *contemporaneous* one. If such stories could be laid a few centuries back, they would do no harm [. . .] But when the heroes and heroines are men and women of like passions with ourselves, and living in our midst, they have all the wicked influence of personal bad company. [. . .] novels now depict everything and everybody, and all kinds of human character may be found on a railway bookstall. Novels are the sermons of this era, and a favorite novelist exerts a deeper and far more extensive influence than any living clergyman; not in the formation of this or that special opinion, but in a subtle and permanent bias and prepossession over the whole character. And when men and women of all ages are constantly under [the influence of] these interesting sermons, it is worse than idle to say that 'nothing comes of it'.

[. . .]

Women are practically affected by novels far more than men are, for the experience of men enables them to dispute or dilute or correct many things said. But a woman's life is greatly influenced by the fiction she reads. She draws her ideas from her favorite books; she tries to speak, and act, and dress like her favorite heroines. How good, then, it must be for an egotistical, selfish girl to have a course of George Eliot's novels for her constant lesson through her characters is that the world was not made for them alone. She knocks the selfishness out of them all, or she punishes them for retaining it. She is also a good teacher for girls self-willed and self-opinionated; for all her good, lovable women need a master and a rule of life; yes, even Romola needed Savonarola. The one thing to be regretted in many of the lighter novels of the day is their kind of heroine. She is not a nice girl. She talks too much, and talks in a slangy, jerky way, that is odiously vulgar. She is frank, too frank, on every subject and occasion. She is contemptuous of authority, even of parental authority, and behaves in a high-handed way about her love affairs. She is, alas! something of a Freethinker. She rides a bicycle, and plays tennis, and rows a boat. She laughs loudly, and dresses in manly fashion, and acts altogether in accord with an epoch that travels its sixty miles an hour. She is very smart and clever, but in her better moments she makes us sigh for the girls who thought their parents infallible and who were reverent church-women – the girls who were so shrinkingly modest, and yet so brave in great emergencies – the girls who were so fully accomplished and so beautiful, and who yet had no higher ambition than to be the dearly loved wife of a noble-hearted man and the good house-mother of happy children.

Amelia E. Barr, 'Good and Bad Mothers', *The North American Review*, Volume 156, Issue 437, April 1893, pp. 408–15

[. . .] if the father be the head and the hands of a family, the mother is the heart. No office in the world is so honorable as hers, no priesthood so holy, no influence so sweet and strong and lasting.

For this tremendous responsibility mother-love has always been sufficient. The most ignorant women have trusted to it; and the most learned have found its potential when all their theories failed. And neither sage men nor wise women will ever devise anything to take the place of mother-love in the rearing of children. If there be other good things present, it glorifies them; if there be no other good thing – it is sufficient. For mother-love is the spirit of self-sacrifice even unto death, and self-sacrifice is the meat and drink of all true and pure affection.

[. . .] how to make home the sweetest spot on earth, a place of love, order and repose, a temple of purity where innocence is respected, and where no one is permitted to talk of indecent subjects or to read indecent books; these are the duties of a good mother: and her position, if so filled, is one of dignity and grave importance. For it is on the hearthstone she gives the fine healthy initial touch to her sons and daughters that is not effaced through life, and that makes them blessed in their generation. [. . .]

But if the grand essential to a good mother be self-denying, self-effacing love, this is a bad era for its development. Selfishness and self-seeking is the spirit of the time, and its chilling poison has infected womanhood, and touched even the sacred principle of maternity. In some women it assumes the form of a duty. They feel their own mental culture to be of supreme importance, they wish to attend lectures and take lessons, and give themselves to some special study.

[. . .] If they have assumed the position of wifehood, it is a monstrous thing to hold themselves degraded by its consequences; or to consider the care of children a waste of their own life. The world can do without learned women, but it cannot do without good wives and mothers; and when married women prefer to be social ornaments and intellectual amateurs, they may be called philanthropists and scholars, but they are nevertheless moral failures, and bad mothers.

'The New Heroines of Fiction', Harper's Bazaar, 1 January 1898

The following article from the popular journal Harper's Bazaar, which appeared in the year before Chopin's novel was published, celebrates the changing representation of women in literature. It is claimed that such literary development is reflective of the changing expectations and demands of women themselves, that women now look for something other than marriage, hence their newly 'realistic' fictional counterparts cease to be merely 'romantic', 'sentimental', 'artificial' creations. But, whilst these more well-rounded female characterisations are lauded, what is still of concern here is their effect on a young female readership. Considering that the influence of these new 'heroines' is presented in favourable terms, it is doubtful that their self-assertion in any way reflects the shocking unconventionality of Chopin's 'new heroine' Edna Pontellier. Note also the allusion to the fictional character being a 'reproduction' of the author and her experiences, which would have damning implications if applied to Chopin and Edna.

Fiction novels especially may not so much represent Life and Nature as they represent what the average person, usually a woman, likes to read. Novels have, within the last forty or fifty years, undergone an extraordinary change, particularly in their heroines. They used to be called ideal, because they were unreal, nothing like them ever having existed on the earth, above the earth, or under the earth. They were all bewilderingly beautiful, wildly romantic, singularly delicate, oppressively sentimental, exceedingly rich, positively ridiculous. How they did talk! Such fustian, such bombast as human tongue never uttered, or human ear never listened to or would listen to if retreat were possible. Descriptions of them in detail were devoured. To-day nobody could be induced to read about them, and they have, as a consequence, gone into everlasting retirement.

The heroine of the present is entirely a distinct creature. She has some relation to nature; she belongs at least to the order of beings we know as women. She is not inevitably beautiful; indeed, she is often plain. She is not opulent in what were formerly thought to be irresistible fascinations. She has an individuality of her own. Some of her qualities may not be attractive at first, but they are brought out, and shown to be consistent with her character. She has some other object eternally in view than marriage. She is not always prepared to fall in love at sight.

[. . .]

The founder of this sort of novel was Charlotte Brontë, who, nearly sixty years since, introduced *Jane Eyre* to an astonished public. The book created a literary revolution, and has had, as everything original invariably has, hundreds and hundreds of imitators. Nevertheless, it continues to be widely and eagerly read, and may be read throughout the coming century. *Jane Eyre* is supposed to have been largely a reproduction of Charlotte Brontë herself, as first novels are apt to be of their authors and such experiences as she had had.

The new heroine is commonly more or less realistic – more rather than less – and generally interesting in proportion to her realism. There is now some prospect, from reading about her in current fiction, of learning something of her sex, in which man has a perennial concern. The novelist of this time tries less to furnish a stimulating story than to furnish fresh personages, at least those having unusual experiences and singular temperaments [. . .]

The extraordinary change in novels and their heroines is due, in a great measure, to the change in women themselves. These have ceased to be the romantic, sentimental, artificial beings they were even thirty years ago, and their reflex in fiction has been discontinued. We will not read of the languishing, empty, mawkish, flavourless Sybils, Angelinas and Arabellas that our mothers and grandmothers hung over and wept over. The heroine of the period is not satisfied to look pretty and obey the fixed rules of etiquette; nor is the actual woman so satisfied either. The actual woman wants to be somebody, to do something, to take some part in life; and she is and does, even if surrounded by luxury and bulwarked by influential friends. It is noticeable how active she is, how useful she tries to make herself, whatever the temptations of wealth and society to render her otherwise.

[. . .] heroines act favorably, as a rule, on feminine readers, and feminine readers, in a way, act favorably on them. That is, what the readers say and do reaches the ears of writers of fiction directly or indirectly – writers are ever on the watch for new subjects, new suggestions, new ideas – and the fictionists incorporate in time their fresh stock of knowledge into their characters.

It is a favorable sign that realism prevails so much in fiction; for, properly understood, it indicates a genuine interest in humanity, and the disposition to aid and advance it. The heroines of the books, before they had appeared there, were heroines without the title in real life.

'French Novels for Public Libraries', *Harper's Bazaar*, 11 April 1896, p. 318

Chopin's French-Creole background together with her identification of French realist author Guy de Maupassant as her major literary influence have determined that her writing is often identified with the kind of 'risqué' foreign literature under discussion in this article. Maupassant is, in fact, mentioned here specifically as the author of some 'unpardonable' stories. *The Awakening* itself was largely condemned on its publication for its boldness and shocking exploration of female sexuality; fears were thus being expressed about the impact such reading material would have if made freely available to impressionable young minds. The author of this article has similar concerns, advocating censorship and strict regulation of the volumes which are permitted onto the shelves of public libraries. Again, this resonates with the publication history of Chopin's novel and explains in some measure the long-standing belief that *The Awakening* was subject to a library ban. This particular story has, however, recently been dismissed by Chopin's biographer, Emily Toth.

The writer of these papers, being trustee of a public library and member of a State Library Association, has been several times urged to suggest in these columns, or elsewhere, a list of French novels which can be freely issued to young people. Granting, for the sake of argument, that there are older people who ought to read everything, good or bad, the French themselves set the example of making certain restrictions for the young; and for public libraries especially, where books are bought with money belonging to the whole community, some such restrictions must be recognized. In our larger cities, where French and German are studied even in the high-schools, it is becoming the practice to include these literatures in purchases for public libraries; and these requests have come from sources as far apart as the Merrimac and the mouth of the Mississippi [. . .]

[. . .] when we think that the greatest French writers have written both good and evil things, and that nobody can read everything, why not select? Grant that when a Frenchman writes, deliberately, [. . .] for youths and maidens, *virginibus puerisque*, he is apt to write something rather namby-pamby, as in Zola's *Le Rêve*; it is also true that when he writes simply for art's sake, as he prefers to do, he may write something that is perfectly unexceptional; he has no prejudice against virtue – nor, perhaps, against vice – what he seeks is art. Probably the most exquisite tribute ever paid in all literature to the force of married love, lighting up poverty, priva-tion, banishment, with a permanent glow of bliss is in Guy de Maupassant's *Le Bonheur* (Happiness); and yet the very volume which contains it has also stories that are unpardonable. By saying that I do not mean first or chiefly that they would injure any pure mind, for they would only disgust it; but the trouble is that they would taint the memory and cling around it, like ugly words we have heard as children, not fully knowing what they meant. If now the same fountain can bring forth sweet waters and bitter, why not fearlessly seek the sweet?

[. . .] Of foreign authors writing in French, or habitually translated, it is safe to name the Genevese tales of Töpffer and the Flemish tales of Hendrik Conscienco: Tolstoi's *La Guerre et la Paix, Les Cosaques*, and *Seratopol*, I myself should add his *Anna Karenina*, which may safely be read by any one who is old enough to read; or Hawthorne's *Scarlet Letter*, the theme in both cases being very painful and the treatment noble. Almost anything of Tourguénief's may be trusted, and his *Terres Vierges* has universal application.

[. . .] in spite of the vague prejudice which lumps together all French novels as evil, it is easy to get together quite a collection of those which are not merely readable – usually more readable than any others – but also reasonably free from moral dynamite. They will, of course, vary somewhat in literary execution; but here also they have the advantage implied in the remark of that admirable critic, the late M. Schérer, who divided all French novels into two classes: those which were written – meaning well written – and those which were not written; but classed all English novels under the latter head.

Arthur Martine, *Martine's Hand-Book of Etiquette and Guide to True Politeness*, New York: Dick & Fitzgerald Publishers, 1866. Reprinted by R.L. Shep, Box 668, Mendocino, Calif. 95460, 1988

An examination of contemporary popular literature reveals nineteenth-century America as a society which is extremely concerned with the maintenance of 'proper' standards of behaviour, particularly for women. Arthur Martine's hand-book is one of many such volumes which offer prescriptive advice on adhering to expectations. His guidance on correct standards of dress, on wifely duty, and on the 'impropriety' of a woman's being alone with a man who is not her husband determine that these extracts are particularly relevant in contextualis-ing the extent to which Edna Pontellier flouts such conventions.

'On Dress'

Lavater has urged that persons habitually attentive to their attire, display the same regularity in their domestic affairs. He also says: 'Young women who neg-lect their toilet and manifest little concern about dress, indicate a general dis-regard of order – a mind but ill adapted to the details of housekeeping – a deficiency of taste and of the qualities that inspire love.'

Hence the desire of exhibiting an amiable exterior is essentially requisite in a young lady, for it indicates cleanliness, sweetness, a love of order and propriety, and all those virtues which are attractive to their associates, and particularly to those of the other sex.

'Visiting'

A well-bred person always receives visitors at whatever time they may call, or whoever they may be; but if you are occupied and cannot afford to be interrupted by a mere ceremony, you should instruct the servant *beforehand* to say that you are 'not at home.' [. . .]

Ladies in the present day are allowed considerable license in paying and receiving visits; subject, however, to certain rules, which it is needful to define. Young married ladies may visit their acquaintances alone; but they may not appear in any public places unattended by their husbands or elder ladies. This rule must never be infringed, whether as regards exhibitions, or public libraries, museums, or promenades; but a young married lady is at liberty to walk with her friends of the same age, whether married or single. Gentlemen are permitted to call on married ladies at their own houses. Such calls the usages of society permit, but never without the knowledge and full permission of husbands.

Ladies may walk unattended in the streets, being careful to pass on as becomes their station – neither with a hurried pace, nor yet affecting to move slowly. Shop-windows, in New York especially, afford great attractions; but it is by no means desirable to be seen standing before them, and most assuredly not alone. Be careful never to look back, nor to observe too narrowly the dresses of such ladies as may pass you. Should any one venture to address you, take no heed, seem not to hear, but hasten your steps. Be careful to reach home in good time. Let nothing ever induce you to be out after dusk, or when the lamps are lighted. Nothing but unavoidable necessity can sanction such acts of impropriety.

Lastly, a lady never calls on a gentleman, unless professionally or officially. It is not only ill-bred, but positively improper to do so. [. . .]

'Domestic Etiquette and Duties'

On the wife especially devolves the privilege and pleasure of rendering home happy. We shall, therefore, speak of such duties and observances as pertain to her. When a young wife first settles in her home, many excellent persons, with more zeal, it may be, than discretion, immediately propose that she should devote some of her leisure time to charitable purposes: such, for instance, as clothing societies for the poor, or schools, or district visiting. We say with all earnestness to our young friend, engage in nothing of the kind, however laudable, without previously consulting your husband, and obtaining his full concurrence. Carefully avoid, also, being induced by any specious arguments to attend evening lectures, unless he accompanies you. Remember that your Heavenly Father, who has given you a home to dwell in, requires from you a right performance of its duties. Win your husband, by all gentle appliances, to love religion; but do not, for the sake even of a privilege and a blessing, leave him to spend his evenings alone. Look often on your marriage ring, and remember the sacred vows taken by you when the ring was given; such thoughts will go far toward allaying many of these petty vexations which circumstances call forth. [. . .]

In all money matters, act openly and honorably. Keep your accounts with the most scrupulous exactness, and let your husband see that you take an honest pride in rightly appropriating the money which he intrusts to you. [. . .]

[. . .] The home department belongs exclusively to the wife; the province of the husband is to rule the house – hers to regulate its internal movements.

'A Social Problem', *Harper's Bazaar*, 30 May 1896, p. 462

In *The Awakening* Edna shocks her husband by neglecting her duty in opting out of the obligatory round of social visiting. Because she is dissatisfied with the imposition on her time and wishes instead to come and go as she pleases and to indulge her desire to paint she decides that she will no longer be 'at home' on Tuesday afternoons for her regular female callers. The article included here expresses similar discontent with the excessive demands of 'visiting' and cites the 'rebellious' actions of women who have decided to modify the arrangements of their social gatherings. Note, however, that the 'rebels' here have merely amended the times of their 'at homes' or re-adjusted their guest lists. There is no suggestion of the outright rejection of 'duty' as practised by Edna – visiting here remains an appropriate and accepted activity for women.

A thoughtful woman remarked, the other day, 'Now that the season is over, it is borne in upon me that afternoon teas are fast changing friends into acquaintances and acquaintances into strangers.' When we only see our friends in their best gowns, and in the society of others, we have to nourish our interest and affection upon what we have known of them under the surface, in times past, and little by little, we grow indifferent and learn to live without them.

Our visiting lists naturally become longer with the passing of the years, since one meets charming new people, and one does not neglect old friends, but the time between sunrise and sunset remains unchanged, and the demands upon us increase as our children grow older, our parents more feeble, and our realization of the sacredness of life and opportunity more keen. Then at the end of the season we find that we have religiously paid the social 'mint, anise, and cumin', have called upon our acquaintances on their 'days' with punctilious courtesy, but those for whom we really care have been almost crowded out of our lives.

We all feel that the receptions known as 'afternoon teas' leave much to be desired. We receive a hurried greeting from our hostess, who has only time perhaps to ask some question showing personal interest, when her attention is claimed by the next comer, and our answer is no longer of consequence. We see familiar faces of friends here and there and hasten to exchange a few words with each, knowing that there is no time for real conversation, and that we have several other 'teas' for that same afternoon, and must not stop too long.

We hurry out of the house, and entering the carriage, sit bolt upright, as though the relaxing of our muscles might retard our progress, and alight at another house, where is repeated the same scene that we have just left. Upon our return home, we have a pleasant sense of having accomplished much in 'checking off' a goodly number of social 'obligations', but to this feeling often succeeds another that is less self-gratulatory. We reflect that society fills life with imaginary duties; that our best selves are dominated and stifled by its petty conventionalities; that our social intercourse is built upon the trivial interests of our lives, and not upon that which can make us any happier by giving us the joys of friendship, or even bringing real relaxation, or any better by developing and ennobling our immortal part.

True, society does not pretend to be a moral teacher. It tells us how to dress, how to behave, and, according to the rigid traditional law of uniformities, dictates how we must endeavour to amuse ourselves and entertain our friends; but why we may not make our very respectful bow to Dame Fashion and her satellites, be careful not too flagrantly to outrage their sense of what is fit, but claim for ourselves a little time to enjoy each other?

A little company of friends have tried the experiment of meeting for an hour once a week at one another's homes, and have kept alive the 'sacred fire' of friendship most successfully. Any good story or bit of fun, any strong or helpful thought, met with in their reading, is treasured to be shared at the 'tea party'. Each member is in turn the hostess, and enjoys the merry rivalry as to who shall have the most delicious sandwiches, or the latest novelty in cake, or in the brewing of that much-abused beverage that serves as title to the little entertainment. They find the hour thus spent together both restful and stimulating.

Another rebel against the all-encroaching demands of general society is a most charming woman who has informed her more intimate friends that she is always to be found at home during one special *morning* in each week. Only those are asked whose coming brings pleasure – a matter of pure friendship, with no hint of social obligation.

Three or four of the ladies are often asked to remain for the dainty but simple luncheon that is served at the usual hour.

[. . .]

Why should we not have the courage of our opinions? We are such spendthrifts, too, of time, and forget to realize that:

'This is *life*, with its golden store,
It comes but once, and it comes no more.'

'What Girls are Doing', *Harper's Bazaar*, 10 April 1897

Both Edna Pontellier, and Chopin herself, are unconventional in that they enjoy walking unaccompanied. This article is included to demonstrate the very eccentric nature of their chosen pastime. Young women wishing to engage in walking for exercise and pleasure are seen here to be organising themselves into groups in order to practise their leisure pursuit. Their walking trips do not take the form of Edna's unaccompanied, unplanned meanderings, but rather the carefully planned structure of a group activity.

The out of town girls are busy getting up walking clubs, which during our short spring season are always enjoyable. It is a very difficult matter in town to arrange any thing like a good walking party, as the distances are so great before you are able to get off into the country. Besides, if the start is made at four o'clock or thereabouts, it is nearly dark before you can get back. So the city girl is arranging to pay various visits to her out of town friends, and therefore to come in for some of the walking parties. The start is made very often from the country-club house if there is one in the neighborhood, and the walkers return there to a dinner, which, as a rule, is a subscription one. Every advantage has to be taken of the few spring days our climate allows us; very early in the season the roads become too dusty and the sun too hot for any real enjoyment in walking. Some of these walking clubs propose to go into the study of botany, and in their rambles to collect specimens of spring flowers and ferns.

'Kissing', *Godey's Lady's Book*, October 1876, p. 385

This interesting piece posits the propriety or otherwise of a 'young lady' permitting her escort to kiss her as a serious subject for public debate. That such a seemingly trivial matter can provoke such concern places into context the shocking nature of the married Edna Pontellier's indulgence in a sexual relationship with Alcée Arobin and her extra-marital romantic encounter with Robert Lebrun.

Two of our New York contemporaries are at present engaged in a little controversy concerning a very sweet and interesting question, viz.: Whether it is right or proper for a young lady who indulges in moonlight strolls to permit her escort to kiss her on the doorsteps. In this controversy we have another singular illustration of the inconsistency of newspapers. The *Sun*, which is usually regarded as the most unblushing of New York dailies, holds up its types in holy horror at the bare idea of a young lady kissing any young man to whom she is not engaged, while the *World*, a virtuous and matronly old fogy, believes and stoutly maintains that in the mouths of sensible and discreet maidens who may be trusted to a 'moonlight stroll' the right to kiss and to receive kisses may also be trusted, not only with perfect impunity, but also with advantage. 'The *Sun* must admit,' says the *World*, 'that the harm which it professes to fear lies not in the kiss itself, but in the intention of the kisser or kissee. Given a kissee of good sense and discretion, qualities enabling her not only to choose a kisser of good and religious motives, but also to receive his kiss with pious and proper intent, then let the kiss be gently but firmly placed where it will do the most good, not hastily and clumsily on the nose, and "if a body kiss a body need a body cry?" We trow not.'

It appears to us that there are two sides, as well as lips, to the question. Granted that there are many forms of kisses, harmless as well as harmful, it is a generally-accepted social rule that no young lady has a right to receive or permit a liberty from a gentleman not a relative which she would not acknowledge in the light of day and in the presence of the world. An accepted lover may, of course, kiss his *fiancée*, but even then a strict sense of delicacy will deter a virtuous young woman from receiving more than a moderate share of these seals of affection. Engage-ments in these modern days, like marriages, very often end in smoke, and a husband always feels more contented if he knows or believes that his wife has not been prodigal of these favors to half a dozen fellows before him. On the whole, therefore, we agree with the *Sun* in this matter.

American girls have an abundance of personal liberty already, too many opportunities, indeed, for permitting the advances of unscrupulous and designing men. Our countrywomen abroad have acquired a reputation for boldness and brusquerie, the result, no doubt, of that lack of strict training which forms a guard to virtue, and so much adorns it. We conclude that, except in the case of a very near relative or a prospective husband, kissing between man and woman is not only improper, but vulgar. We have had quite enough of paroxysmal kissing and all that rubbish in this country already, and the sooner we do away with such false sentiment, the better for our sisters, sweet hearts, wives, and daughters, and for that purity and virtue which ought to be the glory of a nation.

'Smoking in the Street Cars', *The Daily Picayune*, Sunday 28 May 1899, p. 5

This article demonstrates that in 1899 even being in the presence of men who are smoking is widely accepted as being abhorrent to all women. That they may indulge in the habit themselves is, apparently, unthinkable, although, as we have noted, Chopin herself enjoyed smoking.

The smokers on the Carrollton cars line are getting to be a nuisance. They are daily infringing on the space limit allotted to them by the company in accordance with the city ordinances, and the management does not seem to take any steps to prevent this. It seems to me that the city authorities should compel this company to protect the women and children who have to use their cars from this vile nuisance. Frail women, [. . .] are compelled to go to their daily work, sometimes sick and suffering, and are forced to receive in their faces the puffs of smoke which, to them, are nauseating in the extreme. Can't something be done to put a stop to this? Spitting in the street cars has been almost done away with; then why permit so great a nuisance as smoking? Many men do not smoke, do not like tobacco in any form, and no woman smokes. Still, by a limited statute, these are placed in the predicament of being compelled by the management of this company to endure a distasteful odor.

'Bathing and Bathing Costumes', The Delineator, August 1895, pp. 222–4

The following article is concerned with swimming which obviously features significantly in Chopin's novel. Here, however, it is the 'medicinal property' of the salt water which is celebrated, the health benefits which are promoted rather than the intense physical sensations felt by Edna Pontellier. What to Chopin's heroine is the difficult to master yet incredibly liberating act of swimming, is described by the author of The Delineator piece as a mechanical process which can be 'acquired easily enough'. In terms of the advice given on correct swimming attire, the emphasis here is on modesty. Far from Edna's naked plunge into the surf, the range of patterns provided suggests stockings, corsets and the avoidance of 'clinging stuffs [. . .] for obvious reasons'.

A plunge in the surf when the temperature of both air and water favors is one of the delights of Summer which must be experienced to be fully appreciated. If indulged in with moderation great benefit may be derived from surf bathing, not only because of the medicinal property of salt water, but as well on account of the massage of the waves. To those who have mastered the art of swimming the pleasures of the surf are intensified. To be able to move about at will in the water by the aid of a few simple strokes seems a wonderful feat to the uninitiated, its usefulness is universally acknowledged and it is now counted among the fashionable accomplishments. It is probably true that swimming does not come naturally to man, though there are some who maintain that an emergency will often develop the knowledge.

SWIMMING – The art of supporting the body in water can be acquired easily enough if the pupil have confidence in herself and in her instructor. Indeed, without a certain amount of coolness and courage, no sport in which personal safety is involved can either be thoroughly learned or comfortably practiced. Swimming in salt water is far easier than in fresh water. The specific gravity of the former is considerably greater than that of the latter, and the body by displacing a greater weight is the more easily buoyed up, less exertion being required to keep afloat. The various movements made and positions taken in swimming after a while become mechanical, and when once learned are never forgotten. The philosophy of swimming is to give the body motion so as to cause it to ride upon layers of water.

[. . .]

It is unwise to take a sudden plunge into the water upon first coming from the dressing room. Take a turn or two about the beach before entering the water. Twenty minutes should be the limit for robust bathers in water whose temperature is not less than 68 degrees. Eight minutes are considered quite long enough for those who are not strong, and a surf bath should not be taken oftener than every other day. It is well, even when not swimming, to move about in the water, and on leaving it, a bath robe should be, at once, thrown over the body for protection while walking from the beach to the bath house. When the bathing suit is removed, which should be done as quickly as possible, the body should be vigorously rubbed with a coarse bath towel. Everyone knows that bathing immediately after a meal is dangerous. At least two hours should elapse after eating before taking a bath but after coming out of the water some light refreshment may be taken with benefit.

[. . .] Now about proper clothing; clinging stuffs are avoided for obvious reasons, yet the material should be light of weight, and, at the same time, repel the water. Gloria, alpaca, or brilliantine and repellant serge, a wiry woollen fabric with a fine twill, have been recently adopted for bathing costumes and have not been found wanting in excellence. These are principally offered in navy-blue and black. Cravenette, a water proof serge, not unlike the repellant serge, is also used for bathing suits. Black surah silk suits are occasionally seen, but unless the best quality is selected, the material will not wear well and the best quality is decidedly expensive for such a purpose. Flannel, pluette (a water-proof serge) and wide-wale English serge in the indigo dye, still have a large following. Red and mixed gray twilled flannels are also seen, but they are oftener worn by misses or children than by ladies. Canvas bathing shoes are sometimes worn, but they are not generally popular. Black stockings, held up by hose supporters instead of garters are mostly seen, though, at present, there is a fancy for wearing no stockings at all, for which the Trilby craze is perhaps responsible. Stockings are a hindrance to swimmers, for when wet they retard the action of the legs.

Corsets are uncomfortable, yet many bathers are unwilling to dispense with their support. The most practical corset, one designed expressly for bathing, is made of white jean by pattern No. 3285 (copyright), price 10d. or 20 cents. It is cut with gores, laces at the back and buttons in front, extending just to the waist-line. Bones are, of course, inserted, and shoulder straps are provided [. . .]

A ladies' bathing suit may be fashioned from dark-blue brilliantine and fine white flannel by pattern No. 7690 (copyright), price 1s. 6d. or 35 cents. The blouse and drawers make one garment, the body portion being gathered to a square yoke and the drawers either left plain at the bottom or drawn up closely in knickerbocker style. The neck is cut low to accommodate a flannel sailor collar with pointed ends, from which fall tie ends of the same. If a high neck is preferred the sailor collar should be cut with rounding ends. The sleeves are short and puffed, though bishop sleeves with narrow flannel cuffs are provided for. A full short skirt hangs from a belt of flannel over the drawers and near the bottom a band of flannel is decoratively applied.

[. . .]

After each wearing, the bathing suit should be well rinsed in clear, fresh water and hung up to dry. A partially dried suit should never be put on, for aside from its uncomfortable feeling, it chills the body, and may cause illness.

Figure 1

3285   3285

Figure 2

7690   7690   7690

Figure 3

Figures 1, 2 and 3 Illustrations from 'Bathing and Bathing Costumes' (article), *The Delineator*, August 1895, pp. 222–4.

Figure 4 **'Bathing and Bathing Costumes',** *The Delineator,*
        August 1895, p. 123.

The following images (Figures 5–8) demonstrate the many expectations of correct dress which would have been imposed upon a woman of Edna Pontellier's social standing in late nineteenth-century America. As is clear, a wide range of costumes is required for different occasions, all of which are modest and somewhat impractical. The heavy skirts and corseted waists are extremely restrictive and not at all conducive to the free movement required for the walking, the swimming and, in general, the independent lifestyle which Edna Pontellier seeks. The ornateness on display here is indicative of the clothing's symbolic value as a measure of a woman's husband's wealth and social standing. Edna's loosening and removal of such garments throughout the novel indicates her rejection of both physical and figurative limitation.

Figure 5 'Ladies' Afternoon Costume', *The Delineator*, August 1895, p. 124.

Figure 6 'Ladies' Calling Costume', *The Delineator*, May 1895.

Figure 7 'Ladies' Evening Toilette', *The Delineator*, September 1895, p. 257.

Figure 8 'Costumes for Driving and the Races', *Harper's Bazaar*. Library of Congress Collections.

The following sketches are included to give an indication of the role of 'resort bachelor' as it is performed in the text by Robert Lebrun.

AN OBJECT OF INTEREST—
(The only young man in the place.)

A NICE PLACE FOR A BACHELOR—

Figure 9 'Some Summer Sketches', *Harper's Bazaar*, September 23, 1876, p. 613.

A RAIN BEAU—

Figure 9 continued

This sample of newspaper advertisements, promoting summer vacations which echo the novel's Grand Isle resort, is provided to demonstrate the popularity of such leisure travel at the end of the nineteenth century.

◆A Summer ◆Vacation

Can be most enjoyably spent at Milwaukee, Waukesha, Madison, Devil's Lake, Green Lake, Gogebic Lake, Lake Geneva, St Paul, Mineapolis, Lake Minnetonka, White Bear, Duluth, Ashland, Marquette, and the resorts of Wisconsin, Northern Michigan and Minnesota.

Exceptionally fine train service to all points. Low-rate tourist tickets and pamphlets upon inquiry at ticket offices. Ask for tickets via

Chicago & North-Western Ry.

And send for copy of "Hints to tourists" forwarded free upon application to the General Passenger and Ticket Agent.

Chicago Office, 212 Clark St.

H. R. McCULLOUGH.   W. B. KNISKERN
3d V. -P & G.T.M.   G.P. & T.A.
                CHICAGO

THE MIDDLESBORO,
Middlesboro, Ky.
Now open
The ideal summer resort,
near Cumberland Gap.

Magnificent mountain scenery, charming lake, boating, fishing, hunting. Hotel unequalled: 200 elegantly furnished rooms, single or en suite, with private baths. At very moderate rates.

Under the management of H. C. Ferguson, formerly manager Mexican Gulf Hotel. Pass Christian, Miss.

CLARENDON HOTEL
Saratoga Springs, N.Y.

Thoroughly renovated. Cuisine and service unsurpassed. Best family hotel and finest location in Saratoga. Famous Washington Springs situated in Clarendon's private Park.

New York Office Hotel Vendome.
J. A. Nutter, M. P. Robinson, W. J. Aldon.

Figure 10 'Summer Resorts', *The Daily Picayune*, May 28, 1899, p.6.

Robert Grant, 'The Art of Living: The Summer Problem', *Scribner's Magazine*, Vol. 18, Issue 1, July 1895, pp. 48–59

> For the vacation arrangements of the characters in her novel, Kate Chopin drew upon her own life experience. Creole women often spent summers on Grand Isle with their children whilst their husbands remained at home in the city, visiting them only at weekends. Such an arrangement is described here in this article from *Scribner's Magazine* which extols the benefits of escaping the stifling and unhealthy atmosphere of the city in midsummer. The 'Summer Problem' article, however, also hints at the dangers inherent in the family living apart for significant periods of time. It is significant that Chopin chooses Grand Isle, the 'other' space, from which husbands are largely absent, as the setting for Edna's initial 'awakenings'.

What is the good American to do with himself or herself in summer? The busiest worker nowadays admits that a vacation of a fortnight in hot weather is at least desirable. Philanthropy sends yearly more and more children on an outing in August, as one of the best contributions to the happiness and welfare of the poor. The atmosphere of our large cities in midsummer is so lifeless and oppressive that everyone who can get away for some part of the summer plans to do so, and fathers of families find themselves annually confronted by a serious problem.

[. . .] the family man who lives in a large city finds more and more difficulty every year, as the country increases in population, in making up his mind how best to provide for the midsummer necessities of his wife and children. [. . .]

[. . .] The American father has the trick of sending his family out of town for the summer, and staying at home himself. This had its origin probably in his supposed inability to escape from business in the teeth of the family craving to see something of the world outside of their own social acquaintance. Yet he acknowledged the force of the family argument that with such a large country to explore it would be a pity not to explore it; and accordingly he said, 'Go, and I will join you if and when I can.' Paterfamilias said this long ago, and in some instances he has vainly been trying to join them ever since. There are all sorts of trying in this world, and perhaps his has not been as determined as some; nevertheless he has maintained tolerably well the reputation of trying. The Saturday night trains and steamboats all over the country are vehicles, from July first to October first, of an army of fathers who are trying successfully to join their nearest and dearest at the different summer-resorts of the land.

To be separated for three months from one's wife and children, except for a day or two once a fortnight, is scarcely an ideal domestic arrangement, in spite of the fact that it is more or less delightful for the dear ones to meet new people and see new scenes. The American father may not try very hard to leave his city home, but it must be admitted that he has been an amiable biped on the score of the summer question. He has been and is ready to suffer silently for the sake of his family and his business.

Albert Rhodes, 'Suicide', *The Galaxy*, Vol. 21, Issue 2, February 1876, pp. 189–99

This article is one of several such pieces published in popular periodicals of the day. The level of journalistic interest is suggestive of a certain fascination with the issue of an individual's taking of their own life in this time, and the manner in which Edna Pontellier meets her death determines that suicide is a relevant issue in any debate on Chopin's novel. The author of the *Galaxy* article is careful to employ statistics which establish that not only do men and women usually have different reasons for committing suicide but that they also employ diverse means in order to achieve their aim. Interestingly, drowning, Edna Pontellier's choice, is cited as one of the most popular methods for women – their 'usual tendency [. . .] toward the pacific'. But, whilst Chopin presents Edna's decision following from her realisation that she can never achieve real autonomy, this article demonstrates that popular perceptions attribute women's suicide to 'misery', 'seduction', and 'disappointed love'.

Suicide is unknown in animals, and rare in unintelligent peoples. The instinct of self-preservation grows stronger as the intellect grows weaker. It is the head which drives the man to the act; he reasons; and from his reasoning comes death. Man is now better fed, housed, and clothed than ever, and yet he administers his own death-blow more frequently than ever. If civilization is progressive, so is suicide, one marching close behind the other. In the regions of comfort and learning these deaths are the most frequent and in the countries where brigandage and ignorance prevail they are the rarest; and in the homes of civilization this malady of the mind does not attack the humble and the simple so much as the refined and the sensitive. [. . .]

It is hardly necessary to say that if the suicides are to be diminished, the causes must be ascertained as far as may be which produce them, and this can only be done through centralized, official direction. When these are learned then only may remedies be intelligently proposed and carried out. [. . .]

The eighth census, published in 1866, was the last time the Government furnished any extended information on the subject of suicides. In it we are told that in 1850 491 destroyed themselves, which made 17 deaths in 10,000 deaths from known causes, and in 1860 993 persons, the proportion of these in both cases being larger in the South than the North. [. . .]

The following table is furnished showing in each sex the ratio of methods of self-destruction in 10,000 suicides.

	Males	Females
Cutting throat	1,203	759
Firearms	1,929	207
Hanging	4,429	3,862
Strangulation	85	–
Poison	1,646	3,034
Drowning	708	2,138

The table shows the usual tendency toward violent methods on the part of the men, and the usual one toward the pacific on the part of the women. [. . .]

It is difficult to know the real causes of self-killing and official documents must not be too hastily accepted as final on this subject. From such indications as they furnish, leaving aside mental maladies and physical sufferings which affect about equally the two sexes, women appear to be more subject to moral influences, such as disappointed love, betrayal, desertion, jealousy, domestic trouble, and sentimental exaltation of every description, while men are rather affected by trials of a material order, such as misery, business embarassments, losses, ungratified ambition, the abuse of alcohol, the desire to escape from justice, and so on.

[. . .] The principal causes of women's suicide in England and the United States are misery and seduction.

Jessie J. Cassidy, 'The Legal Status of Women', *Political Science Study Series*, Vol. II, No. 4, New York: The National American Woman Suffrage Association, March 1897

Sections of Cassidy's document are included to provide a picture of the very limited financial autonomy and legal status afforded to women in the United States in this period. Note that in the state of Louisiana, the setting for the novel, a woman's control over her own property is permissible 'only by agreement' and that any wages she may earn remain 'In [her] husband's control'. Early in the text Léonce, Edna's husband, is identified as the controller of the family's finances when he fingers the dollar bills in his pocket. Throughout the narrative the issue of female financial autonomy remains a constant concern – Edna's removal from the family home is only made possible by her having 'a little money of [her] own from [her] mother's estate'.

[. . .] In Louisiana and Texas there has been no statutory change, and wages are community property and in the husband's control. In a number of states special acts have granted the wife control of her wages under certain conditions. In Arizona, California, Idaho, Oklahoma, North and South Dakota, they are only her own if she is living separate from her husband; in Georgia, Montana, Nevada, North Carolina, Oregon and Virginia, only if she is separate or is a registered free trader; in Missouri, only if she is not supported by her husband, and in Tennessee, only if she has been permitted by her husband to receive and retain them. (Grayson's Code, 1894.) Thus there are sixteen states where the married woman has not yet secured full legal control of her wages. [. . .] Regarding other property there are five states, Florida, Idaho, Louisiana, Tennessee and Texas, where the husband has control of the wife's property. [. . .]

Property rights of married women

State	Control of property	Power to will property	Control of wages
Alabama	*Partial*, Feb 18, 1895	Code of 1843	Feb 28, 1887
Arizona	Jan 22, 1871	First code, 1864–71	Feb 19, 1881 *Partial*
Arkansas	Constitution, 1874	Constitution, 1874	Constitution, 1874
California	March 21, 1872	March 21, 1872	March 9, 1870, *Partial*
Colorado	Nov 7, 1861	Nov 7, 1861	Nov 7, 1861
Connecticut	April 20, 1877	May session, 1809	April 20, 1877
Delaware	April 9, 1873	March 17, 1875	April 9, 1873
Dist. of Columbia	April 10, 1869	Code of 1857	April 10, 1869
Florida	*In husband's control*	Feb 11, 1881	In code of 1891
Georgia	In code of 1882	In code of 1882	In code of 1882, *Partial*
Idaho	*In husband's control*	In code of 1887	In code of 1887, *Partial*
Illinois	Feb 21, Apr 24, 1861	March 3, 1845	March 24, 1869
Indiana	April 16, Sept 19, 1881	March 3, 1859	May 31, 1879
Iowa	In code of 1873	In code of 1873	April 14, 1870
Kansas	Oct 31, 1868	Oct 31, 1868	Oct 31, 1868
Kentucky	March 15, 1894	March 15, 1894	April 11, 1873
Louisiana	*Only by agreement*	In code of 1889	*In husband's control*
Maine	Since March 22, 1844	In code of 1857	In code of 1857
Maryland	Since June 12, 1860	June 12, 1860	May 13, 1882
Massachusetts	May 5, 1855	May 5, 1855	May 5, 1855
Michigan	Feb 13, 1855	By Constitution of 1850	Feb 13, 1855
Minnesota	March 5, June 1, 1869	March 6, June 1, 1869	March 5, June 1, 1869
Mississippi	In code of 1880	In code of 1880	In code of 1880
Missouri	June 11, 1889	April 17, 1877	March 25, 1875, *Partial*

In the table opposite it has been the intention to give the earliest date when the married woman secured full and absolute control of her property. In many cases, earlier enactments gave only partial control. Where two dates are given, the first is that of the passage of the bill and the second the date when it went into effect. When the special act was not found, the date has been given of the earliest compiled laws that contains the larger power. The name 'code' is used uniformly for Revised Statutes, Compiled Laws, General Laws, etc.; meaning always the compilation of the year given.

Evelyn W. Ordway, 'How the Women of New Orleans Discovered Their Wish to Vote', *Political Science Study Series*, Vol. V, No. 4, New York, March 1900

By the end of the nineteenth century various American women's suffrage organisations were flourishing and gaining significant momentum in their call for the vote. These organisations were, however, primarily based in and active in the North East of the country. Although Elizabeth Cady Stanton, a prime figure in the movement, had visited New Orleans on a speaking tour in 1885, Southern women, perhaps conditioned by a culture in which traditional definitions of femininity prevailed for longer, were less forthcoming in their demands for equal citizenship. As Ordway's document demonstrates, in the Southern states often an added impetus was needed in order to motivate women into demanding their rights.

It was in 1892 that a Woman Suffrage club was first organized in New Orleans with less than a dozen members, and the meetings during that first winter were held in the quietest way at their respective homes, the members avoiding publicity through fear of the opprobrium sure to follow. Seven years later, in June of 1890, at an election held to promote sewerage and drainage, the women bore a prominent part, several thousand, voting – about one-third of all the votes cast, in fact, being contributed by them.

It might be inferred from this that during those seven years there had been a very rapid growth of suffrage sentiment, attended with large and flourishing suffrage clubs. But such was not the fact.

Several months previous to the election many of those who voted would have scouted the idea, saying that they were not interested in politics – that they did not want to vote – and that voting belonged to men. Many did not even know of their newly-acquired right to vote, – how, during the winter of 1898, a few suffragists appeared before the convention for the revision of the State constitution, and obtained – not what they asked for, full suffrage, but a mere morsel, enabling women of Louisiana who are tax-payers to vote on questions relating to the taxation of their property. When the time of the election arrived, however, they showed that they really did want to vote, and, moreover, that they were very much interested in the result of the election. And well they might have been, for the question was one seriously affecting the health and prosperity of New Orleans, – the question whether or not the taxpayers were willing to have imposed an additional yearly tax to provide for a system of sewerage and drainage, and an adequate supply of pure water.

There are about 10,000 taxpaying women in the city, many of them small householders, owning the little homes in which they dwell. Owing to the peculiar situation of New Orleans – lower than the level of the Mississippi river – and to the fact of there being no underground drainage, it is a difficult matter to drain off the rainwater after one of the heavy showers, by no means unusual here. At such times the rear portion of the city is inundated to a greater or less extent, and naturally women living there would be exceedingly glad to have the city possess a good drainage system.

For two successive years previous to the election a rigid and disastrous quarantine against the city, owing to prevalence of yellow fever, had so paralyzed business that property had much depreciated, rents were low and difficult to collect, and many dwellings were unoccupied. The prospect of a greatly improved sanitary condition of the city, which should prevent yellow fever epidemics and banish quarantines, appealed to the financial interest of taxpayers, generally – men and women. Moreover, as housekeepers, the New Orleans women often suffer inconvenience for lack of an adequate supply of clear water. The waterworks – too small by far – are in the hands of a monopoly, which supplies the muddy water of the Mississippi unfiltered, and charges exorbitant rates for it [. . .]

[. . .] One part of the proposition submitted to the taxpayers provided for the transfer of the waterworks to municipal control and for furnishing a plentiful supply of clarified water.

No wonder the women were interested; and thus it happened that when after listening to explanations of the projected enterprise at mass meetings, they were publicly invited – even strongly urged – by the mayor and other prominent men to come forward with their votes, they were found ready and glad to vote. And they were doubly glad afterward when it was found how potent a factor the women's vote had been, and the election returns showed that but for the women an important part of the measure would have been lost.

During the campaign preceding the election for municipal officers, which occurred the following November, very many women showed their interest by attending the meetings, and would have been glad to vote again; for the carrying out of the sewerage and drainage plan was in some measure involved. Both parties made them very welcome, extending invitations through the press, reserving seats for them, and appealing to them to use their influence on each respective side; and many of them, as well as many of the men interested for the success of their party, for the first time sincerely deplored the political disabilities – of Louisiana women.

The obvious moral of all this is, that in time of peace we should prepare for war. Because in the past certain women have not desired to vote, it is no proof that there may not arise an occasion on which they may very much desire to.

Let them make the necessary effort to provide themselves with the RIGHT against the time of need.

From **Charlotte Perkins Gilman, *Women and Economics: A Study of the Economic Relation Between Women and Men***, New York: Prometheus Books, 1994, originally published, Boston: Small, Maynard & Co., 1898

Charlotte Perkins Gilman was a radical social reformer and activist, a prolific writer and tireless lecturer, whose revisionist theories were grounded in the inequality of the gender system. A near contemporary of Chopin, Gilman was equally concerned with women's role and status in nineteenth-century American society. Here, her identification of the wedding band as a symbol of women's dependence and subjugation resonates with Edna Pontellier's actions in Chapter Seventeen of the novel when she takes off her wedding ring, throws it to the floor, and stamps on it, 'striving to crush it'. The two women's written expressions of their concerns, however, differ markedly as is explored in Janet Beer's essay, extracts from which appear later in this volume (**pp. 92–7**). Gilman's polemic style, her advocacy of community housing, childcare facilities, and better employment opportunities for women identify her as a socialist, her efforts, in the main, concentrated on the collective. By contrast, Chopin concerns herself more with an exploration of the conditions of existence of the individual woman.

To the young man confronting life the world lies wide. Such powers as he has he may use, must use. If he chooses wrong at first, he may choose again, and yet again. Not effective or successful in one channel, he may do better in another. The growing, varied needs of all mankind call on him for the varied service in which he finds his growth. What he wants to be, he may strive to be. What he wants to get, he may strive to get. Wealth, power, social distinction, fame, – what he wants he can try for.

To the young woman confronting life there is the same world beyond, there are the same human energies and human desires and ambition within. But all that she may wish to have, all that she may wish to do, must come through a single channel and a single choice. Wealth, power, social distinction, fame, – not only these, but home and happiness, reputation, ease and pleasure, her bread and butter, – all, must come to her through a small gold ring.

[. . .]

We know that it is time to change [. . .] In our present stage of social evolution it is increasingly difficult for women to endure their condition of economic dependence, and therefore they are leaving it. This does not mean that at a given day all women will stand forth free together, but that in slowly gathering numbers, now so great that all the world can see, women in the most advanced races are so standing free. Great advances along social lines come slowly, like the many-waved progress of the tide: they are not sudden jumps over yawning chasms [. . .]

The woman's club movement is one of the most important sociological phenomena of the century, – indeed, of all centuries, – marking as it does the first timid steps toward social organization of these so long unsocialized members of our race. Social life is absolutely conditioned upon organization. The military organizations which promote peace, the industrial organizations which maintain life, and all the educational, religious, and charitable organizations which serve our higher needs constitute the essential factors of that social activity in which, as individuals, we live and grow; and it is plain, therefore, that while women had no part in these organizations they had no part in social life [. . .]

[. . .] now the whole country is budding into women's clubs. The clubs are uniting and federating by towns, States, nations: there are even world organizations. The sense of human unity is growing daily among women. Not to see it is impossible. [. . .] Into this new phase of life comes a new spirit, – the spirit of women such as Elizabeth Cady Stanton and Susan B. Anthony; of Dr. Elizabeth Blackwell and her splendid sisterhood; of all the women who have battled and suffered for half a century, forcing their way, with sacrifices never to be told, into the field of freedom so long denied them.

From **Kate Chopin, Commonplace Book**, reprinted in, Emily Toth and Per Seyersted, eds, *Kate Chopin's Private Papers*, Bloomington and Indianapolis: Indiana University Press, 1998

Toth and Seyersted note that Chopin's Commonplace Book was begun when she was a sixteen-year-old pupil of the Sacred Heart Academy at the urging of one of her teachers, Sister Mary O'Meara. The book served a variety of purposes, including that of confidante, journal and a space in which to compose original literature. Initially it was used to copy out the writings of other authors whom the young Katie O'Flaherty admired. The extracts included here focus particularly on her thoughts on marriage to Oscar Chopin and on the period in which the Commonplace Book became a honeymoon diary documenting experiences of European culture. Chopin's account of their travels in Germany, Switzerland and France reveals that it was at this time that she encountered many unfamiliar codes of behaviour which both shocked, and yet attracted her. She records walking the streets unaccompanied, drinking beer, getting sunburnt, and being tempted to the gambling table, in fact, much of the unconventional behaviour which some thirty years later would be indulged in by her fictional heroine, Edna Pontellier. Seyersted and Toth indicate that they reproduce the text of the Commonplace Book in a form which is close to the original, complete with several errors and misspellings. The following extracts remain true to their principles of reproduction.

May 24th 1870   St. Louis.

Exactly one year has elapsed since my book and I held intercourse, and what changes have occurred! not so much outwardly as within My book has been shut up in a great immense chest buried under huge folios through which I could never penetrate, and I – have not missed it. Pardon me my friend, but I never flatter you.

All that has trans pired between then and now vanishes before this one consideration – in two weeks I am going to be married; married to the right man. It does not seem strange as I thought it would – I feel perfectly calm, perfectly collected. And how surprised every one was, for I had kept it so secret!

June 8th Wednesday.

Tomorrow I will be married. It seems to me so strange that I am not excited – I feel as quiet and calm as if I had one or two years of maiden meditation still before me. I am contented [. . .]

THREE MONTHS ABROAD.

June 9th

My wedding day! How simple it is to say and how hard to realize that I am married, no longer a young lady with nothing to think of but myself and nothing to do. We went to holy Communion this morning, my mother with us, and it gave me a double happiness to see so many of my friends at mass for I knew they prayed for me on this happiest day of my life. The whole day seems now like a dream to me; how I awoke early in the morning before the household was stirring and looked out of the window to see whether the sun would shine or not; how I went to mass and could not read the prayers in my book; afterwards how I dressed for my marriage – went to church and found myself married before I could think what I was doing [. . .] It was very painful to leave my mother and all at home; and it was only at starting that I dis covered how much I would miss them and how much I would be missed. We meet several acquaintances on the cars who congratulated us very extensively, and who could not be brought to realize that they must call me Mrs Chopin and not Miss Katy. They joined us however in consuming a few champagne bottles that had escaped the dire destruction of their companions to meet with a more honorable consummation by the bride and groom. [. . .]

> The diary records the couple's journey through Cincinnati and on to Philadelphia, where they arrived on the 12th. The second city made a less than favourable first impression upon Chopin, who described it as 'gloomy', 'puritanical', and 'miserable'.

13th   The city looked a little less gloomy to day, the stores being all opened and a great many people on the streets. We saw a few pretty girls on Chesnut. St whose chief beauty consisted in the lovely complexions. We were not sorry to take the 6 P.M. train for New York – the ride in the cars was long, but extremely agreeable, and besides we had the honor and pleasure of making the acquaintance of Miss Clafflin, the notorious 'female broker' of New York – a fussy, pretty, talkative little woman, who discussed business extensively with Oscar, and entreated me not to fall into the useless degrading life of most married ladies – but to elevate my mind and turn my attention to politics, commerce; questions of state, &c. &c. I assured her I would do so – which assurance satisfied her quite. – Reached the city at midnight. [. . .]

The Chopins spent two weeks in New York, after which they set sail for the German town of Bremen, from where they travelled on to Cologne and later to Bonn. Chopin records convivial meetings with fellow travelling Americans and the various attractions offered by the very different European cultures she experienced on the journey.

Dear me! I feel like smoking a cigarette – think I will satisfy my desire and open that sweet little box which I bought in Bremen. Oscar has gone to some Halle to witness these Germans' interpretation of a galop – a waltz & c. Tomorrow we take the boat far up the Rhine – perhaps B. will accompany us. I must not forget to note that we travelled on the same train this afternoon with the queen of Prussia, who was going to attend a concert in Rollensburg. I am enchanted with Bonn [. . .]

14   'The Rhine! the Rhine! A blessing on the Rhine' so says Long fellow & so say I. It seems like an exquisite panorama – as I close my eyes, and pass again in fancy Drockenfeld, Godes berg, and the Rolans's ecke. Shall I ever forget the beauties of the beautiful Rhine? The gray & stately ruins, – the churchs peeping out of the dense foliage, & those vineyards upon vineyards sloping to the waters edge.

Wiesbaden.

15th   We left Mayence this afternoon & arrived in Wies baden. What an unpleasant souvenir I retain of Mayence. Let it dwell only in my memory – and I trust even there, not too long. We stroled into the Cursaal to night and watched intently the gambling. It is all as I had pictured – the sang froid of the croupier – the eager, greedy, and in some instances fiendish look upon the faces of the players. I was tempted to put down a silver piece myself – but had not the courage. [. . .]

On 17 June Chopin notes having heard news of the declaration of war between France and Prussia. The honeymoon continues, however, the couple visiting Frankfurt, Heidelberg and Stuttgart before crossing the border into Switzerland and reaching Zurich on 11 August.

I have yet seen no more bautiful situation than that possessed by Zurich. The white houses gleaming on the hills – the mountains surrounding the landscape like a frame work – and more than all – the clear green waters like a mirror reflecting back the hills – the trees that surround it. We went in the evening to the Ton Halle to hear some music, which was only tolerable.

12th   Awoke this morning to find a disagreeable rain falling, which had stopped however when we finished our 10 o'clock breakfast. The sun came out brilliantly and we ventured on a row on the lake. I find myself handling the oars quite like an expert. Oscar took a nap in the afternoon and I took a walk alone. How very far I did go. Visited a panorama which showed the Rigi Kulm in all its grandeur – the only audience being myself and two soldiers. I wonder what people thought of me – a young women stroling about alone. I even took a glass of beer at a friendly little beer garden quite on the edge of the lake; and amused myself for some time feeding the importunate little fish who came up to the surface as tame as chickens to receive their crumbs. [. . .]

> The diary record of the continuing journey through Switzerland with short stays in Berne and Geneva is punctuated with news of the Franco Prussian war[1]. The Chopins travelled to France and made their way to Paris.

Paris

Sunday Sep 4th 1870

What an eventful day for France – may I not say for the world? And that I should be here in the midst of it. This morning my husband and myself rose at about eleven, and after taking our coffee, started of in the direction of the Madelein for mass.

Very sad and very important news had reached Paris during the previous night, from the seat of war. The Emperor was prisoner in the hands of the Prussians – McMahon either wounded or dead, and forty thousand armed men had surrendered! What did it mean? The people on the streets looked sad and pre-occupied. It was now nearly one, & we entered church where mass had not yet commenced. It was also the hour when the Corps Legislativef was going to meet to decide on an important affair of state, and already there were determined looking people marching towards the Chambre. The short mass was soon over. We hastened out and stationed ourselves on the Church steps, from which pos-ition we commanded a splendid view of the entire length of the street up to the Chamber of the Corps Législatif. There were thousands of people forming one great human mass. In the Chamber was an all important question being decided,

---

1   The 1870–1 conflict between France and Prussia which signalled the rise of German military power and imperialism.

and, without, was an impatient populace ~~learning~~ waiting to learn the result. Scarcely an hour passed, when down they came, when down they came, the whole great body, and at once it seemed to pass like an electric flash from one end of Paris to the other – the cry 'Vive la Republic'

I have seen a French Revolution! And astonishing – no drop of blood has been shed – unless I take into account the blood that has paid sad tribute to the Prussian. The Gens' D'Armes have been dispersed, and the Garde National has taken under its care the public buildings and places of the city. Oscar has gone to night on the Boulevards, where men women and children are shouting the Marseilles with an abandon and recklessness purely <u>french</u>. Now, whilst I write, comes to me that strain from the martial air 'Aux Armes, Citoyens! Formons nos Batallions!'

If now they will form their batallions against the Prussian & cease their cry of 'A bas l'Empereur.'

All day they have been tearing down and casting in the dust the Imperial eagles that have spread their wings so proudly over Paris. It cannot but make one sad. We have seen the rude populace running & strutting through the private grounds of the Tuilleries: places that 24 hours ago were looked upon as almost sacred ground. What a nation.

Our stay in Paris was short and of course offered none of those attractions – fascinations – usually held out to visitors. We left on the 10th sep and proceeded to Brest, from which point we took the steamer 'Ville de Paris' for New York, where we arrived after a very stormy & threatening passage; nor did we tarry on our way to St. Louis – where once again I have embraced those dear ones left behind.

2

Interpretations

2

Interpretations

Critical History

Several contemporary reviews, one by the important novelist, Willa Cather, give a flavour of the critical reception afforded to Kate Chopin's *The Awakening* on its publication in 1899. Her art – structure, style, language, imagery – as well as her proficiency as a writer of local colour receives applause, but her subject is condemned. There is a uniformity of tone and substance in contemporary reactions to Chopin's novel; as one reviewer puts it, 'It is sad and mad and bad, but it is all consummate art' (p. 57). So, because the novel was regarded as controversial and shocking on publication, it did not receive very wide distribution or dissemination. However, as Emily Toth, Chopin's most recent biographer, has proved, the novel was not, despite popular mythology, banned, nor was it withdrawn from circulation (Toth, pp. 422–5). Nevertheless, its boldness of subject and design earned it few supporters, the absence of an arbitrating, moralising voice within the narrative compounding, for many readers, the depravity of the plot. There is, therefore, a relative absence of critical attention paid to Chopin's work in the first fifty years of the twentieth century, although there are exceptions to this rule.

Chopin's first biographer, Father Daniel S. Rankin, published his *Kate Chopin and her Creole Stories* in 1932; in this study he paid scant attention to the novel, concentrating instead on her work as a regionalist in her short stories. An important readership for Chopin's work outside the United States, however, was established in 1953 when Cyrille Arnavon translated *The Awakening* into French; this was published together with an appreciation of the writer. Chopin found a sympathetic audience in France as her own work is discernibly influenced by French writers, and most particularly, in the case of her short stories, by Guy de Maupassant. *The Awakening* itself is often compared to *Madame Bovary* by Gustave Flaubert and, indeed, is often called the 'American Bovary'. This was a comparison made from the very beginning and Willa Cather, in her review of the novel, uses the relationship between the texts to demonstrate that Chopin was both morally and artistically wrong to choose what Cather calls 'so trite and sordid a theme' and that she is but a pale imitation of Flaubert. The contemporary theorist, Stephen Heath, however, writing in 1994, sees Chopin as producing a much more sophisticated rendition of *Madame Bovary* in *The Awakening*; the contrast between their analyses of the text provides the most straightforward illustration of the shift in critical approaches to the novel between the nineteenth and late twentieth centuries.

Between 1950 and 1970 a number of influential critics, including Edmund Wilson, Warner Berthoff, Larzer Ziff and Chopin's second biographer and the editor of *The Complete Works of Kate Chopin* (1969), Per Seyersted, contributed significantly to the renaissance of Chopin's work. She began to be included much more widely in surveys of writing from the American South or from the post-Civil War period; the outstanding examples are Wilson's *Patriotic Gore* (1962), Berthoff's *The Ferment of Realism. American Literature, 1884–1919* (1965), and Ziff's *The American 1890s: Life and Times of a Lost Generation* (1966).

The real explosion of critical interest in Chopin's writing, however, came with the serious retrieval of her work and reputation by feminist critics; no one was more influential in this process than Helen Taylor; an extract from her most recent essay on Chopin is included here (**pp. 78–82**). Taylor edited a volume of Chopin's short stories, *Portraits*, in 1979, bringing her work to a British audience for the first time; she also published an extended study of Chopin, *Gender, Race and Region in the Writings of Grace King, Ruth McEnery Stuart, and Kate Chopin*, in 1989. In the United States, the outstanding figure is Cynthia Griffin Wolff, whose essay, 'Thanatos and Eros: Kate Chopin's *The Awakening*' (1973) led the reappraisal of Chopin's work as worthy of the most theoretically sophisticated critical approaches; again extracts from one of her more recent articles are re-published here (see **pp. 73–7**). The critics who have devoted sophisticated and groundbreaking attention to Chopin read like a Who's Who of the most important figures in feminist criticism; to name but few in addition to Taylor and Wolff: Elaine Showalter, the author of *A Literature of Their Own* (1977), Sandra Gilbert and Susan Gubar, joint authors of *The Madwoman in the Attic* (1979), and Ellen Moers, author of *Literary Women* (1977) all recognise and return with fresh insights to Chopin's novel in their work. Their serious consideration of her fiction has led to the inclusion of Chopin amongst the pantheon of the most important American women writers of the nineteenth century. Emily Toth's biography, *Kate Chopin*, published in 1990, has completed the restoration of Chopin to the centre of American letters, and provides the fullest account of Chopin's work and life to date. Toth details Chopin's travels, her houses, her children, her marriage, her possible lovers as well as a critique of her writings and her relationships with her publishers. An extremely useful publication history of Chopin's short stories is included as one of Toth's appendices.

In recent years, interpretations of Chopin's work have encompassed a range of critical approaches, some of the most important of which are represented in this volume. Elizabeth Fox-Genovese and Nancy Walker are amongst those who contextualise Chopin's writing within the American South. Both these critics feature in a collection, *Approaches to Teaching Chopin's The Awakening* (1988), which focuses on the many ways in which the novel is used in the classroom as it has achieved immense popularity in schools, colleges, universities and extra-mural settings. Wendy Martin's *New Essays on The Awakening* (1988), is an important collection, with Martin's introduction and Showalter's 'Tradition and the Individual Talent: *The Awakening* as a Solitary Book' being especially noteworthy.

Lynda S. Boren and Sara deSaussure Davis are the editors of *Kate Chopin Reconsidered: Beyond the Bayou* (1992), which features biographical as well as critical approaches to Chopin's work by such scholars as Heather Kirk Thomas, whose essay provides a useful supplement to Toth's biographical work, Katherine Joslin, who compares the novel to Willa Cather's 1925 novel, *The Professor's House*, Barbara C. Ewell, who discusses the novel in the context of American philosophical ideas of individualism, and Nancy Ellis, who looks at other 'awakenings' which take place in Chopin's short fiction. Bert Bender is the leading exponent of an approach which considers Chopin as a naturalist writer; he has written essays on Chopin and an extended study, *The Descent of Love: Darwin and the Theory of Sexual Selection in American Fiction* (1996), which argues for the broadening of the catchment of American literary Darwinism, extending the group of writers most usually described as naturalists to include the work of Kate Chopin, amongst others. His central thesis advances the particular influence of Charles Darwin's *The Descent of Man and Selection in Relation to Sex* (1871) on Chopin's work. Since the publication of Elizabeth Ammons' study *Conflicting Stories: American Women Writers at the Turn into the Twentieth Century* (1991) increasing attention has been paid to the fact that, as Ammons says, 'The background of *The Awakening* is filled with nameless, faceless black women carefully categorized as black, mulatto, quadroon, and Griffe' (p. 74). Ammons' work is a clear influence on many critics, including Michelle A. Birnbaum, and parts of her essay, 'Alien Hands: Kate Chopin and the Colonization of Race', are re-published here (**pp. 70–73**).

The selection of essays included in this volume is intended to demonstrate cutting-edge scholarship in Chopin studies by some of the most eminent critics of her work. Taylor and Wolff, as already mentioned, led the revival of Chopin's work in the UK and USA respectively, and they continue to produce original work in the area. All the other critics whose work is included here (see bibliography for publication details) represent important strands of Chopin studies although the field is broader than could possibly be included here.

Nineteenth-Century Responses

Contemporary Reviews

C.L. Deyo, *St Louis Post-Dispatch*, 20 May 1899, reprinted in, Margo Culley ed., *The Awakening*, New York: W.W. Norton & Company, 1994, p. 164

There may be many opinions touching other aspects of Mrs. Chopin's novel 'The Awakening,' but all must concede its flawless art. The delicacy of touch of rare skill in construction, the subtle understanding of motive, the searching vision into the recesses of the heart – these are known to readers of 'Bayou Folk' and 'A Night in Acadie.' But in this new work power appears, power born of confidence. There is no uncertainty in the lines, so surely and firmly drawn. Complete mastery is apparent on every page. Nothing is wanting to make a complete artistic whole. In delicious English, quick with life, never a word too much, simple and pure, the story proceeds with classic severity through a labyrinth of doubt and temptation and dumb despair. It is not a tragedy, for it lacks the high motive of tragedy. The woman, not quite brave enough, declines to a lower plane and does not commit a sin ennobled by love. But it is terribly tragic. Compassion, not pity, is excited, for pity is for those who sin, and Edna Pontellier only offended – weakly, passively, vainly offended.

'The Awakening' is not for the young person; not because the young person would be harmed by reading it, but because the young person wouldn't under-stand it, and everybody knows that the young person's understanding should be scrupulously respected. It is for seasoned souls, for those who have lived, who have ripened under the gracious or ungracious sun of experience and learned that realities do not show themselves on the outside of things where they can be seen and heard, weighed, measured and valued like the sugar of commerce, but treas-ured within the heart, hidden away, never to be known perhaps save when exposed by temptation or called out by occasions of great pith and moment. No, the book is not for the young person, nor, indeed, for the old person who has no relish for unpleasant truths. For such there is much that is very improper in it, not to say positively unseemly. A fact, no matter how essential, which we have all agreed shall not be acknowledged, is as good as no fact at all. And it is disturbing – even indelicate – to mention it as something which, perhaps, does play an important part in the life behind the mask.

It is the life and not the mask that is the subject of the story. One day Edna Pontellier, whose husband has vaguely held her dear as a bit of decorative furniture, a valuable piece of personal property, suddenly becomes aware she is a human being. It was her husband's misfortune that he did not make this interesting discovery himself, but he had his brokerage business to think about and brokers deal in stocks, not hearts. It was Mrs. Pontellier's misfortune that another man revealed her to herself, and when the knowledge came it produced profound dissatisfaction, as often happens when love is born in a cage not of its own building. In the beginning she had no thought of wrong-doing, but resentment was hot and made her sullen. Robert Lebrun, whose heart was ensnared before he realized it, went away to Mexico to make money, which was quite the proper thing to do. It would have been the right thing had he gone before it was too late, for then he might have been only a shadowy dream in Edna's life, instead of a consuming reality. This made the poor woman still more discontented. She took to all sorts of foolish fancies to divert her mind. Her children did not help her, for she was not a mother woman and didn't feel that loving babies was the whole duty of a woman. She loved them, but said that while she was willing to die for them she couldn't give up anything essential for them. This sounded clever because it was paradoxical, but she didn't quite know what it meant. She dabbled with brush and canvas. Mademoiselle Reisz told her that to be an artist one must be courageous, to dare and defy. But, unhappily, Mrs. Pontellier was not courageous. So she was not an artist. Mademoiselle Reisz, who was a witch, and knew Robert and Edna better than they knew themselves, did not add, what was really in her mind, that to be a great sinner a woman must be courageous, for great sinners are those who sin for a pure, howbeit unlawful, motive. Edna was not courageous. So she was not a great sinner, but by and by she became a poor, helpless offender, which is the way of such persons – not good enough for heaven, not wicked enough for hell.

Mrs. Pontellier was prepared by unlawful love for unholy passion. Her husband was extinct so far as she was concerned, and the man she loved was beyond her power. She had no anchor and no harbor was in sight. She was a derelict in a moral ocean, whose chart she had never studied, and one of the pirates who cruise in that sea made her his prize. Robert might have saved her from ignoble temptation by supplying a motive for a robust sin, but he was in Mexico and the thought of him only deepened her discontent. The moment came and with it the man. There is always a man for the moment, sometimes two or three. So thought Mrs. Pontellier, and she grew dull with despair. Passion without love was not to her liking and she feared the future. If she had been a courageous woman she would have put away passion and waited for love, but she was not courageous. She let sensation occupy a vacant life, knowing the while that it only made it emptier and more hopeless.

So because she could not forget her womanhood, and to save the remnants of it, she swam out into the sunkissed gulf and did not come back.

It is sad and mad and bad, but it is all consummate art. The theme is difficult, but it is handled with a cunning craft. The work is more than unusual. It is unique. The integrity of its art is that of well-knit individuality at one with itself, with nothing superfluous to weaken the impression of a perfect whole.

Providence Sunday Journal, 4 June 1899, reprinted in Margo Culley, ed., *The Awakening*, New York: W.W. Norton & Company, 1994, p. 166

Miss Kate Chopin is another clever woman, but she has put her cleverness to a very bad use in writing 'The Awakening.' The purport of the story can hardly be described in language fit for publication. We are fain to believe that Miss Chopin did not herself realize what she was doing when she wrote it. With a bald realism that fairly out Zolas Zola,[1] she describes the result upon a married woman who lives amiably with her husband without caring for him, of a slowly growing admiration for another man. He is too honorable to speak and goes away; but her life is spoiled already, and she falls with a merely animal instinct into the arms of the first man she meets. The worst of such stories is that they will fall into the hands of youth, leading them to dwell on things that only matured persons can understand, and promoting unholy imaginations and unclean desires. It is nauseating to remember that those who object to the bluntness of our older writers will excuse and justify the gilded dirt of these latter days.

Chicago Times-Herald, 1 June 1899, reprinted in Margo Culley, ed., *The Awakening*, New York: W.W. Norton & Company, 1994, p. 166

Kate Chopin, author of those delightful sketches, 'A Night in Acadie,' has made a new departure in her long story, 'The Awakening.' The many admirers whom she has won through her earlier work will be surprised – perhaps disagreeably – by this latest venture. That the book is strong and that Miss Chopin has a keen knowledge of certain phases of feminine character will not be denied. But it was not necessary for a writer of so great refinement and poetic grace to enter the overworked field of sex fiction.

The Outlook, 3 June 1899, reprinted in Margo Culley, ed., *The Awakening*, New York: W.W. Norton & Company, 1994, p. 166

The Awakening is a decidedly unpleasant study of a temperament. The author, Kate Chopin, is known as the writer of several faithful stories of Louisiana life. This, too, is faithful enough in its presentation of certain phases of human passion and downward drift of character, but the story was not really worth telling, and its disagreeable glimpses of sensuality are repellent.

---

1   Emile Zola (1840–1902), French author of realistic novels.

St Louis Daily Globe-Democrat, 13 May 1899, reprinted in Margo Culley, ed., *The Awakening*, New York: W.W. Norton & Company, 1994, p. 163

[. . .] At the very outset of the story one feels that the heroine should pray for deliverance from temptation, and in the very closing paragraph, when, having removed every vestige of clothes she 'stands naked in the sun' and then walks out into the water until she can walk no farther, and then swims on into eternity, one thinks that her very suicide is in itself a prayer for deliverance from the evils that beset her, all of her own creating.

It is not a healthy book; if it points any particular moral or teaches any lesson, the fact is not apparent. But there is no denying the fact that it deals with existent conditions, and without attempting a solution, handles a problem that obtrudes itself only too frequently in the social life of people with whom the question of food and clothing is not the all absorbing one. Mrs Pontellier does not love her husband. The poison of passion seems to have entered her system, with her mother's milk. [. . .]

Willa Cather (signed 'Sibert'), **Pittsburgh Leader**, 8 July 1899, reprinted in Margo Culley, ed., *The Awakening*, New York: W.W. Norton & Company, 1994, p. 170

A Creole *Bovary* is this little novel of Miss Chopin's. Not that the heroine is a Creole exactly, or that Miss Chopin is a Flaubert – save the mark! – but the theme is similar to that which occupied Flaubert. There was, indeed, no need that a second *Madame Bovary* should be written, but an author's choice of themes is frequently as inexplicable as his choice of a wife. It is governed by some innate temperamental bias that cannot be diagrammed. This is particularly so in women who write, and I shall not attempt to say why Miss Chopin has devoted so exquisite and sensitive, well-governed a style to so trite and sordid a theme. She writes much better than it is ever given to most people to write, and hers is a genuinely literary style; of no great elegance or solidity; but light, flexible, subtle, and capable of producing telling effects directly and simply. The story she has to tell in the present instance is new neither in matter nor treatment. Edna Pontellier, a Kentucky girl, who, like Emma Bovary, had been in love with innumerable dream heroes before she was out of short skirts, married Léonce Pontellier as a sort of reaction from a vague and visionary passion for a tragedian whose unresponsive picture she used to kiss. She acquired the habit of liking her husband in time, and even of liking her children. Though we are not justified in presuming that she ever threw articles from her dressing table at them, as the charming Emma had a winsome habit of doing. We are told that 'she would sometimes gather them passionately to her heart; she would sometimes forget them.'

At a Creole watering place, which is admirably and deftly sketched by Miss Chopin, Edna met Robert Lebrun, son of the landlady, who dreamed of a fortune awaiting him in Mexico while he occupied a petty clerical position in New Orleans. Robert made it his business to be agreeable to his mother's boarders, and Edna, not being a Creole, much against his wish and will, took him seriously. . . .

The lover of course disappointed her, was a coward and ran away from his responsibilities before they began. He was afraid to begin a chapter with so serious and limited a woman. She remembered the sea where she had first met Robert. Perhaps from the same motive which threw Anna Karenina under the engine wheels, she threw herself into the sea, swam until she was tired and then let go. . . .

Edna Pontellier and Emma Bovary are studies in the same feminine type; one a finished and complete portrayal, the other a hasty sketch, but the theme is essentially the same. Both women belong to a class, not large, but forever clamoring in our ears, that demands more romance out of life than God put into it. Mr. G. Bernard Shaw would say that they are the victims of the over-idealization of love. They are the spoil of the poets, the Iphigenias of sentiment. The unfortunate feature of their disease is that it attacks only women of brains, at least of rudimentary brains, but whose development is one-sided; women of strong and fine intuitions, but without the faculty of observation, comparison, reasoning about things. Probably, for emotional people, the most convenient thing about being able to think is that it occasionally gives them a rest from feeling. Now with women of the Bovary type, this relaxation and recreation is impossible. They are not critics of life, but, in the most personal sense, partakers of life. They receive impressions through the fancy. With them everything begins with fancy, and passions rise in the brain rather than in the blood, the poor, neglected, limited one-sided brain that might do so much better things than badgering itself into frantic endeavors to love. For these are the people who pay with their blood for the fine ideals of the poets, as Marie Delclasse paid for Dumas' great creation, Marguerite Gauthier. These people really expect the passion of love to fill and gratify every need of life, whereas nature only intended that it should meet one of many demands. They insist upon making it stand for all the emotional pleasures of life and art; expecting an individual and self-limited passion to yield infinite variety, pleasure, and distraction, to contribute to their lives what the arts and the pleasurable exercise of the intellect gives to less limited and less intense idealists. So this passion, when set up against Shakespeare, Balzac, Wagner, Raphael, fails them. They have staked everything on one hand, and they lose. They have driven the blood until it will drive no further, they have played their nerves up to the point where any relaxation short of absolute annihilation is impossible. Every idealist abuses his nerves, and every sentimentalist brutally abuses them. And in the end, the nerves get even. Nobody ever cheats them, really. Then 'the awakening' comes. Sometimes it comes in the form of arsenic, as it came to Emma Bovary, sometimes it is carbolic acid taken covertly in the police station, a goal to which unbalanced idealism not infrequently leads. Edna Pontellier, fanciful and romantic to the last, chose the sea on a summer night and went down with the sound of her first lover's spurs in her ears, and the scent of pinks about her. And next time I hope that Miss Chopin will devote that flexible iridescent style of hers to a better cause.

Modern Criticism

Elizabeth Fox-Genovese, '*The Awakening* in the Context of Experience, Culture and Values of Southern Women', *Approaches to Teaching Chopin's The Awakening,* Bernard Koloski, ed., New York: The Modern Language Association of America, 1988, pp. 34–9

Fox-Genovese frames *The Awakening* in its historical, geographical and cultural context in order to address what she identifies as the 'disjuncture' between Chopin's intentions in writing and modern feminist readings of the text. Identifying nineteenth-century women's movements as a primarily northern endeavour she reiterates Chopin's lack of interest in any such organised activity or social reform agenda, and points instead to the author's focus on the individual woman. Whilst noting that 'Chopin's explicit discussion of women's sexuality' placed her in direct conflict with the social mores of the day, Fox-Genovese draws a distinction between Edna's assertion of self as a 'private and psychological matter' and the wider public and social considerations, including women's rights, that Chopin's text does not engage. Situating Chopin firmly within a southern context, this article argues for the impossibility of such a separation in northern culture where, for a woman to 'revolt against her sexual suppression was to call into question her gender role'. According to Fox-Genovese, 'there is reason to believe that Chopin intended her explorations of women's sexual self-awareness to pose less of a threat to the social order of her world than explorations of their social independence would have'.

[. . .] *The Awakening* shocked Chopin's contemporaries for the same reason that it has earned the admiration of recent generations: it candidly acknowledges women's sexual impulses. Modern readers [. . .] tend to view Edna's awakening to her sexuality as logically portending her struggle for liberation. Yet Chopin remains more ambiguous, thus inviting multiple, even contradictory, readings [. . .]

It would be difficult to argue that Chopin intended *The Awakening* to be primarily a polemic against marriage as a social institution, or even primarily a polemic against the social limitations on women's relations as individuals to others. Yet Chopin does hint that late-nineteenth-century marriages cast women as the objects of others rather than as the free subjects of their own fates. Thus she introduces Edna through her husband's gaze and, in a frequently cited line, allows that he regarded her as a 'valuable piece of personal property which has suffered some damage'. This view of marriage permits us to link *The Awakening* to the growing public complaints of some American women against the subordination of women to men within marriage. Yet Chopin, unlike an Elizabeth Cady Stanton or a Charlotte Perkins Gilman, does not let the question rest there. Having allowed for the social dimension, she rapidly reveals the multiple possibilities for happiness and shared understanding between husbands and wives, including Edna and Léonce. [. . .]

[. . .] the ways in which marriage imprisoned women and stunted their development more closely resembled the concerns of northern than of southern women. The differences are subtle, but worth attention. The driving force of the women's movement, narrowly understood as the movement to improve women's social position or rights, came out of the Northeast and its offshoots, the Old Northwest and the Western Reserve, where the movement had been closely and explicitly tied to the antislavery movement. [. . .]

By the period of the Gilded Age, during which Chopin wrote, some southern women of her class were becoming committed to various kinds of social reform, including that of their own social and political status [. . .] Chopin appears to have avoided taking a stand on the relations between what she called women's 'independence' and women's social and political rights, much less on the relations between women's independence and race and class relations in general. That silence provides an important caution against any simple social interpretation of *The Awakening*. Does Chopin, in other words, give any indication that she intends her novel as an intervention in the narrow institutional discussion of women's rights? [. . .] it is difficult to find any systematic rebellion against women's prescribed role in the writings of the first postbellum[1] generations of women writers. Not that those writings lack their share of strong, resourceful, and even, to use Chopin's word, independent women. They simply lack women who challenge the social order in the name of women's individual rights.

[. . .] I have found it useful [. . .] to distinguish between gender and sexuality in assessing Chopin's notion of female independence. The distinction inevitably remains messy, but withal heuristically helpful. For gender can be presented as the social construction of sexuality, and sexuality itself as a dimension of women's private, biologically rooted identity. Gender roles, in this context, consist in what we might call society's views or expectations of women: daughter, wife, mother, nurturer, lady. Gender roles remain deeply hostage to considerations of class and race. Sexuality, in contrast, refers to women's nature or essence, to what women share across class and racial lines, to the eternal woman.

---

1   Relating to the period after the American Civil War.

Complications in the application of this distinction arise because different cultures treat the relations between gender and sexuality differently. With respect to the examples at hand, northern middle-class culture tended to present gender and sexuality as isomorphic. For a northern woman to revolt against her sexual suppression was to call into question her gender role. For a northern woman to challenge the constraints on her gender was, in her community's view if not always in her own, implicitly to assert her sexuality. The egalitarian ideals of northern democracy – republicanism to be precise – imposed the association of gender and sexuality. The private feelings and behavior of middle-class women had implications for the behavior of all women, who, at least in ideology, were assumed to resemble them in both gender and sexual attributes.

[. . .] Chopin did not participate in the heated discussions about women's rights, which she surely viewed as yet another side of the social question. But aspects of her work strongly suggest that she sought, as it were, to write around or above the issue. Neither *The Awakening* nor any of her other writings suggest that she secretly espoused woman suffrage or related causes. To the contrary, everything that she wrote, including *The Awakening*, indicates that she viewed women's independence as a personal more than a social matter [. . .] the constant, underlying current in her writings makes it clear that she took no inconsiderable pride in having attained a sophisticated and independent maturity on her own, within the limitations that her society imposed. In *The Awakening*, she carefully delineates both the possibility for women's happiness within marriage (Mme Ratignolle) and the possibility for their independence from it (Mlle Reisz).

[. . .]

In *The Awakening*, Kate Chopin self-consciously sought to move beyond the specific southern identification of her local-color stories. She surely did not intend her novel as a specific reflection of the values of southern women, parochially defined. Yet today, the novel gains resonance if read [. . .] in historical context. As a novelist, Chopin navigated between specificity of detail and universality of theme. It is difficult not to wonder if she fully understood how firmly that strategy linked her to the emerging modern tradition of southern letters. No social or domestic novelist, she wrote of the female human condition as a full member of that distinctive culture which would also inform the work of William Alexander Percy and William Faulkner.

Nancy Walker, 'The Historical and Cultural Setting', *Approaches to Teaching Chopin's The Awakening*, Bernard Koloski, ed., New York: Modern Language Association of America, 1988, pp. 67–72

Walker's essay offers a consideration of the historical and cultural background against which *The Awakening* is set, focusing on the particularity of the late nineteenth-century world of New Orleans. She argues that the sophistication of this southern metropolis, with its European influences and, 'colorful mixture of cultures', and the 'warm, easygoing' Creole culture, is set in direct opposition with Edna Pontellier's stern Kentuckian Presbyterian background to provide the central tension in the novel. Walker explores the significant religious, political and social differences between the worlds of the American and the Creole, and examines Edna's dilemma in finding herself caught between the two. She is keen to stress that the text is 'far from autobiographical', identifying the sophisticated, worldly and well travelled Chopin as very much a part of the Creole culture with which her inexperienced heroine 'feels at odds and yet to which she is strongly attracted'.

[. . .] In keeping with this atmosphere of social freedom, women in Creole culture, as is evident in *The Awakening*, were far less affected by the Victorian strictures that dictated the behavior of middle-class women in other parts of the country [. . .] Creole women participated fully in the sensuous atmosphere that surrounded them: drinking wine, enjoying music and literature, wearing bright colors, and entertaining lavishly. Well-educated, especially in the arts, these women were acquainted with literary trends, and many were accomplished musicians and painters. Although Creole culture was patriarchal in the extreme, women enjoyed life in ways that those subjected to Edna's father's 'gloom' could not.

[. . .] Early in the novel, Chopin makes clear Edna's distance from the mores of the Creoles summering at Grand Isle: 'Mrs. Pontellier, though she had married a Creole, was not thoroughly at home in the society of Creoles; never before had she been thrown so intimately among them. . . . A characteristic which distinguished [the Creoles] and which impressed Mrs. Pontellier most forcibly was their entire absence of prudery' (Ch. 4). Edna is shocked by Mme Ratignolle's detailed recounting of her childbirth experiences, and she reads 'in secret and solitude' an unnamed novel that the others read and discuss openly (Ch. 4). The gossipy, confidence-sharing ways of the Creoles does not merge easily with Edna's Presbyterian reserve – 'Mrs. Pontellier was not a woman given to confidences' – yet she is seduced by the easy relations of this culture: 'That summer at Grand Isle she began to loosen a little the mantle of reserve that had always enveloped her' (Ch. 7). Significantly, Chopin places the Pontelliers' New Orleans residence not in the Garden District, the 'American' part of the city, but on Esplanade Street (actually, Avenue), at the edge of the French Quarter [. . .] Edna is thus immersed physically in the Creole world, both on Grand Isle and in New Orleans.

Edna's early desire to escape the grimness of her Kentucky home has led to her marriage to Léonce. Beneath her reserve lies a strain of romanticism and rebelliousness that early in her life manifested itself in imagined attachments to a series of unavailable men: the 'dignified and sad-eyed cavalry officer,' the young man in Mississippi who was engaged to someone else, and finally the 'great tragedian' whose picture she kept on her desk. Chopin makes it clear that Edna's marriage is not the result of any such grand passion: 'Her marriage to Léonce Pontellier was purely an accident' (Ch. 7). One of her motives for marrying him, in fact, is her desire to flout the wishes of her father, who violently opposes her marrying a Catholic.

[. . .] Caught between the Puritanical sternness of her father's world and the relaxed familiarity of Creole culture, Edna can belong fully to neither. Mme Ratignolle recognizes Edna's position as an outsider early in the novel when she exhorts Robert Lebrun to stop flirting with her: 'She is not one of us; she is not like us. She might make the unfortunate blunder of taking you seriously' (Ch. 8) [. . .]

Readers of *The Awakening* have tended, correctly, to see Edna as a 'misfit' in several ways. She is not a 'mother-woman' like Mme Ratignolle, nor is she a self-fulfilled artist like Mlle Reisz. She tries to be an artist – with Mlle Reisz's encouragement – but tragically, considering the milieu, fails for lack of sufficient talent and commitment. She feels unconnected to her marriage and wants independence, but divorce is not an option and she does not have the means to be financially independent. In these respects she is a woman who does not belong to her time, but it is equally important to realize that she does not belong to her place.

From **Emily Toth, *Kate Chopin: A Life of the Author of The Awakening*,** London: Random Century, 1990

Three biographies of Kate Chopin have been written: Daniel Rankin's *Kate Chopin and her Creole Stories*, published in 1932, *Kate Chopin: A Critical Biography* by Per Seyersted in 1969, and more recently Emily Toth's account of the author's life from which the following extracts are taken. The particular selections included here are drawn from the first chapter of the text entitled 'A Curious Child' and are provided to give a flavour of the early life of Kate Chopin in St Louis, Missouri. Chapter One of the biography examines her familial relationships, significant events in her young life, such as the death of her father, and the cultural and social influences which may have contributed to the attitudes of the mature writer.

Katie O'Flaherty was a lively, inquisitive child – and something of a brat. Although her first portrait reveals the round, chubby, dimpled darling favored by baby lovers everywhere, she quickly developed a pugnacious streak. A photograph taken in 1855, when she was five, shows her wearing a mismatched vest and checkered dress, and sporting disordered ringlets in a wild variety of lengths. Despite her rigid pose – neck clamps were used for fidgety subjects – Katie O'Flaherty has rebellion in her eye. By that time, Kate was no longer the baby of the family. One little sister, Marie Therese, had already died in infancy, as countless children did in St. Louis's unhealthy and dangerous climate: In 1849, over eight thousand St. Louisans, a third of them children, had died in a devastating cholera epidemic. It was not until two years later, a year after Kate O'Flaherty was born, that city authorities finally drained Chouteau's Pond, a stagnant sewer stuffed with butchers' offal and factory waste, only ten blocks from the O'Flahertys' home.

[. . .] Almost every spring the Mississippi threatened to flood both sides of the river, and St. Louis was notorious for grime: The burning of soft coal for winter fuel blackened the city with a pall so dense that citizens used candles at noon – and everyone coughed incessantly. Every summer people sickened and died in the sultry, brick-baking heat.

Infants who survived their second summer were said to be safe – but by the fall of 1855, Katie O'Flaherty had another baby sister, Jane, who would be too fragile to survive. The crowded O'Flaherty household also included Kate and Jane's seven-year-old brother, Tom; their parents; their grandmother, Athénaïs Charleville Faris; five very young aunts and uncles; Ed. O'Flaherty, a surveyor; and slaves – four in 1855 and six in 1860, ranging in age from six months to sixty-four years. There was also George, Kate's winsome fifteen-year-old half-brother from Thomas's first marriage [. . .]

Katie O'Flaherty's father left the house very early every day: She had spied on the huge black horses, the colorfully clad black footman, and the black and gold family carriage that came each morning to take Thomas O'Flaherty away. She was intrigued. 'Where do you go?' Kate finally asked her father – and one day, over her mother's and grandmother's mild protests, he took her with him.

First they went to mass, at the old cathedral: Her father went to church every morning. Kate was somewhat disappointed – and (according to her son Felix) in later life she could never tell why. The weekday mass did lack the splendor of high mass on Sunday, with very few people, lights, or decorations, and even the holy pictures were hard to see [. . .]

Then her father took her to the levee, a mile-long scene of excitement, with steamboats belching smoke and mule-driven drays, wagons, and carriages racing by, as men jostled and cursed at each other. The steamboats with their gaudy gingerbread trim resembled huge white animals, looming over hogsheads of sugar, bags of coffee, bales of cotton, and barrels from all over the world. Part of the wharf was paved with lumpy bricks, but the rest was steaming black mud, a hazard to a child's tiny slippers. Kate smelled the Mississippi River, and the fish, the mud, the hay, the hides, and the stinking 'fur rows' of pelts brought by trappers. She gawked at the Indians in their colorful clothes, and listened to the organ-grinders and bagpipers, and the musical cries of cigar vendors [. . .] Everything fascinated her – although she would have been too young to understand some of the sights: the drunkards, confidence men, and pickpockets, the homeless, begging children, and the young girls who survived by selling their bodies to steamboatmen.

The outing created a special bond between Kate and her father, who encouraged her curiosity. The trip also inspired Kate O'Flaherty with a lifelong interest in the world that respectable young ladies did not see – and she connected being outdoors with freedom from social restraints. Twenty years later, as a young wife in New Orleans, she described riverfront scenes in her diary, including a cotton 'pickery'; more than forty years later, she wrote The Awakening about a woman who swims out 'where no woman had swum before.' [. . .]

Bert Bender, 'The Teeth of Desire: *The Awakening* **and** *The Descent of Man'*, *American Literature*, Vol. 63, No. 3, September 1991, pp. 459–73

Bender's essay treats *The Awakening* as an example of literary naturalism, a term which, in itself, provokes much critical debate, but which has been broadly defined as the literary representation of human beings governed by their instincts and passions, of characters conditioned and controlled by environment, heredity, instinct, or chance. In this context, Bender examines the influence of Charles Darwin's *The Descent of Man and Selection in Relation to Sex* (1871) on Chopin's writing in general and on *The Awakening* in particular. Darwin's theory of sexual selection, which aligns natural human impulses with those found in the animal kingdom, presents the male of the species as the active agent in competition for available females. In order to be successful, he claims, they are endowed with great passions. The female, by comparison, is defined as passive, devoid of sexual appetites, whose role is to attract the male whilst simultaneously curbing his enthusiasm through her modesty and maternal instinct. In this way, according to Darwinian theory, the number of offspring is moderated and the health and success of the species is ensured. Chopin, Bender argues, was initially attracted to Darwinism by its offer of a 'profoundly liberating sense of animal innocence in the realm of human courtship', but, he notes, 'she quarrelled with his analysis of the female's role in sexual selection'. In her fictions, the article claims, Kate Chopin creates a series of women for whom sexual desire and the freedom actively to select a mate are similarly 'natural' and powerful instincts. Bender argues that many of Chopin's courtship plots are 'studies in natural history according to the logic of sexual selection'. He identifies elements of Darwinian theories in her work and traces her developing engagement and dispute with the hypothesis – particularly with the limitations which Darwin's 'Victorian sensibility' placed upon women – which culminated in her daring creation of Edna Pontellier – the mother who expresses sexual desire.

[. . .]

Many of [Chopin's] stories dramatize the 'law of battle' that dictates 'a struggle between the males for the possession of the female,' but she also resisted its corollaries concerning the female's passive and modest role in sexual relations and the male's physical and mental superiority to the female. Chopin's women often manage in various ways to deny Darwin's definitions of the female's inferiority. And Chopin was particularly interested in Darwin's interpretation of the evolutionary development among 'savage' human beings, whereby the male had 'gained the power of selection' by having kept the female in an 'abject state of bondage.' Although Darwin wrote that 'the civilized nations' were vastly improved in this regard (women now having 'free or almost free choice'), Chopin still felt the bind. And – increasingly throughout the middle and late nineties – her women characters not only reclaim the power to select, but select for their own reasons. Eventually, especially in the case of Edna Pontellier in *The Awakening*, Chopin's women select on the basis of their own sexual desires rather than for the reasons Darwin attributed to civilized women, who 'are largely influenced by the social position and wealth of the men'.

Chopin's ambivalence toward the idea of sexual selection is apparent in [. . .] stories she wrote in 1894, five years after she had completed *At Fault* and four years before she began *The Awakening*. [. . .] Mrs. Baroda (in 'A Respectable Woman') recognizes the sexual desire she feels for her husband's visiting friend and is at first repulsed by these feelings. She is a 'respectable woman.' But Mrs. Baroda will soon become one of the most daring women in American fiction during these years. For when she asks her husband to invite their friend for another visit, declaring that 'I have overcome everything!' and promising that 'this time I shall be very nice to him,' it is clear that she is now determined to select the lover she desires. In creating this woman who not only threatens the institution of marriage but whose motive in sexual selection (her desire) is independent of the drive to propagate the species, Chopin modified Darwin's theory of sexual selection in a way that would have offended his Victorian sensibility. But Chopin did not at this stage in her development dare to depict a mother's desire (as she would in Edna Pontellier).

[. . .]

As a meditation on the Darwinian reality of Edna's life, *The Awakening* begins and ends with the essential fact of motherhood. Edna is of course a mother, but she cannot be like the 'mother-women' she sees at Grand Isle, whose 'wings as ministering angels' identify them as 'the bygone heroine[s] of romance' (Ch. 4). By the end of the novel Dr. Mandelet will refer to this 'illusion' of angelic love as 'Nature[']s . . . decoy to secure mothers for the race,' but this cannot console Edna (Ch. 38). Attending the birth of her friend's child, she had seen this 'little new life' as merely another in the grotesque 'multitude of souls that come and go'; thus she revolts 'against the ways of nature' and finally sees her own children as antagonists (Ch. 37 and 39).

[. . .] Chopin's first pointed reference to the role of sexual selection in Edna's life occurs in Chapter 9. She has already responded to 'the seductive odor of the sea,' but now she will know the 'wonderful power' of music as Darwin described it in both *The Descent of Man* and *The Expression of Emotions in Man and Animals*. Edna's response to Mademoiselle Reisz's piano performance of a piece by Frédéric Chopin is clearly based on a passage from Darwin, the point of which is that music was originally the means by which our 'half-human ancestors aroused each other's ardent passions'.

[. . .] Chopin indicates [. . .] that Edna's developing desire will eventually lead her into the 'abysses of solitude.' When she enters the water on this night, she gathers 'in an impression of space and solitude' from 'the vast expanse of water'; and in her solitary swim she realizes that she might perish 'out there alone.' Moreover, the simultaneous development of her desire and her sense of solitude will eventually lead her to a clearer understanding of her 'position in the universe' as an animal and therefore as a creature empowered to participate fully in the sexual reality as a self-conscious selector (Ch. 6). Her development toward claiming the power to select is gradual, but she takes a first crucial step immediately after her swim by refusing to yield to Mr. Pontellier's 'desire.' And a few days later she awakens more fully to her animal nature after fleeing from an oppressive church service to Madame Antoine's seaside home. Here, awakened from a nap, 'very hungry,' she 'bit a piece' from a loaf of brown bread, 'tearing it with her strong, white teeth' (Ch. 13).

[. . .]

Chopin will force the awakening Edna to endure the frustrations of civilized life, first by having to contend with Robert's sudden departure and the jealousy she feels when Robert writes only to others; and then when she suffers more consciously from the restrictions in her marriage. She rebels against her husband's and society's covenants, refuses to be one of his 'valued . . . possessions,' and stamps on her wedding ring (Ch. 17). And when she obstinately withdraws her normal 'tacit submissiveness' in her marriage (Ch. 19), she takes another of her crucial steps toward claiming her place in the arena of sexual selection. Before she selects a lover, she rejects her husband's sexual advances, leaving him 'nervously' to explain to Dr. Mandelet that her 'notion . . . concerning the eternal rights of women' means that 'we meet in the morning at the breakfast table' (Ch. 22).

[. . .]

In a discussion with Mademoiselle Reisz about the meaning of love, Edna exhibits a wisdom that Chopin will not grant Mademoiselle Reisz, whose 'avoidance of the water' is not only amusing (some of the bathers imagined that 'it was on account of her false hair') but indicative of her essential sexlessness (Ch. 16). Accusing Mademoiselle Reisz of either lying or having 'never been in love,' Edna proclaims, 'do you suppose a woman knows why she loves? Does she select? Does she say to herself: "Go to! Here is a distinguished statesman with presidential possibilities. I shall proceed to fall in love with him . . . [or with] this financier?" ' She admits that she loves Robert when she 'ought not to,' but Chopin's 'ought' refers more to Darwin's theory about why civilized women select (modestly and discriminately, for wealth, etc.) than to the more obvious social prohibition against extramarital love. Edna loves Robert for the same reason that Whitman's imagined woman let her hand descend 'tremblingly from [the young men's] temples': 'Because his hair is brown and grows away from his temples, because he opens and shuts his eyes,' because she likes his 'nose,' 'two lips,' and 'square chin' – in short, because she is 'happy to be alive' (Ch. 26).

In her next meeting with Arobin, then, Edna's 'nature' responds fully and for the first time to a kiss – 'a flaming torch that kindled [her] desire' (Ch. 27). And she will awaken next morning – in the pivotal twenty-eighth chapter – to her post-Whitmanian sense of the 'significance of life, that monster made up of beauty and brutality.' Comprehending life in this new way – 'as if a mist had been lifted from her eyes' – she feels neither shame nor remorse, only 'regret' that 'it was not the kiss of love which had inflamed her, because it was not love which had held this cup of life to her lips' (Ch. 28).

[. . .] Edna's birthday party is a ritual celebration of her entry into the modern sexual reality [. . .]

Edna is now fully awake to her new reality: 'Today it is Arobin,' she tells herself, and 'tomorrow it will be someone else' (Ch. 39). Her desire (like the passion she had felt at the musical performance that night when she was twenty-eight) will rise and fall, 'lashing' her soul 'as the waves daily beat upon her splendid body' (Ch. 9). She knows that the sense of her absolute isolation as a solitary soul will descend inevitably when she forgets even Robert. She will find no peace until she feels the 'soft, close embrace' of the sea, her true element. And in this despair she sees her children as 'antagonists,' for *they* are nature's cause in natural and sexual selection – the force within herself by which love's wing was broken.

Michelle A. Birnbaum, 'Alien Hands: Kate Chopin and the Colonization of Race', American Literature, Vol. 66, No. 2, June 1994, pp. 301–23

Birnbaum's essay considers the role of the nameless and often silent black, quadroon[1], mulatto[2], and Mexican women in the text. Her discussion addresses not only the way in which their labour facilitates Edna's pursuit of personal fulfilment, but also their function as a means of sexual liberation for the white, middle-class heroine. According to Birnbaum, Chopin makes use of the exotic 'otherness' of these marginalised women, the popular perception of them as overtly sexual beings, to eroticise Edna. In choosing to marginalise herself through her rejection of the expectations of her role, for instance in equating her experience of maternity with a kind of slavery, Birnbaum claims that Edna aligns herself with these 'nameless, speechless, shadowy women'. But, as is also discussed here, 'the appropriation of the 'rhetoric of racial oppression' to facilitate escape from gender convention, in fact serves to 'reinforce rather than raze class and race differences'.

It did not go unnoticed [. . .] by Chopin's contemporaries, who commented frequently on her representation of 'these semi-aliens,' the diverse residents of Louisiana, remarking that her characters are an 'exotic, not quite American species.' For Chopin and her readers, there were more images than Aphrodite – no less mythic and much closer to home – in the historical racial types with which she was quite familiar. In other words, Aphrodite was in Chopin's own backyard, for those of the 'warmer' races had been long considered 'well-vers'd in Venus' school.'

Edna locates in racial and ethnic Others a territory necessary for a liberating alterity: in their difference, she finds herself. The white Catholic Creole society is

1   A person with one quarter black ancestry.
2   A person of mixed race.

the most apparent but not the only influence upon Edna (a Protestant Kentuckian). Although Edna admits that she is initially attracted to the 'excessive physical charm of the Creole' (Ch. 7) and to the caresses of Mme. Ratignolle in particular, Creole women in *The Awakening* are also described as emphatically chaste. Edna calls Mme. Ratignolle a 'faultless Madonna', a 'sensuous Madonna' (Ch. 5), whose 'lofty chastity' is in 'Creole women . . . inborn and unmistakable' (Ch. 4). Instead, Edna first discovers the erotic frontiers of the self by exploiting the less visible constructions of sexual difference associated with the blacks, quadroons, and Acadians in the novel.

[. . .]

In one sense 'alien hands,' anatomized and anonymous, simply render domestic services; nameless, speechless, shadowy women manumit Edna from 'responsibility', and, as critics have noted, to that extent her sexual awakening is a white middle-class luxury. But the relation between sex and labor is not simply a matter of economic privilege in *The Awakening*, for Edna's class bias is not her 'chief obstacle to freedom of expression.' Critics have argued that the hierarchical class relations in the novel limit Chopin's feminist project because they interrupt the circuit of female sympathy for those less privileged; however, it is actually Edna's generalized identification with – rather than her alienation from – the marginalized which both affirms her class position and allows her to critique the sexual constraints associated with it. Equating maternity and slavery, for instance, Edna remarks that her children are her 'soul's slavery' (Ch. 39). [. . .]

By initiating her escape from gender convention through the rhetoric of racial oppression, Edna reinforces rather than razes class and race differences. In fact, class distinctions reflect the structuring of racial difference which enables Edna's sexual expression. There is no suggestion that she sympathizes with the vague dissatisfaction of the nannies on Grand Isle, who appear 'disagreeable and resigned' to their caretaking duties (Ch. 7). Edna neglects not so much her children, as Mr. Pontellier insists, but the quadroon nursemaid who tends them. When Mr. Pontellier rhetorically asks 'if it was not a mother's place to look after children, whose on earth was it?' (Ch. 3), neither Edna nor her husband seem to recognize the answer revealed by their daily practice: the quadroon's. Not just of no account, but not accounted for, the quadroon cares for the toddlers morning to night. It is she who accompanies the children to Iberville when Edna begins her affair with Arobin, and she who takes them for the day when Edna escapes with Robert to *Chênière Caminada*. Edna's agency is measured against – indeed is contingent upon – the necessarily mute quadroon.

[. . .]

It is no accident that the quadroon is anonymous; she is in effect absented or, perhaps more accurately, displaced by Edna. The 'sweet, half-darkness' (Ch. 17) that Edna seeks is made possible by the partially visible life of the quadroon, a life which may be entered only by remaining unexposed and little understood. After all, Edna does not really want to know the experience of the people of color she sees dimly on the street; her new identity emerges only in the twilight of junctures, in the illicit coupling of her life to theirs. Assuming the 'far-away meditative air' (Ch. 1) which earlier in the novel characterizes her nanny, Edna takes on and takes over the quadroon's distance from the bourgeois life Edna is eager to leave behind. As a 'little negro girl' sweeps with 'long absent-minded strokes' (Ch. 12), as 'an old *mulatresse*' sleeps 'her idle hours away' (Ch. 36), so Edna is frequently lost in an 'inward maze of contemplation or thought' (Ch. 2) and feels pulled to 'lose [her soul] in mazes of inward contemplation' (Ch. 6). And indirect proportion to her 'awakening,' she becomes absent-minded – daydreaming in company, acting 'idly, aimlessly,' (Ch. 7) humming 'vacantly'.

Thus it is not only that the quadroon's (and the little black girl's and the *mulatresse*'s) physical labor is taken for granted, but that Edna employs as well their tropological potential, their associations with the marginal and, ultimately, with the erotic. In his useful analysis of the figure of the black servant in the visual arts, Sander L. Gilman points out that one of the image's 'central functions in . . . the eighteenth and nineteenth centuries was to sexualize the society in which he or she is found.'[3] [. . .] Edna's sexuality is brought into relief by the quadroon's literary inheritance of sexual conventions. As Hortense Spillers puts it, the 'mulatto in the text of fiction' silently speaks of unsanctioned sex, allowing the 'dominant culture to say without parting its lips that "we have willed to sin." '[4] The relationship between Edna's willingness to 'sin' and the quadroon's is further reinforced by the narrative's own 'vocabulary of signs,' (Gilman, p. 251) signs which provocatively yoke Edna's and the quadroon's mutual distraction, and, thereby, their potential social and sexual deviance.

[. . .]

The erotics of race not only govern the place but afford the principal basis of Edna's awakening. Although Edna finds the Ratignolles 'very French, very foreign', she also decides that they lead a rather 'colorless existence' (Ch. 18). In contrast to Mme. Ratignolle's 'embodiment of every womanly grace and charm' (Ch. 4), Edna's frank arousal leaves her 'unwomanly' in her lack of 'repression in . . . glance or gesture' (Ch. 23); at best, she admits, she is a 'devilishly wicked specimen of the sex' (Ch. 27). Her 'unwomanly' behavior does not unsex her – quite the opposite, it allies her with the putatively feral and libidinous races. The cult of true womanhood (whose tenets of purity, piety, submissiveness and domesticity, Mme. Ratignolle as a 'mother-woman' to some degree represents) sets race against gender; females of the physical and promiscuous race by definition fall outside the bounds of womanhood – as does Edna. Her sexual awakening is couched in the same terms as those conventionally used to define the woman of color in the 1890s. She becomes 'some beautiful, sleek animal waking up in the sun' (Ch. 23); her lover 'appeal[s] to the animalism that stirred impatiently within her' (Ch. 26). Even her dining habits assume a bestial air as she tears at her bread with 'her strong, white teeth' (Ch. 8). Chopin writes of a similar animal in

3 [Birnbaum's note.] Sander L. Gilman, 'Black Bodies, White Bodies: Toward An Iconography of Female Sexuality in Late Nineteenth-Century Art, Medicine, and Literature', in 'Race', *Writing and Difference*, ed. Henry Louis Gates Jr (Chicago: Univ. of Chicago Press, 1986), 228.

4 [Birnbaum's note.] Hortense J. Spillers, ' "The Tragic Mulatta": Neither/Nor – Toward An Alternative Model,' in *The Difference Within: Feminism and Critical Theory*, ed. Elizabeth Meese and Alice Parker (Philadelphia: J. Benjamins, 1989), 168.

'Emancipation: A Life Fable' (1869), often referred to as a precursor to *The Awakening*. Basking in the sun, a beast with 'strong limbs,' 'handsome flanks,' and 'sleek sides' escapes its caged and well-fed life. Written only four years after the Civil War, the vignette employs antislavery discourse – rejection of the cage's dubious protection – in order to critique the sheltered confines of the bourgeois marriage. Joining woman and beast, Chopin finds deliverance from Victorian convention in felinity. [. . .] Awakening to this new and more colorful identity, even Edna's skin is illumined with 'myriad living tints', in contrast to the alabaster cast of the more conventional Mme. Ratignolle. The tan which her husband complains at the outset of the novel burns Edna almost 'beyond recognition' (Ch. 1) is not only a rebuttal of the 'fair lady' image but a foreshadowing of her awakening into a 'native' sexuality.

[. . .]

Edna may be transformed by the white subsumption of the Other, but women like Mariequita or the quadroon or the 'black woman' do not and cannot change in the novel. Precisely because Edna's break with gender constraints is dependent upon representations of racial and ethnic difference, those differences – in order to be available in the first place – must remain intact.

[. . .] racial figuration is intimately involved in the warranty and production of [Edna's] 'self.' To the extent such troping is in a sense 'productive' as well as repressive, race is constitutive of Edna's new identity. In this light, the racial politics of womanhood in Chopin's novel must complicate, if not compromise, our celebration of a nineteenth-century white woman's sexual liberation.

Cynthia Griffin Wolff, 'Un-Utterable Longing: The Discourse of Feminine Sexuality in *The Awakening*', *Studies in American Fiction*, Vol. 24, No. 1, 1996, pp. 3–22

In *The Awakening* Wolff identifies a series of silences, gaps and absences, difficulties in communication and failures in understanding – from the parrot who speaks 'a language which nobody understood', to Edna's incomprehension of the French tongue of the Creole, and her immersion of herself in music and the sounds of the sea, 'forms of "communication" that do not require words'. She also points to characteristics of the text which may be termed 'modernist', 'the strong spareness of the prose and the "minimalism" of a narrative whose absences are at least as important as its action'. Wolff interprets these aspects of the novel as Chopin's representation of the impossibility of articulating female sexual desire in her nineteenth-century society. In establishing a contextual framework for this inability to express desire Wolff examines the pressures placed upon women by the dominant discourses of medical science and religion. She cites the rhetoric of William Acton, the 'acknowledged expert on the nature of women's sexuality' who defined women as asexual and passionless, and also the teachings of the Protestant church that deemed public speaking by women as improper. Both of these discourses are related to the novel and to the heroine – in Edna's 'stern Presbyterian' background, and in Léonce Pontellier's pathologising of his wife's unconventional behaviour through his seeking advice from Dr Mandelet.

[. . .]

The official 'scientific' and 'medical' view can be stated quite simply: an average woman (a 'decent' woman) possesses no sexual feelings whatsoever. Thus it is not enough to say that *The Awakening* is a novel about repression (that is, about a situation in which a woman possesses sexual feelings, but is prohibited from acting upon them). It is, instead, a novel about a woman whose shaping culture has, in general, refused her right to speak out freely; this is, moreover, a culture that construes a woman's self-expression as a violation of sexual 'purity' and a culture that has denied the existence of women's libidinous potential altogether – has eliminated the very concept of sexual passion for 'normal' women.

[. . .]

Of course there was an escape hatch (infinitesimal and insufficient). After all, men and women did marry, did have sexual intercourse, doubtless did (sometimes) enjoy their love-making, and did (occasionally) find ways to discuss the intimate elements of their relationship [. . .]

Medical and psychological experts concluded that although women had no sexual drives *per se*, they often possessed a passionate desire to bear children: such ardor was both 'normal' and (inevitably) sexual. On these terms, then, sexual activity – even moderate sexual 'desire' – was appropriate in 'normal' women. However, a profound displacement or confusion was introduced by this accommodation: the language of feminine sexuality became inextricably intertwined with discourse that had to do with child-bearing and motherhood.

[. . .]

This definition of feminine sexuality radically displaced a woman's passionate desires: unlike males, who were permitted to 'possess' their sexuality and were consequently allowed to experience passion directly and as a part of the 'self,' females were allowed access to sexuality only indirectly – as a subsidiary component of the desire for children. It was literally unimaginable that any 'decent' woman would experience sexual appetite as an immediate and urgent drive, distinct from all other desires and duties. In emotional terms, men 'owned' their libido; however, women's libido was 'owned' by their prospective children.

Any woman would find this concatenation of denials and demands unbalancing; however, in Edna's case, the already vexed situation is heightened by a severe conflict of cultures. In a society where the actual experiences of women were diverse and the normative pronouncements were stringent, Chopin has constructed a novel where extremes converge to demonstrate the malignant potential of these normative attitudes, and she marks the summer at Grand Isle as the moment when crisis begins. Reared as a Presbyterian in Kentucky, Edna has been married to a Creole for many years. Nonetheless, she has never become 'thoroughly at home in the society of Creoles; [and] never before had she been thrown so intimately among them' (Ch. 4). It is not that these people do not have a rigorous sexual code: their customs follow the boundary conditions that Acton and his fellow theorists postulated. However, far from being Bible-bound, sober, and staid, so long as they remain within the rules of this code, Creoles permit themselves an extraordinary freedom of sensual expression. Thus a lusty carnal appetite in men is taken for granted. (Robert has his affair with the Mexican girl, everyone knows about it, and no one thinks to disapprove.) However, the case of Creole women is different, for their sexuality may exist only as a component of 'motherhood.' Nevertheless, so long as they accept this model, women, too, may engage in a sumptuous sexual life. Mme. Ratignolle, the 'sensuous Madonna,' embodies the essence of ardor and voluptuary appetite thus construed. Such a system imposes penalties (Adèle's accouchement is one specific marker for the price to be paid); however, within these limiting conditions, the Creole world is more densely erotic than any community Edna has encountered. It revels frankly and happily in the pleasures of the flesh – not merely enjoying these delights with undisguised zest, but discussing them in public with no shame at all. Edna can recognize the inherent 'chastity' of such people, but their habits nonetheless embarrass her profoundly:

> Madame Ratignolle had been married seven years. About every two years she had a baby. At that time she had three babies, and was beginning to think of a fourth one. She was always talking about her 'condition.' Her 'condition' was in no way apparent, and no one would have known a thing about it but for her persistence in making it the subject of conversation. (Ch. 4)

A late twentieth-century reader may innocently suppose that Adèle's preoccupation is purely maternal. The full truth is quite otherwise: in the discourse of the day, Adèle has elected to flaunt her sexuality – to celebrate both her ardor and her physical enjoyment. Robert enters the festive, flirtatious moment by recalling the 'lady who had subsisted upon nougat during the entire –,' and is checked only by Edna's blushing discomfort.

All such instances of candor unsettle Mrs. Pontellier. This strange world, with its languorous climate and frankly sensuous habits, is a world where 'normal,' 'respectable' women openly vaunt pleasures that are unfamiliar to Edna Pontellier. She is fascinated, stimulated, eventually profoundly aroused. And although she is bewildered by these new sensations, once having been touched by them, she becomes unwilling to pull away. Much of the novel, then, is concerned with Edna's quest for a viable and acceptable mode of owning and expressing her sexuality: first by locating the defining boundaries for these feelings and thus being able to *define* and *name* what she feels inside herself; second by finding some acceptable social construct which will permit her to *enact* what she feels in the outside world and to make an appropriate, vital, and affirming connection between the 'me' and the 'not-me.'

[. . .] Like Adèle, Léonce is acquainted with no discourse of feminine sexuality other than some variant on the language of 'motherhood.' This conflation is revealed in the first intimate scene between Léonce and Edna. Léonce has returned from an evening of card-playing, jolly at having won a little money – 'in excellent humor . . . high spirits, and very talkative' (Ch. 3). To be sure, he does not 'court' his wife; yet he is scarcely brutal or coarse, and his gossipy, somewhat preoccupied manner as he empties his pockets might be that of any long-married man. Indeed, it is *Edna's* unapproachable manner that disrupts the potential harmony of the moment. There is nothing peculiar about the 'action' of this scenario, nor is it difficult to read the subtext: Léonce would like to conclude his pleasant evening with a sexual encounter; his wife is not interested.

The real oddity has to do with language. Although the couple falls into a kind of argument over their differing inclinations, sex itself is never mentioned. Instead, when Léonce chooses to rebuke his wife (presumably for her passional indifference to him), he employs a vernacular of 'motherhood' to do so. 'He reproached his wife with her inattention, her habitual neglect of the children. If it was not a mother's place to look after children, whose on earth was it?' (Ch. 3). With this alienated discourse, neither party can talk about the real source of unhappiness, and sexual harmony within the marriage is threatened or compromised. Léonce at least has 'acceptable' alternatives (for example, we should probably not suppose that he is celibate during his long absences from home). Edna has none – not even the satisfaction of being able to define the exact nature of her despondency.

[. . .]

In some primitive way, silence also is Edna's only appropriate reaction to society's way of defining female sexuality: for if women were imagined to have no sexual feelings, not to speak would (ironically) be the way to 'communicate' this absence. Yet not to speak has an annihilating consequence: it is, in the end, not to be – not to have social reality. One can never affirm 'self' merely through silence and fantasy – can never forget that vital connection between the 'me' and the 'not-me' that validates identity [. . .]

Indeed, the dispassionate tone of Chopin's novel may be related to the complexity of Edna's quest, for Edna cannot 'solve' her problem without an extraordinary feat of creativity. She must discover not merely a new vernacular with which to name her feelings – not merely a new form of plot that is capable of containing them – but also an 'audience' that both comprehends and esteems the story she might ultimately tell. Thus the true subject of *The Awakening* may be less the particular dilemma of Mrs. Pontellier than the larger problems of female narrative that it reflects; and if Edna's poignant fate is in part a reflection of her own habits, it is also, in equal part, a measure of society's failure to allow its women a language of their own.

[. . .]

It is troubling that the narrative formulations to which Edna is habitually drawn are so formulaic, that they decline to attempt some model of feminine initiative or some assertion of explicitly feminine passion. She configures her outing with Robert as 'Sleeping Beauty' (' "How many years have I slept?" she inquired' [Ch. 13]). [. . .] Arobin pursues Edna by pretending that casual sexuality is some fuller, more 'sincere' emotion (he is careful never to mention love). And although his practiced style invites 'easy confidence,' it is also filled with 'effrontery' (Ch. 25) – with the desire to treat her as no more than a 'beautiful, sleek animal waking up in the sun' (Ch. 23). [. . .] Thus the aftermath of their consummation is not an affirmation of identity for Edna, but another form of maiming – a cascade of simple sentences in largely parallel form to configure alienation and disintegration – the novel's shortest, most mutilated chapter. Less than half a page. These lay bare the harsh realities of existence, 'beauty and brutality,' and conclude with nothing but a 'dull pang of regret because it was not the kiss of love which had inflamed her' (Ch. 28).

By the time Robert returns, Edna [. . .] has gained the courage to speak forbidden discourse in the hope of inventing a new kind of narrative. 'I suppose this is what you would call unwomanly,' she begins, 'but I have got into a habit of expressing myself. It doesn't matter to me, and you may think me unwomanly if you like' (Ch. 36). They return to her little house, and when Robert seems to doze in a chair, she rewrites the sleeping beauty story by reversing their roles and awakening *him* with a kiss, 'a soft, cool, delicate kiss, whose voluptuous sting penetrated his whole being. . . . She put her hand up to his face and pressed his cheek against her own. The action was full of love and tenderness' (Ch. 36).

[. . .]

After the delivery, [of Adèle's baby] Edna's still-fragile emergent self is shaken. In response to Dr. Mandelet's queries, she once again shrugs away from language: 'I don't feel moved to speak of things that trouble me.' Her desires continue to trail a fairy-tale hope of absolute happiness: 'I don't want anything but my own way' (Ch. 38). Still her anticipated reunion with Robert fortifies her. She foresees the opportunity to resume their love-making; and she believes there will be a 'time to think of everything' (Ch. 38) on the morning to follow, a chance to fashion the story of their life together. However, she has refused to consider his weakness and his fondness for illusions. Thus she is unprepared for the letter she finds: 'I love you. Good-by – because I love you' (Ch. 38). In the end, Edna has discovered no partner/audience with whom to construct her new narrative, and she cannot concoct one in solitude.

[. . .]

So Edna has failed. Or rather, being a woman with some weaknesses and no extraordinary strengths, Edna has chosen the only alternative she could imagine to the ravaging social arrangements of her day. [. . .] However, we must not overlook the fact that if her heroine faltered, Kate Chopin fashioned a splendid success. *The Awakening* is the new narrative that Mrs. Pontellier was unable to create: not (it is true) a story of female affirmation, but rather an excruciatingly exact dissection of the ways in which society distorts a woman's true nature. The ruthless contemporary reviews leave no doubt that Kate Chopin had invented a powerful (and thus threatening) discourse for feminine sexuality. And although the novel was forced to languish (like yet another 'sleeping beauty') largely unread for three quarters of a century, the current respect it enjoys is a belated affirmation of Kate Chopin's success.

Helen Taylor, 'Walking through New Orleans: Kate Chopin and the Female Flâneur', *Symbiosis*, Vol. 1, No. 1, April 1997, pp. 69–85

Helen Taylor looks beyond Chopin's reputation as a writer of rural, regional, and 'local colour' stories to consider her as an urban writer and critic, examining her literary engagement with the southern city of New Orleans. Taylor discusses the nineteenth-century city in terms of its being, 'defined and organised around *male* mobility, work, pleasure and sexuality', and as a problematic space for women, who were denied the freedom of the urban streets. 'Women "on the street", she claims, 'were defined as prostitutes or creatures of dubious virtue.' As Taylor notes, in literature and the popular imagination, the 'emblematic figure of the flâneur' – the unaccompanied stroller, the observer of the 'spectacle' of the city – is invariably masculine. Through a consideration of two works – the 1896 story 'Athénaïse' and *The Awakening* – Taylor examines Chopin's appropriation of this traditionally masculine 'flâneur' figure for her heroines – for Athénaïse who, 'revels in the anonymity of walking streets where no-one recognises her', and for Edna Pontellier who, 'consumes the pleasures of the city, walking alone as she wishes'.

[. . .]

The city of New Orleans is at the very heart of *The Awakening*, and is the site of Edna Pontellier's most dramatic and revolutionary self-revelations and independent actions. It is not the place where that awakening is initiated, nor is it the place in which she resolves her dilemma of how or whether to live. Grand Isle, an island which until the great hurricane was a vacation centre, site of leisure consumption for the white Creole community into which Edna had married, is the Edenic arena in which nature and natural forces begin to transform her: the warmth of the sun, the pleasures of the sea on the body, the sexual attraction to Robert Lebrun and a new physical restlessness and claustrophobia. As in stories set in Natchitoches Parish, the seductiveness of landscape and forbidden eroticised relationships arouse the woman to a keen new sense of possibility.

In some writing about Chopin, too stark a division is made between the worlds and experiences of Grand Isle and New Orleans. Western thought too easily sets up rural and urban as oppositional, with the rural perhaps too readily conceived of as natural, pastoral and untainted while the urban is unnatural, corrupt, and diseased. It is easy to see *The Awakening* as a warning to women not to take holiday romances too seriously when they return to the humdrum realities and tedious constrictions of quotidien urban existence. Like 'Athénaïse', *The Awakening* plays with these oppositions between urban and rural, and with yet another set of oppositions between Catholic French Creole and Protestant English-speaking Presbyterian. The French Creoles inhabit both rural and urban worlds, and (in keeping with the historic defensiveness, and desire for clear demarcation of the Creole community) make artificial distinctions between them.

The city intrudes constantly into Grand Isle life, as working husbands and daily newspapers arrive by boat along with boxes of bon-bons from Vieux Carré shops. Women and children, sent to the island in summer retreat from the city's heat, discomfort and disease, are joined by their men who drink together at Klein's Club, read market reports, then leave thankfully for 'a lively week in Carondelet Street' (Ch. 3). The only men left behind are the young feckless or between-jobs, like Robert Lebrun, whose summer labour is annually to engage a married woman's affections. The Creoles understand this to be light summer flirtation. For them, the pastoral retreat versus urban reality binary divide holds good, and must be upheld for the sake of social cohesion. With characteristic lightness of touch, Chopin gives us a clear picture of an ethnic grouping fighting for an autonomy and identity we know had been steadily eroding since the Louisiana Purchase.[1] For Protestant Edna, this clear demarcation line does not exist, since she is an outsider ('She is not one of us', Adèle warns Robert). Born into a Presbyterian Kentucky family with a strict sense of duty and a tendency to emotional repression, she has married into a close-knit Creole community which observes strict social and marital rules but in other ways is emotionally open and flexible.

The Frenchness of this community is emphasised throughout the novel. The French language is used to such an extent that many editions give footnote translations of phrases and sentences (particularly heavy in the first half of the book when Creole dialogue dominates). Furthermore, there are references to French writing (Daudet, the Goncourts, and a shocking unnamed novel circulated at Grand Isle that has to be French). French piano music and a French ditty 'Si tu savais' move Edna to tears, while Mrs Highcamp tells Victor Lebrun saucily that her daughter would be charmed to talk French and sing French songs with him. Paris is the city Pontellier plans to take Edna for painting lessons. Edna herself cannot speak French well, while her husband – whose paragon status is semi-parodic – speaks French to perfection and, unlike the Ratignolles (the idealised Creole couple), English without an accent. The Ratignolles appeal to Edna, but largely in terms of their difference: 'There was something which Edna thought very French, very foreign, about their whole manner of living' (Ch. 18).

Throughout Chopin's work, France and Frenchness are used as signifiers of desire, the illicit, and sexual pleasure. In her first published story, 'A Point at Issue', tongues wag with the separation of Professor Faraday and his wife Eleanor. Eleanor spends time in Paris: 'And in Paris, of all places, to leave a young woman alone! Why not at once in Hades?'. Though riding in a carriage with the artist who is painting her portrait as a gift for her husband, Eleanor is assumed – this

---

1 In 1803, Thomas Jefferson and the Emperor Napoleon negotiated the sale of a significant part of the North American continent. The Louisiana Purchase, approved by treaty in April 1803, is often described as the most significant real estate transaction in the history of civilization. Involving over 800,000 square miles of land, at the price of four cents per acre, the territory would eventually form a part of fifteen American states: Louisiana, Arkansas, Missouri, Iowa, North Dakota, Texas, South Dakota, New Mexico, Nebraska, Kansas, Wyoming, Minnesota, Oklahoma, Colorado and Montana.

being Paris – to be engaged in an adulterous liaison [. . .] The French language is used with sensuous, poetic and erotic effect throughout *The Awakening*, suggesting the exotic appeal of Creole culture for a woman who significantly cannot speak that language well.

And, like that European city of sophisticated pleasures, New Orleans is also a city of performances. A city, like Paris, of theatre, opera and street promenading, it is a place where the Creole upper class hold soirées musicales and 'at homes', and where the name of Alcée Arobin is used on lawyer firm's letterheads and shingle so that the playboy may (in his own words) 'assume the virtue of an occupation if he has it not' (Ch. 30). It is also a city in which appearances are maintained performatively, as in Mr Pontellier's expensive city gifts sent during the week to Grand Isle, and his elaborate arrangements to have the Esplanade Street house refurbished to conceal the fact his wife had moved out. Edna suspects the Creole mother-women masquerade in feminine guise (Adèle assiduously sewing winter garments in summer, listening with exaggerated interest to her husband at midday dinner) and it is her refusal to so masquerade, her desire to 'daily [cast] aside that fictitious self which we assume like a garment with which to appear before the world' (Ch. 19), that makes her so threatening to women as well as men. No wonder Robert takes flight, especially after she has reproached him with selfishness and assured him she has 'got into a habit of expressing [herself]' which he would call 'unwomanly' (Ch. 36). Indeed, Edna's 'womanliness' has undergone considerable shifts. In terms of performative identities, Edna's transformation/awakening literally embodies the shifting nature of gender identity within the novel. Victor Lebrun is only one who notices how different Edna looks in New Orleans: 'The city atmosphere has improved her. Some way she doesn't seem like the same woman' (Ch. 20).

So what is it about New Orleans that has 'improved' her? I would suggest that Edna's progress within the city is signalled through a series of walks. Emotionally if not physically alone, unattached and relatively anonymous (though we know at least one friend, Dr Mandelet, has observed her), she explores the meaning of femininity within an urban context. Her mother-in-law takes the children away for some country life so they won't be 'wholly "children of the pavement" ' (Ch. 20), recalling Benjamin's 'botanizing on the asphalt' or the figure of 'notorious gambler' Hector (in 'In and Out of Old Natchitoches') and indeed Alcée Arobin, that most feckless of flâneurs. But Edna could never be a child, or woman of the pavement, a botanizer or a gambler (though she plays at all these). She leaves the city for a different reason. She goes to the Gulf because those 'allurements of city life' (Ch. 34) Victor and Mariequita are discussing as she arrives at Grand Isle prove in the end illusory for an eroticised adult woman.

Unlike Mlle Reisz (an urban survivor) Edna makes an uneasy and demanding observer of life. She masquerades as flâneur, but without the easy anonymity and marginality of Baudelaire's classic Frenchman. She shares the flâneur's irresponsibility and openness to erotic encounter. She 'go[es] and com[es] as it suited her fancy . . . lending herself to any passing caprice' (Ch. 19) but hardly with the relaxed indifference of her lover Arobin. Walter Benjamin notes the delight of the city-dweller as 'not so much love at first sight as love at last sight',[2] and Edna finds lingering in her memory and sometimes disturbing her 'the glance of strange eyes' (Ch. 23) on the street. Having walked alone to the Lebruns', she permits a dangerous erotic intimacy with Robert's young brother Victor, who visits the city from his home on Grand Isle for 'occasional relaxation' (Ch. 20), the salacious details of which he begins to share with Edna. It is significant that Victor whispers his tale to a fully-comprehending Edna while saying he cannot think of telling her since, as a woman, she could not comprehend such things. It is the playfulness here around gender identity and erotic narrative that engages and amuses the previously prudish and shockable Edna.

Finally, like many a male flâneur, she consumes the pleasures of the city: walking alone as she wishes, taking food and coffee at an off-the-beaten-track *mulatresse*'s garden, and buying bonbons at a confectioner's for the children in Iberville. Although New Orleans is a walker's city, and other women walk to one another's houses, Edna alone performs the role of flâneur regardless of who might see her. Compare her insouciance with the care taken by the heavily pregnant Adèle, whose only recorded urban walk is taken 'avoiding the too public thoroughfares' (Ch. 33). Note also that no woman can play flâneur for long. She is accompanied on her walks by Arobin, from the Esplanade Street house to the pigeon-house, Robert from Mlle Reisz's and later the suburban garden to her new home, and from Adèle's childbirth by Dr Mandelet who sends away his carriage in order to accompany her home and offer kindly patriarchal advice. Her most significant walk (even then accompanied by a – significantly nameless – servant) is Edna's walk to Adèle's childbirth scene, an act that is decisive in defining her fate. After she leaves, Robert too leaves forever, and it is this final blow which leads to her last, and this time solitary, trip to Grand Isle and death.

[. . .]

Chopin chose to write and to live in a city rather than a small town or rural area. After her mother's death, she stayed in St Louis, and rarely left thereafter. But although she sets some stories and parts of *At Fault* there, St Louis does not provide her with the resonant historical, cultural, symbolic landscape of New Orleans. Her perspective on that city rarely moves into controversial and difficult areas; the uneasy and often violent cohabitation of different ethnic and racial groups before and after the Civil War is alluded to but never foregrounded (as it was by her contemporaries George W. Cable and Grace King). Her New Orleans is a feminised site of consumerism rather than production; of individual spatial relationships rather than political landscapes; of eroticism rather than racial and physical danger. It is a city of secretiveness and suggestion – the very qualities that were central to Chopin's own life and indeed her allusive work. And of course it is very much a city of the street, full of spectacular, olfactory and musical delights. New Orleans was a walker's heaven, as the young married Kate Chopin and the fictional Edna Pontellier discovered. But, like other nineteenth-century cities, it

<hr>

2   [Taylor's note.] Walter Benjamin, *Charles Baudelaire: A Lyric Poet in the Era of High Capitalism* (London: New Left Books, 1973), 45.

also tried to refuse those delights of the street to respectable women. The desire for, and pleasure in walking and a freedom of movement, were central to this writer and many of her key characters. But she, and they, could only play at having the freedom of the streets, perform the role of flâneur (a term which is firmly a masculine noun). Despite being celebrated as a feminine city, Parisian-style 'Queen of the Mississippi' New Orleans was a perilous site for women in public space. A white woman's sexuality, racial and biological destiny meant that to be *on* the streets suggested, however indirectly, to be *of* the streets. In the end, Athénaïse was much safer back with her dull husband on Cane River; by contrast, Edna gained the freedom of the city for a while then, recognizing the limits of that freedom in terms of her race, class and gender, left town rather than going meekly home, and swam to her death. Chopin transformed that European figure of the solitary, disillusioned, aimless male flâneur into a complex, 'daring and defying' female walker who symbolically challenged the gendered meanings of *fin-de-siècle* urban space. For this alone she deserves recognition as a significant figure in the history of urban fiction.

Donald Pizer, 'A Note on Kate Chopin's *The Awakening* as Naturalistic Fiction', Southern Literary Journal, 33, No. 2 (2001), pp. 5–13

In common with Bert Bender, Pizer considers Chopin's novel as an example of naturalistic fiction which he describes as 'the principal innovative movement in American fiction of the 1890s'. Pizer defines literary naturalism as the drama-tisation of 'the limitations placed upon the human will by the biological and social realities within which the will attempts to find its way', and, like Bender, he draws on Darwinian theories in his examination of the text. The focus here is placed particularly upon Edna's inability to overcome the biological in-stincts of motherhood despite her repeated rejections of the socially imposed expectations of the role.

[. . .] even at Grand Isle, an apparently ideal matrix for Edna's act of redefinition of her identity, her natural and social worlds also send clear messages, ignored by her at this time, that she will find her efforts to establish a fully independent and self-expressive life circumscribed and eventually thwarted by the conditions in which she must live. Edna's friend and confidante, Adèle Ratignolle, is clearly a foil to Edna in that she glories in the role of 'mother-woman'. Despite Edna's rejection of this role, the irrefutable similarity between the two figures is that they are both women and mothers – that though Edna may reject [. . .] the socially-constructed role of a mother's total absorption in her children, she has not escaped the biologically essentialist act of giving birth to children and thus finding within herself the protective emotions of a mother.

[. . .] In the fourth chapter of his *Descent of Man*, Darwin discusses 'social instincts' at length, and on several occasions includes the 'maternal instinct' among them, as in his comment that 'a young and timid mother urged by the maternal instinct will, without a moment's hesitation, run the greatest danger for her own infant'. He sums up, with particular pertinence for Edna, that 'it is far from strange that an instinct so strong and so greatly admired, as maternal love, should, if disobeyed, lead to the deepest misery'. Here, as elsewhere, Darwin makes a distinction between the biological origin of a human characteristic ('an instinct so strong') and its reinforcement ('so greatly admired') by society. It is this distinction which engages Chopin in her depiction of Edna. Although Edna can dismiss the Victorian idealization of the 'mother-woman', she is unable to counter the instinctive hold that her children have upon her.

[. . .] In the New Orleans portion of *The Awakening*, Edna attempts, with increasing breadth and intensity, to make operative in her life the rebirth she had experienced at Grand Isle. In doing so, she unconsciously adopts many of the means for achievement of female emancipation advocated by the New Woman movement of the 1890s. In general, her effort involves freeing herself from the restrictions imposed on women by the conventions of a middle-class marriage while simultaneously discovering vehicles for the creation of her economic, sexual, and spiritual self-sufficiency. [. . .]

In the end, Edna fails in this effort at self-determination of body and soul because she is unable to overcome the biological and social limitations which were present within herself and her world at Grand Isle and which now, as she seeks to test their limits, express their full intractability. Her children have been conveniently away for much of the period of her new life in New Orleans, but she is unable to dismiss them from her thoughts. [. . .]

[. . .] Edna is called [. . .] to aid in the imminent accouchement of Adèle, a melodramatic interruption which, like much melodrama in naturalistic fiction, feeds into several significant themes. One such theme is the reminder expressed by Adèle's childbearing that to be a woman is indeed to embody and express a form of biological destiny. [. . .]

[. . .] Despite her claim to Robert that 'nothing else in the world [other than their love] is of any consequence,' her children, through her act of bearing them and then loving them, are of great consequence to her and constitute an insurmountable obstacle in her effort to live a free and independent existence. She tells Dr. Mandelet, ' "I want to be let alone. Nobody has any right – except children, perhaps – and even then, it seems to me – or it did seem –." She felt that her speech was voicing the incoherency of her thoughts, and stopped abruptly' (Ch. 38). Mandelet, 'grasping her meaning intuitively', expresses openly the concept that Nature is a powerful determinant force in the lives of women. Youthful love, he claims, 'seems to be a provision of Nature, a decoy to secure mothers for the race' [. . .]

[. . .] despite her belief that she has awakened to a need and capacity to escape the confining roles of wife and mother, Edna remains trapped in these roles and can only escape them, she believes, in death. As she swims further and further into the Gulf, 'she thought of Léonce and the children. They were part of her life. But they need not have thought that they could possess her, body and soul' (Ch. 39). They have indeed not 'possessed' her in her 'awakened' state in the sense of controlling her belief that she has an existence other than that of wife and mother.

But they have led to her destruction, as depicted by Chopin, because she has not been able to overcome the hold which the biology of motherhood and the social codes of marriage have had both on her emotions and the beliefs and actions of others within the areas of life in which she functions. [. . .]

Elisabeth Le Blanc, 'The Metaphorical Lesbian: Edna Pontellier in *The Awakening*', Tulsa Studies in Women's Literature, Vol. 15, Part 2 (1996), pp. 289–307

In her consideration of *The Awakening*, Le Blanc engages with a range of lesbian theories claiming that 'the true power of the novel cannot be fully realized unless it is read not only as a feminist text, but also as a lesbian text'. Drawing on the work of Bonnie Zimmerman, Le Blanc defines the 'metaphorical lesbian' as one who is 'not "really" a lesbian but could be', one who disrupts the conventions of heterosexuality and patriarchy, who 'positions herself outside these institutions' and 'exposes their gaps and contradictions'. Reading Edna Pontellier as such a figure she notes her rejection of the conventional role of wife and mother, the suggestions of eroticism in her relationships with Adèle Ratignolle and Mademoiselle Reisz, and her physical appearance, which she argues, 'transcend[s] traditional gender descriptions' and demonstrates aspects of androgyny. Like Cynthia Griffin Wolff, Elisabeth Le Blanc identifies Edna's inability to articulate her emotions, but she understands this as a failure of language to express lesbian desire. Here, whilst the ambiguity of the ending is acknowledged, a possible reading is offered which celebrates the triumph of Edna as 'metaphorical lesbian' finally joining with the sea, her 'figurative female lover' in a 'sensually erotic encounter'.

[. . .] Grand Isle [. . .] is organized entirely around the comfort, concerns and privilege of men. The important businessmen are pampered and entertained by adoring wives and children on weekends [. . .] the fact that the author lumps these 'ministering angels' together as a group suggests an identity that is imposed, not natural. When she singles out one of the mother-women, Adèle, she explicitly invokes Petrarchan conventions, traditionally masculine codes of female beauty, in her description [. . .] Adèle simply is the 'myth of woman,' the 'angel of the house.' [. . .]

It is only in her interactions with the metaphorical lesbian Edna Pontellier, only when we see her through Edna's eyes, that Adèle moves from constructed ideal to individual subject. Even as Adèle's touch initiates Edna's awakening, Edna's physical presence and natural reserve inspire Adèle's wry wit and gentle irony. In their scenes together, Adèle's personality takes on an ironic edge ordinarily suppressed in her performance of adoring spouse and devoted *maman*.

[. . .] Edna's reevaluation results in a gradual construction of spaces – physical, cultural, psychological – that allow her to establish a (lesbian) identity separate from her social world [. . .] Certainly Edna sets herself apart in a psychological space outside her family by defying Léonce's demands, stamping upon her wedding ring, relinquishing household duties and ignoring her receiving day, refusing to be present at her sister's marriage [. . .] declining to join Léonce in New York, and sending her children off to their grandmother's Iberville plantation. But she also tries to establish a position, a space within her culture, from which she can question its norms and constitute herself as an active subject [. . .] Thus Edna maintains a subversive presence in the patriarchy [. . .] allow[ing] her to challenge an ordinarily male-dominated space. [. . .]

We can see Edna's woman-identification in minor details – her open admiration of Mariequita, the artistic inspiration her housemaid provides, her appreciation of Madame Antoine's stories and maternal ministrations, her fondness for the company and conversation of Madame Lebrun. But it is Edna's relationships with Adèle Ratignolle and Mademoiselle Reisz that exemplify the possibilities of the lesbian continuum as a reconstructive strategy. It is through these relationships, rather than her faltering and doomed connections to men, that Edna begins to perceive herself as a subject unrestricted by the confines of patriarchy [. . .] Edna's first attraction to Adèle is erotic [. . .] Adèle's first caress, a clasp of the hand, melts the startled Edna's habitual coolness and paves the way for her sensual and sexual awakening. Edna becomes attached to Adèle the person – as sister, as friend, 'lover' – even as she rejects Adèle the mythical 'woman.'

Edna's woman-identified experience takes another form in her relationship with Mademoiselle Reisz. What Adèle initiates, the pianist nurtures and oversees. It is her music that opens Edna to a sense of 'the unlimited' [. . .] As Edna's awakening progresses, her contacts with Mademoiselle 'stir' and provoke her as nothing else can [. . .]

Edna's desire is boundless, her yearnings vast. Her erotic potential, once triggered, seems to have a life of its own, seeking release in something as unlimited as itself and finding only temporary (and unfulfilling) outlets in Alcée and Robert. Edna most nearly accesses the power of the erotic not with men, but through her art, through her female friends, and most significantly through the sea [. . .]

As Edna's metaphorical lesbian lover, the sea is perhaps the only source of fulfilment equal to her 'unrequited longing' [. . .] The sea offers a sense of possibility that Edna feels with an intensity she cannot recapture elsewhere.

Stephen Heath, 'Chopin's Parrot', *Textual Practice*, Vol. 8, No. 1, Spring 1994, pp. 11–32

Comparisons have often been made between Chopin's *The Awakening* and Gustave Flaubert's *Madame Bovary*. In this wide-ranging essay, Stephen Heath traces the similarities and differences between the two, exploring how Chopin 'rewrites and transforms' the earlier work as, 'Emma Bovary becomes Edna Pontellier, and the married woman moves once more to suicide after weariness in marriage and knowledge of an adulterous passion'. Heath notes, however, the added sophistication of representation which the later writer, who is well informed in all of the major intellectual concerns of the day – who is a reader of 'Darwin, Huxley and Spencer' – brings to her text. For example, he discusses the way in which the unconventional behaviour of both heroines is pathologised – both being perceived as hysterical. But in having Dr Mandelet note that Edna may require the expertise of 'an inspired psychologist', Heath suggests Chopin anticipates the work of Freud whose theories were just beginning to emerge: 'In Emma Bovary's world there is no understanding; in Edna's a glimmering: her doctor at least shows some comprehension, even if still ultimately held in the conventions of what Freud himself will continue to call "the riddle" of woman.'

Heath traces many themes and influences in Chopin's text, from psychoanalysis and evolutionary theory to the suggestion of lesbianism in the figure of Mademoiselle Reisz; from the impact of music on Chopin's life, and on Edna's, to the importance of story telling throughout the text and the frequent inability to comprehend or articulate emotion. Throughout there is an interweaving of corresponding elements in Flaubert's novel – shared characteristics of the heroines, shared features of plot and of imagery. Both novels, Heath notes, contain images of birds and the motif of flight – Emma Bovary 'would have liked to escape from life and fly away in an embrace', Mademoiselle Reisz speaks to Edna of 'the bird that would soar above the level plain of tradition and prejudice'. And the parrot – the shrill voice of the bird, 'so detested by Chopin', and, Heath claims, by Flaubert, opens the novel with 'a language which nobody understood' thus articulating the 'problem of representation that Chopin faces'. The text closes with a different sound – 'the voice of the sea' – one to which the newly awakened Edna is attuned, and with which she identifies. Heath categorises both *Madame Bovary* and *The Awakening* as examples of 'women's modernism', identifying Chopin's text as an extension of and continuation of her precursor's modernist project. He notes that in the later text – 'between the two, parrot and sea, there is the whole process – the substance – of Chopin's writing, the difficult course of Edna's desire for herself, reaching out "for the unlimited".'

[. . . Chopin's] 'Creole Bovary', as Willa Cather called it, contains numerous traces of Flaubert's novel, providing Chopin with elements for the elaboration of her new account. So, for example, Robert, one of Edna's admirers, has a tobacco pouch [. . .] that recalls the one belonging to the Viscount over which Emma dreams after the Vaubyessard ball; his feelings undeclared, Robert departs for Mexico much as Léon does for Paris, leaving Edna like Emma with 'her whole existence . . . dulled'; Alcée, another admirer, shares the same male attitudes as Rodolphe, Emma's seducer; Edna's father, with his military background and penchant for outlandish drinks, matches Emma's old-soldier father-in-law who astounds the peasantry with his kirsch toddies; as schoolgirls, Edna and Emma were both drawn to religion and Edna's later infatuation with a tragedian brings the memory of Emma's response to the thrilling tenor Lagardy [. . .]

In the story Freud tells, it is women who are civilization's disturbing paradox: women lay the foundations of civilization 'by the claims of their love' but soon come into opposition with it by their poor capacity to achieve the required instinctual sublimations, their pull towards the interest of the family and sexual life (this at the same time that they are seen as possessing 'a weaker sexual instinct' and tending to 'severely neurotic' over-refinement). Civilization, indeed, is 'increasingly the business of men' [. . .]

Chopin tells the same story, only with a different perspective, making the woman central and so disturbing the account of her disturbance. Léonce is exactly Freud's husband: doing the work of civilization, away in business, absorbed in his newspaper, spending the evenings with the New Orleans club men around the billiard tables at Klein's hotel, estranged from Edna whom he leaves to her own devices, save only from time to time to remonstrate about her 'neglect' of the children [. . .] or complain about her not looking after her appearance [. . .] Edna, however, is not quite Freud's woman, is surplus to his truth of her, beginning to 'recognize her relations as an individual to the world within and about her' (Ch. 6), coming to 'a flaming, outspoken revolt against the ways of Nature' (Ch. 37). The social-sexual question is articulated through the writing of Edna in such a way as to engender, before Freud, another truth, another representation. No wonder that Léonce is nervous at his sexual dispossession. Edna, like Emma Bovary, is a married woman and a mother, but, like her again, not a 'mother-woman' – 'women who idolized their children, worshipped their husbands, and esteemed it a holy privilege to efface themselves as individuals and grow wings as ministering angels' (Ch. 4). [. . .] Madame Ratignolle *is* the 'mother-woman': 'Madame Ratignolle had been married seven years. About every two years she had a baby. At that time she had three babies, and was beginning to think of a fourth one. She was always talking about her "condition" ' (Ch. 4). She and her husband come with the memory of *Madame Bovary*'s Homais family: same profession, Monsieur Ratignolle a chemist too; same scene of preparing potions at the pharmacy glimpsed through the heroine's eyes; same flourishing family [. . .] The memory, however, underlines the difference. Homais is grotesquely stupid, his wife a mere cipher, the admiring bearer of his brood; Madame Ratignolle is well to the fore and, despite the Homaisian complacency of much of her speech, stands as a pole of attraction in the story. Edna and Chopin acknowledge her as 'the embodiment of every womanly grace' and respond to her 'excessive physical charm' (Ch. 7).

[. . .] Edna voices and acts out a dissatisfaction with marriage and a seeking after independence of self [. . .] As Mr Pontellier reports to the Doctor, Edna refuses to go to her sister's wedding for the reason that 'a wedding is one of the most lamentable spectacles on earth' (Ch. 22) [. . .] Marriage is merely unthinking compliance, part of 'the daily treadmill of the life which has been portioned out to us' (Ch. 11), with the image there at once expressing Edna's experience and stating an overall narrative perspective of things. *The Awakening* follows *Madame Bovary* into marital disillusion and Edna like Emma turns to conjugally illicit passions, Léon and Rodolphe becoming Robert and Alcée.

Flaubert's psychology of female sexuality as depicted in Emma depends,
[. . .] on his notion of the belated arousal of women's senses and Chopin with
Edna somewhat follows this. Married, a mother, Edna on Grand Isle knows
a new strength of desire with Robert, which is then set ablaze by Arobin's
kiss: 'the first kiss of her life to which her nature had really responded' (Ch.
27). The language is that of awakening sensuousness, the first stirrings of a
newly impassioned being. [. . .] Above all, it is expressed by the sea, whose sonor-
ous murmur accompanies and runs beyond the story's terms, the novelistic
doings of marriage and adultery. The sea *speaks*: 'The voice of the sea is seductive; never ceasing, whispering, clamoring, murmuring, inviting the soul to
wander for a spell in abysses of solitude. . . . The voice of the sea speaks to the
soul. The touch of the sea is sensuous, enfolding the body in its soft, close
embrace' (Ch. 6); words which are repeated when Edna swims out to her end
(Ch. 39).

The voice of the sea takes over, finally, a book which began with quite
another voice, that of a parrot, one of the species so detested by Chopin: 'A
green and yellow parrot, which hung in a cage outside the door, kept repeating
over and over: *"Allez-vous-en! Sapristi!"* [. . .] The parrot interferes with Mr
Pontellier reading his newspaper, as later it interrupts the entertainments-
evening performance by the twins, who in turn are also there at the start, heard
just after the parrot playing a duet from "Zampa" upon the piano' (Ch. 1), the
same piece they are playing at the evening. The psittacine repetition moves from
parrot to twins (precisely) and duet (precisely again) and then out to the general
social world of the story with its animated voices, incessant chatter, monotonous talk, all the platitudinousness that Flaubert copied out and that Chopin
can too, to similar effect, leaving the reader unsure at times as to the irony or
not, distance or assent, and so creating a new mode, unsettling of discursive
certainties.

[. . .]

The parrot/sea couple, let me note in closing, is not just particular to Chopin
but resonates more widely. Writing *To the Lighthouse* (1927), *her* great
exploration of identity and the tensions around marriage and maternity and art
and women's life, Virginia Woolf wishes strongly that 'the sea . . . be heard
through it'.[1] It *is*, there through all the weave of characters' shifting thoughts
and feelings; but then these inevitably bring with them the possible loss of the
sea's voice, quickly covered by the given voices, the repetition 'over and over'
of the common sense. The book's own reflection on this – itself within the
terms again of this moment of Western literary history from Flaubert on – is
yet another parrot, the one which puzzles Mrs Ramsay as she ponders the
family of her guest Minta Doyle: 'How did she exist in that portentous atmosphere where the maid was always removing in a dust-pan the sand that the
parrot had scattered, and the conversation was almost entirely reduced to the

---

1   [Heath's note.] Diary entry for 27 June 1925, Anne Oliver Bell (ed.), *The Diary of Virginia Woolf*,
     Vol. III (Harmondsworth: Penguin, 1982), 34.

exploits ... of that bird?'² – Woolf and Chopin's question in writing too: how does *she* exist?

Ivy Schweitzer, 'Maternal Discourse and the Romance of Self-Possession in Kate Chopin's *The Awakening*', Boundary II, Vol. 17, Part 1, 1990, pp. 158–86

Schweitzer identifies the search for self and the conflict between the individual and society as a common concern in American literature – but one which is essentially a male concern. Considering *The Awakening* alongside other texts such as Hawthorne's *The Scarlet Letter*, she examines how such assertions of selfhood are problematised by the fact of maternity. 'Kate Chopin's *The Awakening*', Schweitzer argues, 'raises many genre questions about the differences in a romance written by a woman, and, most specifically, it raises the question of whether a mother may be the hero of romance.' Schweitzer employs a range of feminist theories in her essay, and engages with the complex presentations of maternity within the novel. She recognises 'the competing versions of motherhood at work' – the oppressive demands and responsibilities attached to the role of mother, but also 'the metaphors of self-birth and the seductive, maternal sea which liberate [Edna'.] She defines Edna's early awakenings to herself as a sexual being as 'universal' and not merely 'gender specific', noting that the Pontellier children are often absent, allowing their mother the freedom to 'realize her position in the universe as a human being, and to recognize her relations as an individual to the world within and about her'. But she notes how motherhood and individuality also seem 'mutually exclusive', Edna's children ultimately becoming 'antagonists' who will thwart her attempts at self-realisation. Schweitzer discusses the models of individuality which are available to Edna. Apart from Mademoiselle Reisz, who simultaneously attracts and repulses her, all of these models are male. She argues that through her relationship with Robert Lebrun, Edna, in fact, begins to 'act[s] out the pattern of the male hero of romance, defining herself as self through her desire for another'. But she also highlights how this assumption of male subjectivity, and the quest for self, is again interrupted and undermined by a stark reminder of the woman as mother when Edna attends the birth of Adèle's child.

[. . .] It is curious that the children loom so large in [Edna's] final meditations, because they appear to make so little demand on her time and attention throughout the story. As the wife of a successful Creole financier, Edna has several servants, one of whom, the mute and dreamy quadroon nurse, follows her two boys

2 [Heath's note.] Stella McNichol (ed.), Virginia Woolf, *To the Lighthouse* (1927) (Harmondsworth: Penguin, 1992), 63–4.

around incessantly. For the last half of the story, the children are not even present, having been sent off to live with Edna's mother-in-law in the suburb of Iberville. Yet, in her mind, they have become the slavedrivers of her soul, seeking to possess it, just as the white slaveholders possessed the bodies of the quadroon's ancestors. For all of her adolescent self-containment and the apparent freedom of her adult and socially privileged position, Edna does not feel she possesses herself.

At the same time, the text also recuperates motherhood by using birth as the metaphor for Edna's awakening. The chaotic beginning of her new 'world' of sensations and impressions is hyperbolized as an annunciation of the birth of wisdom by the Holy Ghost (Ch. 6), which foreshadows her own 'virgin birth' at the end. Her final gesture of autonomy, her self-authorized death, is also figured in terms of birth: 'How strange and awful it seemed to stand naked under the sky! how delicious! She felt like some new-born creature, opening its eyes in a familiar world that it had never known' (Ch. 39). Here Edna's unfettered physical response to the sensuousness of the familiar world renovates it and generates herself. In images now conventional in women's literature, she gives birth to herself as a creature which has become its own mother. Note that the narrator does not specify the gender of this creature nor its humanity. Edna's final responses to the world are purely physical. Elsewhere in the story, Dr Mandelet, an old family friend consulted by Edna's husband about her 'morbid condition,' finds 'no repression in her glance or gesture. She reminded him of some beautiful, sleek animal waking up in the sun' (Ch. 13), a description the narrator endorses for the emergence of Edna's sexual nature in her affair with Arobin. Edna as 'new-born creature' has reversed the usual developmental process and the conventional plot structure by metaphorizing and integrating the mother function and by turning an ending into a beginning. [. . .]

The utter difference between these two versions of motherhood is brought out in the violent juxtaposition of the final metaphor of self-engendering and Edna's account of her own children's births. In the penultimate scene, as she attends her friend Adèle's delivery, 'Edna began to feel uneasy. She was seized with a vague dread. Her own like experiences seemed far away, unreal, only half remembered. She recalled faintly an ecstasy of pain, the heavy odor of chloroform, a stupor which had deadened sensation, and an awakening to find a little new life to which she had given being, added to the great unnumbered multitude of souls that come and go' (Ch. 37). Edna's passivity and her unthinking compliance in the deadening of her sensations stand in stark contrast to the vibrant woman hungry for sensual experience she becomes. Her awakening from this forced sleep brings vagueness, not the sharp, sometimes poignant, clarity of her subsequent awakenings around which the text is structured. Only oxymoron, the figure of self-contradiction, can describe her experience of giving birth. Her existential revulsion is clinched in her reaction to Adèle's labor: 'With an inward agony, with a flaming, outspoken revolt against the ways of Nature, she witnessed the scene [of] torture' (Ch. 37). From the mother's perspective, birth is a horrendous imposition, a scene not from a domestic, but from an overtly explicit gothic romance. Adèle's justification of women's suffering, whispered to Edna as she leaves, 'Think of the children, Edna. Oh think of the children! Remember them!'

(Ch. 37) is precisely what Edna does as she evaluates her situation during the midnight vigil which follows.

[. . .] As the gap narrows between her outer conformity and her inner rebellion, she begins not only to demand her rights as an individual and give voice to her thoughts and emotions, but to act upon them – as a romantic hero must, but a mother in this world cannot.

As Edna listens more attentively to the voices within her and compares them to the reality without, she discovers that her world provides her with only two options for her development, options which are gender-coded and extreme. She can resign herself to her 'fate' as a woman, a position in this text always modified by the role of 'mother', or she can demand her practical and existential freedom as an individual, a freedom to explore the range of her desires conventionally reserved for men [. . .]

The alternative to the 'soul's slavery' of the 'mother-woman' is clearly represented by Mademoiselle Reisz, 'a disagreeable little woman, no longer young, who had quarrelled with almost everyone, owing to a temper which was self-assertive and a disposition to trample upon the rights of others' (Ch. 9). Antisocial, asexual, and non-maternal, Mademoiselle Reisz is an accomplished musician who, at the expense of intimacy and attachment, pursues a career and achieves the individuation and autonomy Gilligan[1] defines as masculine. Her position outside of motherhood and community grants her certain privileges, that is, the masculine privilege to ignore or override the rights of others in the name of a higher, abstract end [. . .]

[. . .] As a woman tied by biology, class, and circumstances to the fate of being eternally reproductive, Edna struggles to disengage herself from this self-sacrificing repetition, to produce a self, herself a speaking 'I.'

[. . .]

Ultimately, Edna rejects the masculine autonomy achieved by Mademoiselle Reisz because it is disconnected from the body. The misanthropic, self-possessed little musician makes music which shakes her audience, but seems to leave her untouched. She is cold and sexless, even unnatural. With something of a voyeur's appetite for vicarious pleasure, she raves about Edna's physical beauty while envying her sensibility and vibrant responses to life. Unlike Edna, her relationship to the physical world is one of scorn and disdain. Although she summers at Grand Isle, she avoids water and never swims in the sea [. . .]

By contrast, Edna has awakened slowly over the course of the novel to her physical nature, her sensuality, and her right to enjoy them. The ultimate irony is that, along with all her other mimicry of masculine freedom, the satisfaction of her desire shatters her romantic illusions as she is forced to accept her sexual nature in her affair with Arobin. Experiencing passion separate from love, a split between the physical and emotional 'natural' to men but 'unnatural' and forbidden for women, she understands the rupture upon which her being has been founded. Still holding on to a dream of merger with Robert, in which passion and

1 Carol Gilligan, *In a Different Voice: Psychological Theory and Women's Development*, Cambridge: Harvard University Press, 1982.

love might also merge, she is confronted with the stark reminder of that part of her physical nature she has tried to ignore in her flight to freedom – her mother-hood. Her children are a responsibility she cannot evade. This shocking realiz-ation, coupled with the shattering of her romantic illusions, sends her back to the beach at Grande Isle where she will 'elude' the tyranny of the children, that is, an overwhelming maternal responsibility which amounts, in her eyes, to a soul-killing self-sacrifice [. . .]

Janet Beer, 'Walking the Streets: Women out Alone in Kate Chopin's New Orleans', 2004

In this essay Kate Chopin is compared with her contemporary, Charlotte Perkins Gilman; both wrote about women in cities and in particular the risks taken when women claim freedom of movement in an urban environment. Gilman spent time working at Hull House in Chicago, a settlement house pro-viding services for immigrants founded by the social reformer and activist, Jane Addams and her associate Ellen Gates Starr in 1889; this experience brought Gilman into contact not only with the community that the house served but with some of the most active and intellectually dynamic social critics of the day. Chopin eschewed any kind of 'good works' but she did, nevertheless, have views on the constraints put upon women which chimed with those of Gilman, and this essay considers some of their similarities alongside their considerable dif-ferences. Gilman and Chopin in some ways demonstrate quite neatly the two, not obviously compatible, versions of the 'New Woman' current at the turn of the century; Chopin the liberated, sexually frank, cigarette smoking, open-minded woman, and Gilman the reforming, severely intellectual bluestocking, concerned to regulate and reform the world as ordered by men.

Kate Chopin never ceased to celebrate the urban and in particular New Orleans. She shamelessly romanticised her adoptive city, eulogising its potential as a place of erotic as well as social excitement for any number of her protagonists. Her portrait of the city of New Orleans where 'Up – away up, over the narrow street between the tall houses, the stars were blazing. The air was mild and caressing, but cool with the breath of spring and the night' (Ch. 38), could not, however, form a sharper contrast to the picture offered by Charlotte Perkins Gilman, in her account of the city of Chicago: chilly, downtown Chicago. Let Gilman share the Little Hell experience with you: 'The loathly river flowed sluggishly near by, thick and ill-smelling; Goose Island lay black in the slow stream. Everywhere a heavy dinginess; low, dark brick factories and gloomy wooden dwellings often below the level of the street; foul plank sidewalks, rotten and full of holes; black mud underfoot, damp soot drifting steadily down over everything.'[1] [. . .]

---

1   Charlotte Perkins Gilman, *The Living of Charlotte Perkins Gilman* (1935; Madison: University of Wisconsin Press, 1990), 184–5.

Contemporaries, influenced by life in different cities and attaching equally different meanings to the female body at large in urban surroundings [. . .] Chopin and Gilman express the contingencies of life on the streets for women. The manner, however, in which they expound the body politics of the city streets, provides an opportunity to illustrate prevalent but contradictory ideas of the 'New Woman' in the 1890s. Both these writers have been described as 'New Women' – for different and distinct reasons. Charlotte Perkins Gilman fulfils all the stereotypical attributes of the bluestocking, adhering to sensible shoes and hats, working at Hull House and elsewhere as an active social reformer, lecturing to audiences on a range of socially and morally uplifting topics. Gilman also, however, exhibits a number of the less attractive characteristics of the intellectually advanced 'New' woman – those like Olive Schreiner, Sarah Grand and Jane Addams – characteristics here described by Sally Ledger: 'New Woman writers of the fin de siecle were usually . . . stalwart supporters of heterosexual marriage, they had little or no conception of female sexual desire . . . and often had a considerable investment in eugenic and other imperialist discourses.'[2] Kate Chopin, on the other hand, eschewed good causes and social reformers; her art, again in Sally Ledger's words, 'approximated to the "feminine" "modern" style', Chopin's writing representing 'one (thoroughly sexualised) version of the New Woman' (p. 97). Chopin's literary influences were emphatically European rather than American, and, according to Per Seyersted, Chopin's second biographer, the only firm facts we have about Kate Chopin's library are that it contained the novel, *Elizabeth and Her German Garden* and, more significantly, a few issues of *The Yellow Book*.[3] Both Chopin and Gilman laid claim to new freedoms, particularly the freedom to walk the city streets, but they wished to put such freedoms to radically different uses.

To start with their common ground, however, both Charlotte Perkins Gilman and Kate Chopin loved physical exertion: 'With right early training I could easily have been an acrobat,' (p. 64) Gilman announces in her autobiography. 'I always feel so sorry for women who don't like to walk' says Chopin's Edna Pontellier, 'they miss so much – so many rare little glimpses of life; and we women learn so little of life on the whole' (Ch. 36). The freedom of the woman to move in the wider world is a concern that they share, both writing in the 1890s and challenging the male possession of the streets and the restricted and restrictive range of signification attached to the woman who goes out alone. As Gilman says, again in her autobiography:

A stalwart man once sharply contested my claim to this freedom to go alone. 'Any true man,' he said with fervor, 'is always ready to go with a

---

2   Sally Ledger, *The New Woman: Fiction and Feminism at the fin de siecle* (Manchester: Manchester University Press, 1997), 6.
3   Per Seyersted, *Kate Chopin: A Critical Biography* (Baton Rouge: Louisiana State University Press, 1969), 206. Henry Harland, an American writer, was the Literary Editor of *The Yellow* Book and Aubrey Beardsley, the illustrator, its Art Editor. The magazine was published in London by John Lane: The Bodley Head, between 1894 and 1897.

women at night. He is her natural protector.' 'Against what?' I inquired. As a matter of fact, the thing a woman is most afraid to meet on a dark street is her natural protector. Singular. Personally I have never known fear, except in dreams, that paralyzing terror born of indigestion. (p. 72)

Indigestion does not feature heavily in Chopin's tales of New Orleans; never afraid of indulgence, but seemingly strangers to excess, her protagonists savour the delights of French and Creole cuisine, crisp table linen and sparkling glasses; food consumed indoors in intimate spaces where the married woman and the man who would be her lover may dine unobserved: 'the quiet little restaurant that he knew and liked, with its sanded floor, its secluded atmosphere, its delicious menu, and its obsequious waiter'[4] in the story 'Athénaïse', or out of doors where yet another married woman invites the man she wishes were her lover to share the food perfectly prepared and served on 'a little green table, blotched with the checkered sunlight that filtered through the quivering leaves overhead' (Ch. 36) [. . .] It is through consumption that the woman's relationship with the city of New Orleans is expressed in Chopin's fiction, for it is in the consuming pleasures that the woman is both situated and stimulated in New Orleans – in matters of eating, drinking, smoking and sex. Conversely, it is in an attempt to bring about the prohibition of consumption, or the less desirable results of consumption, that Gilman goes out upon the streets, rehabilitation of the street as a safe space for women is her aim.

On matters of consumption, therefore, the two women occupy radically different positions – in Gilman's writing there is only one kind of drinker and one kind of smoker – loud red-faced men who – at best – abuse their wives and – at worst – lurk in railway stations or department stores looking for young women to deflower and sell into the white-slave trade. In Chopin, civilised men and women enjoy French wines and cigarettes, even the odd 'Egyptian cigarette', the sensual pleasure of consumption is one of the things which is celebrated in the city of New Orleans – and particularly in the stories 'In and Out of Old Natchitoches' and 'Athénaïse' and the novel, *The Awakening*. Women enjoy such pleasures on very precise terms, however. They enjoy them in the company of suitable men; any sign that they might be enjoying them without restraint, alone, in the company of women or with men known to be womanisers or gamblers, and they have overstepped the boundary between permitted and forbidden pleasures.

Gilman's treatise on the condition of women in America, *Women and Economics*, published in 1898, the year before *The Awakening*, is clear on the reasons why women are not at large in the city; economic dependence makes their presence out of doors and unattended suspicious. There are simply no legitimate reasons why a woman should be alone in the street; as Gilman says, this is 'a natural consequence of our division of labor on sex-lines, giving to woman the home and to man the world in which to work'[5] and, when this division of space

---

4   Per Seyersted, ed. *The Complete Works of Kate Chopin* (Baton Rouge: Louisiana State University Press, 1969), 447.

5   Charlotte Perkins Gilman, *Women and Economics* (1898; New York: Harper Torchbooks, 1966), 225.

cannot hold, it leads to what Gilman describes as the 'full flower of the sexuo-economic relation, – prostitution' (p. 171). Gilman's writings have only three types of women inhabiting the streets and they are all working women: prostitutes, working class factory or shop girls – easy prey for pimps and slavers – and female vigilantes – middle-aged women who haunt railway stations and other public spaces from which girls, fresh from the country or recently emigrated, need to be rescued from the hands of unscrupulous men. Chopin's working women in New Orleans are landladies, servants, a single artist and prostitutes. In the short short story 'Doctor Chevalier's Lie' the dead prostitute at the heart of the fabrication is a 'handsome girl, who was too clever to stay in an Arkansas cabin, and who was going away to seek her fortune in the big city' (*Complete Works*, p. 147). [. . .]

Chopin has a few women venture out onto the streets of New Orleans but they are maverick; they are transgressive women occupying liminal spaces, women emboldened by personal crisis to take steps which would otherwise be beyond their power. Athénaïse, treating New Orleans as a refuge from the physical proximity of a husband she finds repellent, moves around the city with fear and trepidation lest she should be identified by anyone she knows from the country; clinging to the arm of Monsieur Gouvernail, well-known inciter of mysterious but powerful sexual feelings in the bosoms of otherwise 'respectable' women, she samples the delights which New Orleans has to offer, gaining access to tastes and pleasures she has never before experienced in quite the way they are offered in the city. New Orleans in Chopin's fiction is the place where women grow up; but they are also eventually forced to grow down – to a sense of the paucity of their opportunities. It is the experience of the city which completes their fate. [. . .] As a part of this awakening to her 'duty', however, this young woman has learnt how to feel, how to be aroused by the sensual pleasures offered as consumables in the city but not connoting anything other than the drag of household responsibilities in the country. Athénaïse's desire is imitative, like Edna Pontellier's; she learns how to become aroused by choosing from the menu of everyday activity – walking, eating, conversation, sexual attraction – activities which are, however, about consumption in the city as opposed to production in the country and thus are converted to pleasure from duty. Trips to the lake, meals in intimate restaurants, walks along busy streets, these are only important because they take place in the city. The circumstances of quotidian existence in Natchitoches Parish are converted, for Athénaïse, to decadent events in New Orleans.

Edna Pontellier's dinner party, a feast with Swinburnian pretensions toward the dissolute, carries the full weight of signification of her new attitude toward consumption. It is Gouvernail, yet again, who is given the task of critiquing the mood through a literary reference:

There was a graven image of Desire
Painted with red blood on a ground of gold. (Ch. 30)

Across the Atlantic, in Marie Corelli's 1895 novel, *The Sorrows of Satan*, the female protagonist – 'a harpy and vulture of vice' comes to blame not only New

Woman fiction but the poetry of Swinburne for her monstrous sexual appetites and general decadence. From the bored housewife, uninterested in the details of household management – whether the chops are burnt and the food generally unfit for any self-respecting breadwinner, or the dress-making patterns for winter combinations for small bodies are cut out and ready to assemble – Edna becomes a table dresser of decadent proportions, a hostess superstar with cocktails matching the décor, food and drink that tantalise the palate just as she tantalises her guests with the mystery of the inspiration behind her new-found sensual awareness. This awakened sensuality is given full rein in the city as she walks, talks, gambles, eats and drinks in the public spaces of New Orleans, but its very expression contains the seeds of its own destruction as she realises not the extent but the limits upon her city life.

The restraints of the city for the woman are actually made manifest in the absence of an adequate language with which to articulate the inspiration and purpose of Edna's wanderings. There are three types of discourse available to express female activity which deviates from the norm: the first is the medical and Léonce Pontellier's instant response to Edna's absences from the house, her mysterious comings and goings and abandonment of her 'at home', is to discuss her as a case with Dr Mandelet, whose response, having seen her 'walking along Canal Street, the picture of health,' (Ch. 22), is to assume that she is having an affair with Alcée Arobin. When pathology fails, art may be diagnosed; Mademoiselle Reisz is permitted greater licence than other women both to practice her art and to be anti-social and ill-tempered. Edna's passing desire to be a painter gives her a certain degree of freedom from overt scrutiny and certain rules of conduct for bourgeois wives, but it is not an ambition she can sustain so artistic licence fails as a means to express her difference. The third discourse is, of course, the language used to describe a woman who is no better than she ought to be and this is the fate which Edna foresees and forestalls by her swim to her death. As Charlotte Perkins Gilman knew all too well, there are few lexical spaces for the woman out alone – and the role that Gilman's mature women play on the streets, that of social reformer – is not a role which Edna, refuser of maternity and pursuer of pleasure would even consider. Edna's awakening sensuality aspires, from the very beginning, to make her outward life consonant with her inner desires; she wants her body to be fully acknowledged in her way of life. She seeks to cast off the restraints of fashionable clothing and patterns of social organisation. Her sexual attraction toward Robert finds its first expression in her fascination with the rhythm of his walk: 'Again she watched his figure pass in and out of the strips of moonlight as he walked away.' (Ch. 10) Her walking, once she regains the city, is mimetic of masculine freedom of association; she kicks over the traces of domestic responsibility by walking, taking street cars, visiting the unfashionable, trying to walk off her physical restlessness, her newly charged sexuality, in the streets of New Orleans.

In both Chopin's New Orleans and Gilman's Chicago, female sexuality becomes material in the street. For the purposes of Gilman's social mission, women at large are eroticised as victims of predatory males or sanitised by their role as moral policewomen, sometimes literally as in her story, 'His Mother' where the middle-aged heroine becomes a detective, a salaried employee complete with a police badge concealed inside her coat. [. . .]

In common with other Chopin heroines, Athénaïse has to pack up her newly awakened sensuality and take it back to the country. The street into which Madame Ratignolle, once her pregnancy becomes advanced, will not venture except under cover of darkness, can only tolerate a strictly limited set of inter-pretations of female sexuality and the respectable woman cannot maintain that definition if she claims too much urban licence. It is the grim realisation of her contingent status, as mother not sexual subject, that haunts Edna Pontellier's final night in the city:

> Despondency had come upon her there in the wakeful night, and had never lifted. There was no one thing in the world that she desired. There was no human being whom she wanted near her except Robert; and she even realized that the day would come when he, too, and the thought of him would melt out of her existence, leaving her alone. The children appeared before her like antagonists who had overcome her; who had overpowered her and sought to drag her into the soul's slavery for the rest of her days. But she knew a way to elude them. She was not thinking of these things when she walked down to the beach. (Ch. 39)

Chopin's new woman, unable to locate an autonomous space in the city, accepts defeat in a return to nature, in death. Gilman's Ellen Burrell, having ensnared her own son, white slaver and pimp, in a police trap, commits herself to 'a long life in trying to do good enough to make up for her own share in his evil.'[6] One new woman surrenders herself to sensation, the other surrenders her son to the authorities; New Orleans and Chicago providing the city spaces in which two uncompromising configurations of the so-called new woman of the fin de siecle find utterance.

---

6   Denise D. Knight, ed. *'The Yellow Wallpaper' and Selected Short Stories of Charlotte Perkins Gilman* (London: Associated University Presses, 1994), 80.

Key passages

Introduction

The Awakening has its own unique style; it is written in a lyrical, sensuous language which is, in a number of ways, closer to poetry than to prose. The chapters are sometimes only one paragraph long; sometimes they extend to three or four pages. The organisation of the text does not conform to that which most of us would find familiar in the nineteenth-century novel in terms of length and detail. This text relies on other means to establish scene, setting and character. Some individuals depicted in the novel have a representative function, for example, the woman in black who seems to dog Edna's footsteps on Grand Isle, or the lovers who fail to be unobtrusive everywhere they go. The commentary here also gives an account of the role of the major players in the story of Edna Pontellier's awakening and pays particular attention to the catalytic effect of her friendships with Mademoiselle Reisz and Madame Ratignolle, looking in detail at her encounters with these women. Mademoiselle Reisz figures throughout the text as a representative of the woman who has managed to find a role for herself outside the conventional constraints of marriage and motherhood. She is an artist but her life is not glamorised by Chopin; rather the opposite, as Mademoiselle Reisz is portrayed as ugly and bad-tempered, living in inconvenient and insalubrious accommodation, and pursuing her independent existence at the cost of friends, family and comfort. The life she leads gives Edna an insight into the kind of maverick existence of the woman artist. Madame Ratignolle, similarly, has a presence as a richly rounded character but also as a symbol of the most stereotypical 'mother-woman', a warm and fluffy individual, devoted to the care and support of her husband and children to the exclusion of all else. She is an entirely domestic creature and as such stands in sharp contrast to Edna Pontellier.

To understand the tenor of Chopin's novel it is best to look at complete chapters; in this way the interest and excitement of her highly original style is not fractured. She structures the text in short sections and so it is possible to engage with an individual chapter as a lyrical whole. Whilst it is not practical or appropriate to include every chapter, gaps in continuity are addressed by commentary provided in headnotes.

To work with unbroken text has the additional advantage of allowing extensive commentary on the structure, themes and language of the novel. The selection of chapters here was guided by the desire to foreground all of the major thematic strains in the novel. It is possible, in this way, to trace the development of Edna's awakening from beginning to end, highlighting Chopin's use of rhetorical devices like repetition, symbolism and hyperbole. It is also possible to look at the circular structure of the text, highlighting in particular the figurative language which provides so much of the atmosphere as well as the narrative drive of the novel. A good example of the structural importance of the symbolic in the novel is Chopin's use of birds: the novel opens with a caged bird, Mademoiselle Reisz tells Edna 'The bird that would soar above the level plain of tradition and prejudice must have strong wings', and as Edna walks to her death a bird with a broken wing is circling overhead.

The commentary draws attention to important issues such as social class, ethnicity and Creole custom and practice, all of which link to the material provided in other parts of the volume which gives the historical and social background to the text. Debates in the magazines and journals of the day which address the control and containment of women are taken up and woven into the text of *The Awakening* by Chopin. For instance, in her unconventional portrayal of women smoking or women walking she can be seen to be responding to contemporary concerns about such activities whilst also making a point about individual freedom. Chopin manages to place serious questions about the fundamental principles of family life – particularly marriage and motherhood – and of religious beliefs and practices, at the heart of the novel without ever sermonising or making direct authorial interventions. The headnotes make clear the function and significance of the various strands which are held together in the very fabric of the narrative.

Key Passages

Chapter One

In this first, brief chapter, Chopin manages to communicate a great deal of information about the life of her heroine, Edna Pontellier, whilst also establishing many of the dominant themes in the novel.

The image of the caged bird with which the novel opens has often been commented upon. References to flight and entrapment recur throughout the text resonating symbolically with the predicament of Edna Pontellier; for instance, as she walks to her death at the end of the novel a bird with a broken wing circles down to the water before her. Also introduced here is the language of possession; Mr Pontellier is said to look at his sunburnt wife 'as one looks at a valuable piece of personal property which has suffered some damage'. As Edna returns from the sea she puts her wedding ring back on, taking it from her husband 'silently'. This is the first in a series of removals and restorations of the clothes and jewellery which signify her position as a married woman. Léonce Pontellier is here delineated, as he will be throughout the novel, as a man absorbed by the world of business, the company of men, financial autonomy and the pursuit of extra-familial pleasures. He is described here and elsewhere as a generous man but one who is largely absent.

Robert Lebrun, seen for the first of many times returning from the beach with Mrs Pontellier, is set up as a ladies' man; he admits 'quite frankly' that he prefers the company of women in general and Mrs Pontellier in particular. In Creole society the role of resort bachelor was deemed to be harmless to married women; there are intimations here, however, that the intimacy between Robert and Edna will take an inappropriate turn. Many of the other people introduced here have important structural roles but are not fleshed out as characters. The woman 'telling her beads' shadows Edna throughout her time on Grand Isle, counting off her prayers whilst Edna moves further and further away from the teachings of the church. The Farival twins are young girls on the threshold of womanhood, encouraged to parade their accomplishments but to remain otherwise silent. Similarly the 'quadroon nurse' and her charges, the Pontellier children, are described, but remain substantially in the background; in other words, Edna's distance as a mother is reflected in the organisation of the narrative.

A green and yellow parrot, which hung in a cage outside the door, kept repeating over and over:

'*Allez vous-en! Allez vous-en! Sapristi!*[1] That's all right!'

He could speak a little Spanish, and also a language which nobody understood, unless it was the mocking-bird that hung on the other side of the door, whistling his fluty notes out upon the breeze with maddening persistence.

Mr. Pontellier, unable to read his newspaper with any degree of comfort, arose with an expression and an exclamation of disgust. He walked down the gallery and across the narrow 'bridges' which connected the Lebrun cottages one with the other. He had been seated before the door of the main house. The parrot and the mocking-bird were the property of Madame Lebrun, and they had the right to make all the noise they wished. Mr. Pontellier had the privilege of quitting their society when they ceased to be entertaining.

He stopped before the door of his own cottage, which was the fourth one from the main building and next to the last. Seating himself in a wicker rocker which was there, he once more applied himself to the task of reading the newspaper. The day was Sunday; the paper was a day old. The Sunday papers had not yet reached Grand Isle. He was already acquainted with the market reports, and he glanced restlessly over the editorials and bits of news which he had not had time to read before quitting New Orleans the day before.

Mr. Pontellier wore eye-glasses. He was a man of forty, of medium height and rather slender build; he stooped a little. His hair was brown and straight, parted on one side. His beard was neatly and closely trimmed.

Once in a while he withdrew his glance from the newspaper and looked about him. There was more noise than ever over at the house. The main building was called 'the house,' to distinguish it from the cottages. The chattering and whistling birds were still at it. Two young girls, the Farival twins, were playing a duet from 'Zampa' upon the piano. Madame Lebrun was bustling in and out, giving orders in a high key to a yard-boy whenever she got inside the house, and directions in an equally high voice to a dining-room servant whenever she got outside. She was a fresh, pretty woman, clad always in white with elbow sleeves. Her starched skirts crinkled as she came and went. Farther down, before one of the cottages, a lady in black was walking demurely up and down, telling her beads. A good many persons of the *pension*[2] had gone over to the *Chênière Caminada*[3] in Beaudelet's lugger to hear mass. Some young people were out under the water-oaks playing croquet. Mr. Pontellier's two children were there – sturdy little fellows of four and five. A quadroon nurse followed them about with a far-away, meditative air.

Mr. Pontellier finally lit a cigar and began to smoke, letting the paper drag idly from his hand. He fixed his gaze upon a white sunshade that was advancing at snail's pace from the beach. He could see it plainly between the gaunt trunks of the water-oaks and across the stretch of yellow camomile. The gulf looked far

---

1   'Get out! Get out! Damn it!'
2   A small hotel.
3   A Creole resort island, like Grand Isle, situated in Jefferson Parish, Louisiana.

away, melting hazily into the blue of the horizon. The sunshade continued to approach slowly. Beneath its pink-lined shelter were his wife, Mrs. Pontellier, and young Robert Lebrun. When they reached the cottage, the two seated themselves with some appearance of fatigue upon the upper step of the porch, facing each other, each leaning against a supporting post.

'What folly! to bathe at such an hour in such heat!' exclaimed Mr. Pontellier. He himself had taken a plunge at daylight. That was why the morning seemed long to him.

'You are burnt beyond recognition,' he added, looking at his wife as one looks at a valuable piece of personal property which has suffered some damage. She held up her hands, strong, shapely hands, and surveyed them critically, drawing up her lawn sleeves above the wrists. Looking at them reminded her of her rings, which she had given to her husband before leaving for the beach. She silently reached out to him, and he understanding, took the rings from his vest pocket and dropped them into her open palm. She slipped them upon her fingers; then clasping her knees, she looked across at Robert and began to laugh. The rings sparkled upon her fingers. He sent back an answering smile.

'What is it?' asked Pontellier, looking lazily and amused from one to the other. It was some utter nonsense; some adventure out there in the water, and they both tried to relate it at once. It did not seem half so amusing when told. They realized this, and so did Mr. Pontellier. He yawned and stretched himself. Then he got up, saying he had half a mind to go over to Klein's hotel and play a game of billiards.

'Come go along, Lebrun,' he proposed to Robert. But Robert admitted quite frankly that he preferred to stay where he was and talk to Mrs. Pontellier.

'Well, send him about his business when he bores you, Edna,' instructed her husband as he prepared to leave.

'Here, take the umbrella,' she exclaimed, holding it out to him. He accepted the sunshade, and lifting it over his head descended the steps and walked away.

'Coming back to dinner?' his wife called after him. He halted a moment and shrugged his shoulders. He felt in his vest pocket; there was a ten-dollar bill there. He did not know; perhaps he would return for the early dinner and perhaps he would not. It all depended upon the company which he found over at Klein's and the size of 'the game.' He did not say this, but she understood it, and laughed, nodding good-by to him.

Both children wanted to follow their father when they saw him starting out. He kissed them and promised to bring them back bonbons and peanuts.

Chapter Two

The economic and social position of Robert Lebrun is established here as much inferior to the Pontelliers, although it is made clear that his mother earns a good living from the summer resort. Whilst Mr Pontellier is set up as a paternalistic figure to both his wife and Robert, their youthfulness, self-absorption and vanity are gently mocked; they are also said to resemble each other physically. Robert's oft-vaunted ambition to go to seek his fortune in Mexico is introduced both to demonstrate his general indecisiveness and to anticipate an actual development in the plot. In broader terms this enables Chopin to refer to a wider, predominantly masculine, theme in American literature, that of escape, of making a fresh start in an unknown land. This is a course of action ultimately unavailable to Edna Pontellier.

Mrs. Pontellier's eyes were quick and bright; they were a yellowish brown, about the color of her hair. She had a way of turning them swiftly upon an object and holding them there as if lost in some inward maze of contemplation or thought. Her eyebrows were a shade darker than her hair. They were thick and almost horizontal, emphasizing the depth of her eyes. She was rather handsome than beautiful. Her face was captivating by reason of a certain frankness of expression and a contradictory subtle play of features. Her manner was engaging.

Robert rolled a cigarette. He smoked cigarettes because he could not afford cigars, he said. He had a cigar in his pocket which Mr. Pontellier had presented him with, and he was saving it for his after-dinner smoke.

This seemed quite proper and natural on his part. In coloring he was not unlike his companion. A clean-shaved face made the resemblance more pronounced than it would otherwise have been. There rested no shadow of care upon his open countenance. His eyes gathered in and reflected the light and languor of the summer day.

Mrs. Pontellier reached over for a palm-leaf fan that lay on the porch and began to fan herself, while Robert sent between his lips light puffs from his cigarette. They chatted incessantly: about the things around them; their amusing adventure out in the water – it had again assumed its entertaining aspect; about the wind, the trees, the people who had gone to the *Chênière*; about the children playing croquet under the oaks, and the Farival twins, who were now performing the overture to 'The Poet and the Peasant.'

Robert talked a good deal about himself. He was very young, and did not know any better. Mrs. Pontellier talked a little about herself for the same reason. Each was interested in what the other said. Robert spoke of his intention to go to Mexico in the autumn, where fortune awaited him. He was always intending to go to Mexico, but some way never got there. Meanwhile he held on to his modest position in a mercantile house in New Orleans, where an equal familiarity with English, French and Spanish gave him no small value as a clerk and correspondent.

He was spending his summer vacation as he always did, with his mother at Grand Isle. In former times, before Robert could remember, 'the house' had been a summer luxury of the Lebruns. Now, flanked by its dozen or more cottages, which were always filled with exclusive visitors from the '*Quartier Français*,'[1] it

---

1   The French quarter of New Orleans.

enabled Madame Lebrun to maintain the easy and comfortable existence which appeared to be her birthright.

Mrs. Pontellier talked about her father's Mississippi plantation and her girlhood home in the old Kentucky blue-grass country.[2] She was an American woman, with a small infusion of French which seemed to have been lost in dilution. She read a letter from her sister, who was away in the East, and who had engaged herself to be married. Robert was interested, and wanted to know what manner of girls the sisters were, what the father was like, and how long the mother had been dead.

When Mrs. Pontellier folded the letter it was time for her to dress for the early dinner.

'I see Léonce isn't coming back,' she said, with a glance in the direction whence her husband had disappeared. Robert supposed he was not, as there were a good many New Orleans club men over at Klein's.

When Mrs. Pontellier left him to enter her room, the young man descended the steps and strolled over toward the croquet players, where, during the half-hour before dinner, he amused himself with the little Pontellier children, who were very fond of him.

Chapter Three

Again Mr Pontellier is characterised by the money in his pocket. The dynamics of the family relationship, established in the opening chapter, are embellished by his tipsy accusations of Edna's neglect – of both him and the children. Chopin makes judicious use of cliché: as he stumbles in late from the bar, he expects the full attention of 'the sole object of his existence'. Léonce's haranguing of his wife, however, precipitates an emotional reaction which she is seemingly helpless to control. Chopin's manner of describing Edna's despair is in the passive voice, a mode to which she returns time and time again when articulating a sense of Edna's disengagement from the realities of her everyday life (see the discussion of Chapter Six, pp. 112–13). Her feelings are given voice as a general sense of 'oppression', as 'a shadow, like a mist passing across her soul's summer day' rather than as a specific and direct expression of anger or upset at her husband's treatment of her. Chopin does not allow this scene to become over-sentimental or melodramatic as she dispels the mood by reference to the mosquitoes which drive Edna indoors and normality is resumed the next day as Mr Pontellier leaves for the city, dispensing gifts along the way.

It was eleven o'clock that night when Mr. Pontellier returned from Klein's hotel. He was in an excellent humor, in high spirits, and very talkative. His entrance awoke

2   A region of central Kentucky noted for its lush blue-grass and the breeding of thoroughbred racehorses.

his wife, who was in bed and fast asleep when he came in. He talked to her while he undressed, telling her anecdotes and bits of news and gossip that he had gathered during the day. From his trousers pockets he took a fistful of crumpled bank notes and a good deal of silver coin, which he piled on the bureau indiscriminately with keys, knife, handkerchief, and whatever else happened to be in his pockets. She was overcome with sleep, and answered him with little half utterances.

He thought it very discouraging that his wife, who was the sole object of his existence, evinced so little interest in things which concerned him, and valued so little his conversation.

Mr. Pontellier had forgotten the bonbons and peanuts for the boys. Notwithstanding he loved them very much, and went into the adjoining room where they slept to take a look at them and make sure that they were resting comfortably. The result of his investigation was far from satisfactory. He turned and shifted the youngsters about in bed. One of them began to kick and talk about a basket full of crabs.

Mr. Pontellier returned to his wife with the information that Raoul had a high fever and needed looking after. Then he lit a cigar and went and sat near the open door to smoke it.

Mrs. Pontellier was quite sure Raoul had no fever. He had gone to bed perfectly well, she said, and nothing had ailed him all day. Mr. Pontellier was too well acquainted with fever symptoms to be mistaken. He assured her the child was consuming at that moment in the next room.

He reproached his wife with her inattention, her habitual neglect of the children. If it was not a mother's place to look after children, whose on earth was it? He himself had his hands full with his brokerage business. He could not be in two places at once; making a living for his family on the street, and staying at home to see that no harm befell them. He talked in a monotonous, insistent way.

Mrs. Pontellier sprang out of bed and went into the next room. She soon came back and sat on the edge of the bed, leaning her head down on the pillow. She said nothing, and refused to answer her husband when he questioned her. When his cigar was smoked out he went to bed, and in half a minute he was fast asleep.

Mrs. Pontellier was by that time thoroughly awake. She began to cry a little, and wiped her eyes on the sleeve of her *peignoir*.[1] Blowing out the candle, which her husband had left burning, she slipped her bare feet into a pair of satin *mules* at the foot of the bed and went out on the porch, where she sat down in the wicker chair and began to rock gently to and fro.

It was then past midnight. The cottages were all dark. A single faint light gleamed out from the hallway of the house. There was no sound abroad except the hooting of an old owl in the top of a water-oak, and the everlasting voice of the sea, that was not uplifted at that soft hour. It broke like a mournful lullaby upon the night.

The tears came so fast to Mrs. Pontellier's eyes that the damp sleeve of her *peignoir* no longer served to dry them. She was holding the back of her chair with

---

1   Woman's dressing gown.

one hand; her loose sleeve had slipped almost to the shoulder of her uplifted arm. Turning, she thrust her face, steaming and wet, into the bend of her arm, and she went on crying there, not caring any longer to dry her face, her eyes, her arms. She could not have told why she was crying. Such experiences as the foregoing were not uncommon in her married life. They seemed never before to have weighed much against the abundance of her husband's kindness and a uniform devotion which had come to be tacit and self-understood.

An indescribable oppression, which seemed to generate in some unfamiliar part of her consciousness, filled her whole being with a vague anguish. It was like a shadow, like a mist passing across her soul's summer day. It was strange and unfamiliar; it was a mood. She did not sit there inwardly upbraiding her husband, lamenting at Fate, which had directed her footsteps to the path which they had taken. She was just having a good cry all to herself. The mosquitoes made merry over her, biting her firm, round arms and nipping at her bare insteps.

The little stinging, buzzing imps succeeded in dispelling a mood which might have held her there in the darkness half a night longer.

The following morning Mr. Pontellier was up in good time to take the rockaway[2] which was to convey him to the steamer at the wharf. He was returning to the city to his business, and they would not see him again at the Island till the coming Saturday. He had regained his composure, which seemed to have been somewhat impaired the night before. He was eager to be gone, as he looked forward to a lively week in Carondelet Street.[3]

Mr. Pontellier gave his wife half of the money which he had brought away from Klein's hotel the evening before. She liked money as well as most women, and accepted it with no little satisfaction.

'It will buy a handsome wedding present for Sister Janet!' she exclaimed, smoothing out the bills as she counted them one by one.

'Oh! we'll treat Sister Janet better than that, my dear,' he laughed, as he prepared to kiss her good-by.

The boys were tumbling about, clinging to his legs, imploring that numerous things be brought back to them. Mr. Pontellier was a great favorite, and ladies, men, children, even nurses, were always on hand to say good-by to him. His wife stood smiling and waving, the boys shouting, as he disappeared in the old rockaway down the sandy road.

A few days later a box arrived for Mrs. Pontellier from New Orleans. It was from her husband. It was filled with *friandises*,[4] with luscious and toothsome bits – the finest of fruits, *patés*, a rare bottle or two, delicious syrups, and bonbons in abundance. Mrs. Pontellier was always very generous with the contents of such a box; she was quite used to receiving them when away from home. The *patés* and fruit were brought to the dining-room; the bonbons were passed around. And the

---

2 A four-wheeled horse-drawn carriage.
3 A New Orleans street in the business district.
4 Delicacies.

ladies, selecting with dainty and discriminating fingers and a little greedily, all declared that Mr. Pontellier was the best husband in the world. Mrs. Pontellier was forced to admit that she knew of none better.

Chapter Four

As is often the case when describing marital relationships or gendered roles Chopin uses cliché to great ironic effect. This technique is deployed very effectively in the depiction of Adèle Ratignolle, 'mother-woman' par excellence, who is rendered as 'the bygone heroine of romance and fair lady of our dreams'. Her total devotion to the wants and needs of husband and children stands in stark contrast to Edna Pontellier's more casual approach to her domestic duties, an opposition reinforced by the opening description of Edna's boys, their toughness and independence.

As has been previously established, the fact that Edna comes from Kentucky, and is therefore not of Creole descent or training, defines her as an outsider. The inhabitants of the Louisiana Chopin portrays, consider themselves to be more French than American; Edna, therefore, is a 'foreigner' who, it is clear, does not really understand the terms upon which men and women interact in Creole society. Nowhere is this more evident than in her reaction to the free and frank discussions of childbirth that take place in mixed company. Unlike Adèle, Edna is not effusive in praise of children or husband, but merely matter of fact; when faced with a risqué novel, for instance, she cannot express herself at all in public but must hide away to read it. The absence of inhibition amongst the Creoles is, it is made clear, maintained alongside a strict adherence to conventional morality, neither of which codes of behaviour are recognised by Edna.

It would have been a difficult matter for Mr. Pontellier to define to his own satisfaction or any one else's wherein his wife failed in her duty toward their children. It was something which he felt rather than perceived, and he never voiced the feeling without subsequent regret and ample atonement.

If one of the little Pontellier boys took a tumble whilst at play, he was not apt to rush crying to his mother's arms for comfort; he would more likely pick himself up, wipe the water out of his eyes and the sand out of his mouth, and go on playing. Tots as they were, they pulled together and stood their ground in childish battles with doubled fists and uplifted voices, which usually prevailed against the other mother-tots. The quadroon nurse was looked upon as a huge encumbrance, only good to button up waists and panties and to brush and part hair; since it seemed to be a law of society that hair must be parted and brushed.

In short, Mrs. Pontellier was not a mother-woman. The mother-women seemed to prevail that summer at Grand Isle. It was easy to know them, fluttering about with extended, protecting wings when any harm, real or imaginary, threatened their precious brood. They were women who idolized their children, worshiped their husbands, and esteemed it a holy privilege to efface themselves as individuals and grow wings as ministering angels.

Many of them were delicious in the rôle; one of them was the embodiment of every womanly grace and charm. If her husband did not adore her, he was a brute, deserving of death by slow torture. Her name was Adèle Ratignolle. There are no words to describe her save the old ones that have served so often to picture the bygone heroine of romance and the fair lady of our dreams. There was nothing subtle or hidden about her charms; her beauty was all there, flaming and apparent: the spun-gold hair that comb nor confining pin could restrain; the blue eyes that were like nothing but sapphires; two lips that pouted, that were so red one could only think of cherries or some other delicious crimson fruit in looking at them. She was growing a little stout, but it did not seem to detract an iota from the grace of every step, pose, gesture. One would not have wanted her white neck a mite less full or her beautiful arms more slender. Never were hands more exquisite than hers, and it was a joy to look at them when she threaded her needle or adjusted her gold thimble to her taper middle finger as she sewed away on the little night-drawers or fashioned a bodice or a bib.

Madame Ratignolle was very fond of Mrs. Pontellier, and often she took her sewing and went over to sit with her in the afternoons. She was sitting there the afternoon of the day the box arrived from New Orleans. She had possession of the rocker, and she was busily engaged in sewing upon a diminutive pair of night-drawers.

She had brought the pattern of the drawers for Mrs. Pontellier to cut out – a marvel of construction, fashioned to enclose a baby's body so effectually that only two small eyes might look out from the garment, like an Eskimo's. They were designed for winter wear, when treacherous drafts came down chimneys and insidious currents of deadly cold found their way through key-holes.

Mrs. Pontellier's mind was quite at rest concerning the present material needs of her children, and she could not see the use of anticipating and making winter night garments the subject of her summer meditations. But she did not want to appear unamiable and uninterested, so she had brought forth newspapers, which she spread upon the floor of the gallery, and under Madame Ratignolle's directions she had cut a pattern of the impervious garment.

Robert was there, seated as he had been the Sunday before, and Mrs. Pontellier also occupied her former position on the upper step, leaning listlessly against the post. Beside her was a box of bonbons, which she held out at intervals to Madame Ratignolle.

That lady seemed at a loss to make a selection, but finally settled upon a stick of nougat, wondering if it were not too rich; whether it could possibly hurt her. Madame Ratignolle had been married seven years. About every two years she had a baby. At that time she had three babies, and was beginning to think of a fourth one. She was always talking about her 'condition.' Her 'condition' was in no way apparent, and no one would have known a thing about it but for her persistence in making it the subject of conversation.

Robert started to reassure her, asserting that he had known a lady who had subsisted upon nougat during the entire – but seeing the color mount into Mrs. Pontellier's face he checked himself and changed the subject.

Mrs. Pontellier, though she had married a Creole, was not thoroughly at home in the society of Creoles; never before had she been thrown so intimately among them. There were only Creoles that summer at Lebrun's. They all knew each other, and felt like one large family, among whom existed the most amicable relations. A characteristic which distinguished them and which impressed Mrs. Pontellier most forcibly was their entire absence of prudery. Their freedom of expression was at first incomprehensible to her, though she had no difficulty in reconciling it with a lofty chastity which in the Creole woman seems to be inborn and unmistakable. Never would Edna Pontellier forget the shock with which she heard Madame Ratignolle relating to old Monsieur Farival the harrowing story of one of her *accouchements*,[1] withholding no intimate detail. She was growing accustomed to like shocks, but she could not keep the mounting color back from her cheeks. Oftener than once her coming had interrupted the droll story with which Robert was entertaining some amused group of married women.

A book had gone the rounds of the *pension*. When it came her turn to read it, she did so with profound astonishment. She felt moved to read the book in secret and solitude, though none of the others had done so – to hide it from view at the sound of approaching footsteps. It was openly criticized and freely discussed at table. Mrs. Pontellier gave over being astonished, and concluded that wonders would never cease.

Chapter Six

This chapter is both short and lyrical and registers the first point at which the narrative is not advanced by action or description; instead, Edna's interior consciousness is explored, again in the passive voice. The passive voice is used where the subject of the verb is apparently not an active agent but is a recipient of the action. The effect of using this form is almost to remove free will from Edna; feelings over which she has little control seem to arise unbidden. Chopin refers us back to the tearful scene with Léonce as a way of indicating that there have been repeat incidents of her bout of seemingly inexplicable weeping, without having to go into detail. Without aggrandising the significance of Mrs Pontellier's growing feelings of uncertainty, Chopin nevertheless manages to convey a sense of the cataclysmic effect of such a personal crisis by using language which encompasses the heights and depths of both nature and supernature as Edna begins to 'realize her position in the universe as a human being'.

The sea as a motif makes its first symbolic appearance in this chapter. The sea is clearly associated with the confusion and excitement of the re-birth of Edna

---

1   Childbirths.

as an individual, both literally when she learns to swim (see discussion of Chapter Ten, **pp. 118–22**) and metaphorically as she emerges from this period in her life having been opened up to all kinds of new sensations. Chopin's language is indeed sensational: supplicatory, tactile and intimate, it establishes a rhythm of sensuality and experimentation. The search for self-fulfilment is fraught with danger but the attractions are many, as is made plain by Chopin: 'The touch of the sea is sensuous, enfolding the body in its soft, close embrace' – a sentence which is repeated verbatim in the final chapter as Edna walks down to the sea for her final swim.

Edna Pontellier could not have told why, wishing to go to the beach with Robert, she should in the first place have declined, and in the second place have followed in obedience to one of the two contradictory impulses which impelled her.

A certain light was beginning to dawn dimly within her – the light which, showing the way, forbids it.

At that early period it served but to bewilder her. It moved her to dreams, to thoughtfulness, to the shadowy anguish which had overcome her the midnight when she had abandoned herself to tears.

In short, Mrs. Pontellier was beginning to realize her position in the universe as a human being, and to recognize her relations as an individual to the world within and about her. This may seem like a ponderous weight of wisdom to descend upon the soul of a young woman of twenty-eight – perhaps more wisdom than the Holy Ghost is usually pleased to vouchsafe to any woman.

But the beginning of things, of a world especially, is necessarily vague, tangled, chaotic, and exceedingly disturbing. How few of us ever emerge from such beginning! How many souls perish in its tumult!

The voice of the sea is seductive; never ceasing, whispering, clamoring, murmuring, inviting the soul to wander for a spell in abysses of solitude; to lose itself in mazes of inward contemplation.

The voice of the sea speaks to the soul. The touch of the sea is sensuous, enfolding the body in its soft, close embrace.

Chapter Seven

This chapter is written in a comparatively expansive style; a great deal of information about Edna's past is communicated through both direct and indirect means. One of the most arresting features of Chopin's writing is the straightforwardness of her descriptions of the sensual. It is significant that Edna's arousal to a heightened awareness of her own body and sexual potential is in the company of Madame Ratignolle. Her inhibitions are broken down by the 'excessive physical charm of the Creole', so that from an opening which declares Edna to be 'not a woman given to confidences', she arrives at a point where the 'unaccustomed taste of candor . . . muddled her like wine, or like a first breath of freedom'. Whilst stopping short of the suggestion that Edna is feeling same-sex desire, Chopin leaves us in no doubt that the homo-erotic stimulus is perhaps the most important factor in her awakening.

In the background, a pair of lovers are enjoying the freedom of the summer, 'exchanging their hearts' yearnings beneath the children's tent' and, like the woman in black, they will reappear throughout the narrative, reminding the reader of the courtship rituals of youth. As Edna opens up to her friend, recounting experiences of childhood and adolescence, and in particular, feelings of sexual bewilderment, so she makes connections between her youthful infatuations and her current state of uncertainty. As elsewhere in the text, Chopin makes much of the detail of the women's clothing: their dress, individual style and physical type is communicative of more than fashion choice, it also speaks of their attitude to home and family. Edna's difference from the crowd is emphasised so that we are not surprised when her marriage is described not in terms of romantic fulfilment or passion but as taking her into 'the world of reality' where her husband and children are sometimes loved and sometimes forgotten. The spell cast by Edna's confessions to Madame Ratignolle is broken by Robert's arrival with the Pontellier and Ratignolle children in tow; the lovers are dislodged as the children reassume their rightful place in the tent and in the order of things.

Mrs. Pontellier was not a woman given to confidences, a characteristic hitherto contrary to her nature. Even as a child she had lived her own small life all within herself. At a very early period she had apprehended instinctively the dual life – that outward existence which conforms, the inward life which questions.

That summer at Grand Isle she began to loosen a little the mantle of reserve that had always enveloped her. There may have been – there must have been – influences, both subtle and apparent, working in their several ways to induce her to do this; but the most obvious was the influence of Adèle Ratignolle. The excessive physical charm of the Creole had first attracted her, for Edna had a sensuous susceptibility to beauty. Then the candor of the woman's whole existence, which every one might read, and which formed so striking a contrast to her own habitual reserve – this might have furnished a link. Who can tell what metals the gods use in forging the subtle bond which we call sympathy, which we might as well call love.

The two women went away one morning to the beach together, arm in arm, under the huge white sunshade. Edna had prevailed upon Madame Ratignolle to leave the children behind, though she could not induce her to relinquish a diminutive roll of needlework, which Adèle begged to be allowed to slip into the depths of her pocket. In some unaccountable way they had escaped from Robert.

The walk to the beach was no inconsiderable one, consisting as it did of a long, sandy path, upon which a sporadic and tangled growth that bordered it on either side made frequent and unexpected inroads. There were acres of yellow camomile reaching out on either hand. Further away still, vegetable gardens abounded, with frequent small plantations of orange or lemon trees intervening. The dark green clusters glistened from afar in the sun.

The women were both of goodly height, Madame Ratignolle possessing the more feminine and matronly figure. The charm of Edna Pontellier's physique stole insensibly upon you. The lines of her body were long, clean and symmetrical; it was a body which occasionally fell into splendid poses; there was no suggestion of the trim, stereotyped fashion-plate about it. A casual and indiscriminating observer, in passing, might not cast a second glance upon the figure. But with more feeling and discernment he would have recognized the noble beauty of its modeling, and the graceful severity of poise and movement, which made Edna Pontellier different from the crowd.

She wore a cool muslin that morning – white, with a waving vertical line of brown running through it; also a white linen collar and the big straw hat which she had taken from the peg outside the door. The hat rested any way on her yellow-brown hair, that waved a little, was heavy, and clung close to her head.

Madame Ratignolle, more careful of her complexion, had twined a gauze veil about her head. She wore dogskin gloves, with gauntlets that protected her wrists. She was dressed in pure white, with a fluffiness of ruffles that became her. The draperies and fluttering things which she wore suited her rich, luxuriant beauty as a greater severity of line could not have done.

There were a number of bathhouses along the beach, of rough but solid construction, built with small, protecting galleries facing the water. Each house consisted of two compartments, and each family at Lebrun's possessed a compartment for itself, fitted out with all the essential paraphernalia of the bath and whatever other conveniences the owners might desire. The two women had no intention of bathing; they had just strolled down to the beach for a walk and to be alone and near the water. The Pontellier and Ratignolle compartments adjoined one another under the same roof. Mrs. Pontellier had brought down her key through force of habit. Unlocking the door of her bath-room she went inside, and soon emerged, bringing a rug, which she spread upon the floor of the gallery, and two huge hair pillows covered with crash, which she placed against the front of the building.

The two seated themselves there in the shade of the porch, side by side, with their backs against the pillows and their feet extended. Madame Ratignolle removed her veil, wiped her face with a rather delicate handkerchief, and fanned herself with the fan which she always carried suspended somewhere about her person by a long, narrow ribbon. Edna removed her collar and opened her dress at the throat. She took the fan from Madame Ratignolle and began to fan both herself and her companion. It was very warm, and for a while they did nothing but exchange remarks about the heat, the sun, the glare. But there was a breeze blowing, a choppy, stiff wind that whipped the water into froth. It fluttered the skirts of the two women and kept them for a while engaged in adjusting, readjusting, tucking in, securing hair-pins and hat-pins. A few persons were sporting some distance away in the water. The beach was very still of human sound at that hour.

The lady in black was reading her morning devotions on the porch of a neighboring bath-house. Two young lovers were exchanging their hearts' yearnings beneath the children's tent, which they had found unoccupied. Edna Pontellier, casting her eyes about, had finally kept them at rest upon the sea. The day was clear and carried the gaze out as far as the blue sky went; there were a few white clouds suspended idly over the horizon. A lateen sail was visible in the direction of Cat Island, and others to the south seemed almost motionless in the far distance.

'Of whom – of what are you thinking?' asked Adèle of her companion, whose countenance she had been watching with a little amused attention, arrested by the absorbed expression which seemed to have seized and fixed every feature into a statuesque repose.

'Nothing,' returned Mrs. Pontellier, with a start, adding at once: 'How stupid! But it seems to me it is the reply we make instinctively to such a question. Let me see,' she went on, throwing back her head and narrowing her fine eyes till they shone like two vivid points of light. 'Let me see. I was really not conscious of thinking of anything; but perhaps I can retrace my thoughts.'

'Oh! never mind!' laughed Madame Ratignolle. 'I am not quite so exacting. I will let you off this time. It is really too hot to think, especially to think about thinking.'

'But for the fun of it,' persisted Edna 'First of all, the sight of the water stretching so far away, those motionless sails against the blue sky, made a delicious picture that I just wanted to sit and look at. The hot wind beating in my face made me think – without any connection that I can trace – of a summer day in Kentucky, of a meadow that seemed as big as the ocean to the very little girl walking through the grass, which was higher than her waist. She threw out her arms as if swimming when she walked, beating the tall grass as one strikes out in the water. Oh, I see the connection now!'

'Where were you going that day in Kentucky, walking through the grass?'

'I don't remember now. I was just walking diagonally across a big field. My sunbonnet obstructed the view. I could see only the stretch of green before me, and I felt as if I must walk on forever, without coming to the end of it. I don't remember whether I was frightened or pleased. I must have been entertained. Likely as not it was Sunday,' she laughed; 'and I was running away from prayers, from the Presbyterian service, read in a spirit of gloom by my father that chills me yet to think of.'

'And have you been running away from prayers ever since, *ma chère?*' asked Madame Ratignolle, amused.

'No! oh, no!' Edna hastened to say. 'I was a little unthinking child in those days, just following a misleading impulse without question. On the contrary, during one period of my life religion took a firm hold upon me; after I was twelve and until – until – why, I suppose until now, though I never thought much about it – just driven along by habit. But do you know,' she broke off, turning her quick eyes upon Madame Ratignolle and leaning forward a little so as to bring her face quite close to that of her companion, 'sometimes I feel this summer as if I were walking through the green meadow again; idly, aimlessly, unthinking and unguided.'

Madame Ratignolle laid her hand over that of Mrs. Pontellier, which was near her. Seeing that the hand was not withdrawn, she clasped it firmly and warmly. She even stroked it a little, fondly, with the other hand, murmuring in an undertone, '*Pauvre chérie.*'[1]

The action was at first a little confusing to Edna, but she soon lent herself readily to the Creole's gentle caress. She was not accustomed to an outward and spoken expression of affection, either in herself or in others. She and her younger sister, Janet, had quarreled a good deal through force of unfortunate habit. Her older sister, Margaret, was matronly and dignified, probably from having assumed matronly and housewifely responsibilities too early in life, their mother having died when they were quite young. Margaret was not effusive; she was practical. Edna had had an occasional girl friend, but whether accidentally or not, they seemed to have been all of one type – the self-contained. She never realized that the reserve of her own character had much, perhaps everything, to do with this. Her most intimate friend at school had been one of rather exceptional intellectual gifts, who wrote fine-sounding essays, which Edna admired and strove to imitate; and with her she talked and glowed over the English classics, and sometimes held religious and political controversies. Edna often wondered at one propensity which sometimes had inwardly disturbed her without causing any outward show or manifestation on her part. At a very early age – perhaps it was when she traversed the ocean of waving grass – she remembered that she had been passionately enamored of a dignified and sad-eyed cavalry officer who visited her father in Kentucky. She could not leave his presence when he was there, nor remove her eyes from his face, which was something like Napoleon's, with a lock of black hair falling across the forehead. But the cavalry officer melted imperceptibly out of her existence.

At another time her affections were deeply engaged by a young gentleman who visited a lady on a neighboring plantation. It was after they went to Mississippi to live. The young man was engaged to be married to the young lady, and they sometimes called upon Margaret, driving over of afternoons in a buggy. Edna was a little miss, just merging into her teens; and the realization that she herself was nothing, nothing, nothing to the engaged young man was a bitter affliction to her. But he, too, went the way of dreams.

She was a grown young woman when she was overtaken by what she supposed to be the climax of her fate. It was when the face and figure of a great tragedian began to haunt her imagination and stir her senses. The persistence of the infatuation lent it an aspect of genuineness. The hopelessness of it colored it with the lofty tones of a great passion.

The picture of the tragedian stood enframed upon her desk. Any one may possess the portrait of a tragedian without exciting suspicion or comment. (This was a sinister reflection which she cherished.) In the presence of others she expressed admiration for his exalted gifts, as she handed the photograph around and dwelt upon the fidelity, of the likeness. When alone she sometimes picked it up and kissed the cold glass passionately.

1   Poor dear.

Her marriage to Léonce Pontellier was purely an accident, in this respect resembling many other marriages which masquerade as the decrees of Fate. It was in the midst of her secret great passion that she met him. He fell in love, as men are in the habit of doing, and pressed his suit with an earnestness and an ardor which left nothing to be desired. He pleased her; his absolute devotion flattered her. She fancied there was a sympathy of thought and taste between them, in which fancy she was mistaken. Add to this the violent opposition of her father and her sister Margaret to her marriage with a Catholic, and we need seek no further for the motives which led her to accept Monsieur Pontellier for her husband.

The acme of bliss, which would have been a marriage with the tragedian, was not for her in this world. As the devoted wife of a man who worshiped her, she felt she would take her place with a certain dignity in the world of reality, closing the portals forever behind her upon the realm of romance and dreams.

But it was not long before the tragedian had gone to join the cavalry officer and the engaged young man and a few others; and Edna found herself face to face with the realities. She grew fond of her husband, realizing with some unaccountable satisfaction that no trace of passion or excessive and fictitious warmth colored her affection, thereby threatening its dissolution.

She was fond of her children in an uneven, impulsive way. She would sometimes gather them passionately to her heart; she would sometimes forget them. The year before they had spent part of the summer with their grandmother Pontellier in Iberville. Feeling secure regarding their happiness and welfare, she did not miss them except with an occasional intense longing. Their absence was a sort of relief, though she did not admit this, even to herself. It seemed to free her of a responsibility which she had blindly assumed and for which Fate had not fitted her.

Edna did not reveal so much as all this to Madame Ratignolle that summer day when they sat with faces turned to the sea. But a good part of it escaped her. She had put her head down on Madame Ratignolle's shoulder. She was flushed and felt intoxicated with the sound of her own voice and the unaccustomed taste of candor. It muddled her like wine, or like a first breath of freedom.

There was the sound of approaching voices. It was Robert, surrounded by a troop of children, searching for them. The two little Pontelliers were with him, and he carried Madame Ratignolle's little girl in his arms. There were other children besides, and two nurse-maids followed, looking disagreeable and resigned.

The women at once rose and began to shake out their draperies and relax their muscles. Mrs. Pontellier threw the cushions and rug into the bath-house. The children all scampered off to the awning, and they stood there in a line, gazing upon the intruding lovers, still exchanging their vows and sighs. The lovers got up, with only a silent protest, and walked slowly away somewhere else.

The children possessed themselves of the tent, and Mrs. Pontellier went over to join them.

Madame Ratignolle begged Robert to accompany her to the house; she complained of cramp in her limbs and stiffness of the joints. She leaned draggingly upon his arm as they walked.

Chapter Ten

This is a pivotal chapter in the narrative. As Edna walks towards the sea, her head is full of thoughts of Robert, but once she enters the water and swims for the first time she is overwhelmed by the grandeur of her experience, 'reaching out for the unlimited in which to lose herself'. Robert is forgotten in the exultation of the experience of swimming but as she leaves the water she is immediately brought back down to earth by Léonce's comments on her achievement. Her land-life encloses and curtails the freedom she experiences in the sea although Robert is subsequently able to penetrate her mood as they return to the house. Chopin's description of Edna's fear of drowning, where a 'vision of death smote her soul', is clearly proleptic of the end of the narrative, but it also communicates a sense of the momentousness of the changes which she is undergoing. Her belated success in learning to swim is presented alongside her similarly belated sexual awakening, as she and Robert experience the 'first-felt throbbings of desire'. As Edna watches Robert 'pass in and out of the strips of moonlight' it becomes apparent to her that she can no longer deny her feelings for him.

At all events Robert proposed it, and there was not a dissenting voice. There was not one but was ready to follow when he led the way. He did not lead the way, however, he directed the way; and he himself loitered behind with the lovers, who had betrayed a disposition to linger and hold themselves apart. He walked between them, whether with malicious or mischievous intent was not wholly clear, even to himself.

The Pontelliers and Ratignolles walked ahead; the women leaning upon the arms of their husbands. Edna could hear Robert's voice behind them, and could sometimes hear what he said. She wondered why he did not join them. It was unlike him not to. Of late he had sometimes held away from her for an entire day, redoubling his devotion upon the next and the next, as though to make up for hours that had been lost. She missed him the days when some pretext served to take him away, from her, just as one misses the sun on a cloudy day without having thought much about the sun when it was shining.

The people walked in little groups toward the beach. They talked and laughed; some of them sang. There was a band, playing down at Klein's hotel, and the strains reached them faintly, tempered by the distance. There were strange, rare odors abroad – a tangle of the sea smell and of weeds and damp, new-plowed earth, mingled with the heavy perfume of a field of white blossoms somewhere near. But the night sat lightly upon the sea and the land. There was no weight of darkness; there were no shadows. The white light of the moon had fallen upon the world like the mystery and the softness of sleep.

Most of them walked into the water as though into a native element. The sea was quiet now, and swelled lazily in broad billows that melted into one another and did not break except upon the beach in little foamy crests that coiled back like slow, white serpents.

Edna had attempted all summer to learn to swim. She had received instructions from both the men and women, in some instances from the children. Robert had pursued a system of lessons almost daily, and he was nearly at the point of discouragement in realizing the futility of his efforts. A certain ungovernable dread hung about her when in the water, unless there was a hand near by that might reach out and reassure her. But that night she was like the little tottering, stumbling, clutching child, who of a sudden realizes its powers, and walks for the first time alone, boldly and with over-confidence. She could have shouted for joy. She did shout for joy, as with a sweeping stroke or two she lifted her body to the surface of the water.

A feeling of exultation overtook her, as if some power of significant import had been given her to control the working of her body and her soul. She grew daring and reckless, overestimating her strength. She wanted to swim far out, where no woman had swum before.

Her unlooked-for achievement was the subject of wonder, applause, and admiration. Each one congratulated himself that his special teachings had accomplished this desired end.

'How easy it is!' she thought. 'It is nothing,' she said aloud; 'why did I not discover before that it was nothing. Think of the time I have lost splashing about like a baby!' She would not join the groups in their sports and bouts, but intoxicated with her newly conquered power, she swam out alone.

She turned her face seaward to gather in an impression of space and solitude, which the vast expanse of water, meeting and melting with the moonlit sky, conveyed to her excited fancy. As she swam she seemed to be reaching out for the unlimited in which to lose herself.

Once she turned and looked toward the shore, toward the people she had left there. She had not gone any great distance – that is, what would have been a great distance for an experienced swimmer. But to her unaccustomed vision the stretch of water behind her assumed the aspect of a barrier which her unaided strength would never be able to overcome

A quick vision of death smote her soul, and for a second of time appalled and enfeebled her senses. But by an effort she rallied her staggering faculties and managed to regain the land.

She made no mention of her encounter with death and her flash of terror, except to say to her husband, 'I thought I should have perished out there alone.'

'You were not so very far, my dear; I was watching you,' he told her.

Edna went at once to the bath-house, and she had put on her dry clothes and was ready to return home before the others had left the water. She started to walk away alone. They all called to her and shouted to her. She waved a dissenting hand, and went on, paying no further heed to their renewed cries which sought to detain her.

'Sometimes I am tempted to think that Mrs. Pontellier is capricious,' said Madame Lebrun, who was amusing herself immensely and feared that Edna's abrupt departure might put an end to the pleasure.

'I know she is,' assented Mr. Pontellier; 'sometimes, not often.'

Edna had not traversed a quarter of the distance on her way home before she was overtaken by Robert.

'Did you think I was afraid?' she asked him, without a shade of annoyance.

'No; I knew you weren't afraid.'

'Then why did you come? Why didn't you stay out there with the others?'

'I never thought of it.'

'Thought of what?'

'Of anything. What difference does it make?'

'I'm very tired,' she uttered, complainingly.

'I know you are.'

'You don't know anything about it. Why should you know? I never was so exhausted in my life. But it isn't unpleasant. A thousand emotions have swept through me to-night. I don't comprehend half of them. Don't mind what I'm saying; I am just thinking aloud. I wonder if I shall ever be stirred again as Mademoiselle Reisz's playing moved me to-night. I wonder if any night on earth will ever again be like this one. It is like a night in a dream. The people about me are like some uncanny, half-human beings. There must be spirits abroad to-night.'

'There are,' whispered Robert. 'Didn't you know this was the twenty-eighth of August?'

'The twenty-eighth of August?'

'Yes. On the twenty-eighth of August, at the hour of midnight, and if the moon is shining – the moon must be shining – a spirit that has haunted these shores for ages rises up from the Gulf. With its own penetrating vision the spirit seeks some one mortal worthy to hold him company, worthy of being exalted for a few hours into realms of the semi-celestials. His search has always hitherto been fruitless, and he has sunk back, disheartened, into the sea. But to-night he found Mrs. Pontellier. Perhaps he will never wholly release her from the spell. Perhaps she will never again suffer a poor, unworthy earthling to walk in the shadow of her divine presence.'

'Don't banter me,' she said, wounded at what appeared to be his flippancy. He did not mind the entreaty, but the tone with its delicate note of pathos was like a reproach. He could not explain; he could not tell her that he had penetrated her mood and understood. He said nothing except to offer her his arm, for, by her own admission, she was exhausted. She had been walking alone with her arms hanging limp, letting her white skirts trail along the dewy path. She took his arm, but she did not lean upon it. She let her hand lie listlessly, as though her thoughts were elsewhere – somewhere in advance of her body, and she was striving to overtake them.

Robert assisted her into the hammock which swung from the post before her door out to the trunk of a tree.

'Will you stay out here and wait for Mr. Pontellier?' he asked.

'I'll stay out here. Good-night.'

'Shall I get you a pillow?'

'There's one here,' she said, feeling about, for they were in the shadow.

'It must be soiled; the children have been tumbling it about.'

'No matter.' And having discovered the pillow, she adjusted it beneath her head. She extended herself in the hammock with a deep breath of relief. She was not a supercilious or an over-dainty woman. She was not much given to reclining in the hammock, and when she did so it was with no cat-like suggestion of voluptuous ease, but with a beneficent repose which seemed to invade her whole body.

'Shall I stay with you till Mr. Pontellier comes?' asked Robert, seating himself on the outer edge of one of the steps and taking hold of the hammock rope which was fastened to the post.

'If you wish. Don't swing the hammock. Will you get my white shawl which I left on the window-sill over at the house?'

'Are you chilly?'

'No; but I shall be presently.'

'Presently?' he laughed. 'Do you know what time it is? How long are you going to stay out here?'

'I don't know. Will you get the shawl?'

'Of course I will,' he said, rising. He went over to the house, walking along the grass. She watched his figure pass in and out of the strips of moonlight. It was past midnight. It was very quiet.

When he returned with the shawl she took it and kept it in her hand. She did not put it around her.

'Did you say I should stay till Mr. Pontellier came back?'

'I said you might if you wished to.'

He seated himself again and rolled a cigarette, which he smoked in silence. Neither did Mrs. Pontellier speak. No multitude of words could have been more significant than those moments of silence, or more pregnant with the first-felt throbbings of desire.

When the voices of the bathers were heard approaching, Robert said good-night. She did not answer him. He thought she was asleep. Again she watched his figure pass in and out of the strips of moonlight as he walked away.

Chapter Eleven

The events of this chapter may seem, at first, to be insignificant, but a number of precedents are established. Stimulated by her first unaided swim, Edna refuses to retire for the night, resisting her husband's imprecations and making it plain to him that she will not listen to his demands. The pattern – of refusal by Edna, threats from Léonce, further refusal from Edna, followed by Léonce backing down before finding a way to keep up appearances whilst salvaging some self-respect – is set here and will be repeated, most notably in the case of Edna's decision to move into the pigeon house.

As in Chapter Three, the site of her small rebellion against her husband's authority is the porch, not the interior of the house. In a novel which is very much taken up with establishing the idea of gendered space, the fact that Edna removes herself from the marital bedroom, and later, from the marital home, in order to register defiance is significant.

'What are you doing out here, Edna? I thought I should find you in bed,' said her husband, when he discovered her lying there. He had walked up with Madame Lebrun and left her at the house. His wife did not reply.

'Are you asleep?' he asked, bending down close to look at her.

'No.' Her eyes gleamed bright and intense, with no sleepy shadows, as they looked into his.

'Do you know it is past one o'clock? Come on,' and he mounted the steps and went into their room.

'Edna!' called Mr. Pontellier from within, after a few moments had gone by.

'Don't wait for me,' she answered. He thrust his head through the door.

'You will take cold out there,' he said, irritably. 'What folly is this? Why don't you come in?'

'It isn't cold; I have my shawl.'

'The mosquitoes will devour you.'

'There are no mosquitoes.'

She heard him moving about the room; every sound indicating impatience and irritation. Another time she would have gone in at his request. She would, through habit, have yielded to his desire; not with any sense of submission or obedience to his compelling wishes, but unthinkingly, as we walk, move, sit, stand, go through the daily treadmill of the life which has been portioned out to us.

'Edna, dear, are you not coming in soon?' he asked again, this time fondly, with a note of entreaty.

'No; I am going to stay out here.'

'This is more than folly,' he blurted out. 'I can't permit you to stay out there all night. You must come in the house instantly.'

With a writhing motion she settled herself more securely in the hammock. She perceived that her will had blazed up, stubborn and resistant. She could not at that moment have done other than denied and resisted. She wondered if her husband had ever spoken to her like that before, and if she had submitted to his command. Of course she had; she remembered that she had. But she could not realize why or how she should have yielded, feeling as she then did.

'Léonce, go to bed,' she said. 'I mean to stay out here. I don't wish to go in, and I don't intend to. Don't speak to me like that again; I shall not answer you.'

Mr. Pontellier had prepared for bed, but he slipped on an extra garment. He opened a bottle of wine, of which he kept a small and select supply in a buffet of his own. He drank a glass of the wine and went out on the gallery and offered a glass to his wife. She did not wish any. He drew up the rocker, hoisted his slippered feet on the rail, and proceeded to smoke a cigar. He smoked two cigars; then he went inside and drank another glass of wine. Mrs. Pontellier again declined to accept a glass when it was offered to her. Mr. Pontellier once more seated himself with elevated feet, and after a reasonable interval of time smoked some more cigars.

Edna began to feel like one who awakens gradually out of a dream, a delicious, grotesque, impossible dream, to feel again the realities pressing into her soul. The physical need for sleep began to overtake her; the exuberance which had sustained and exalted her spirit left her helpless and yielding to the conditions which crowded her in.

The stillest hour of the night had come, the hour before dawn, when the world seems to hold its breath. The moon hung low, and had turned from silver to copper in the sleeping sky. The old owl no longer hooted, and the water-oaks had ceased to moan as they bent their heads.

Edna arose, cramped from lying so long and still in the hammock. She tottered up the steps, clutching feebly at the post before passing into the house.

'Are you coming in, Léonce?' she asked, turning her face toward her husband.

'Yes, dear,' he answered, with a glance following a misty puff of smoke. 'Just as soon as I have finished my cigar.'

Chapter Sixteen

Mademoiselle Reisz, like Madame Ratignolle, carries symbolic as well as literal weight in the narrative. Her life, as a single woman dedicated to her art, provides an alternative model to that of the married woman but also provides an insight into the difficulties of having chosen an independent life. Even though Edna is trying to escape from the constraints of her marriage, her behaviour exhibits all kinds of dependencies, seeking the company of Robert's mother, looking at photographs of him as a child, reading his letters, wishing to hear herself spoken about; she even goes so far as to quiz her husband about his encounter with Robert in New Orleans. The note sent to Madame Lebrun is the first in a series of letters written by Robert to other people which are subsequently read by Edna. The fact that her relationship with Robert, whilst he is away in Mexico, is conducted at one remove, resonates with the stifled nature of her emotional life, in that 'She had all her life long been accustomed to harbor thoughts and emotions which never voiced themselves.' That the Pontellier children interest Edna only when she is looking for a distraction is further evidenced here and is followed by an important articulation of her distinctiveness: whilst agreeing with Madame Ratignolle that she would give her life for her children, she dissents from the injunction that all women should be self-sacrificing.

'Do you miss your friend greatly?' asked Mademoiselle Reisz one morning as she came creeping up behind Edna, who had just left her cottage on her way to the beach. She spent much of her time in the water since she had acquired finally the art of swimming. As their stay at Grand Isle drew near its close, she felt that she could not give too much time to a diversion which afforded her the only real pleasurable moments that she knew. When Mademoiselle Reisz came and touched her upon the shoulder and spoke to her, the woman seemed to echo the thought which was ever in Edna's mind, or, better, the feeling which constantly possessed her.

Robert's going had some way taken the brightness, the color, the meaning out of everything. The conditions of her life were in no way changed, but her whole existence was dulled, like a faded garment which seems to be no longer worth wearing. She sought him everywhere – in others whom she induced to talk about him. She went up in the mornings to Madame Lebrun's room, braving the clatter of the old sewing-machine. She sat there and chatted at intervals as Robert had done. She gazed around the room at the pictures and photographs hanging upon the wall, and discovered in some corner an old family album, which she examined with the keenest interest, appealing to Madame Lebrun for enlightenment concerning the many figures and faces which she discovered between its pages.

There was a picture of Madame Lebrun with Robert as a baby, seated in her lap, a round-faced infant with a fist in his mouth. The eyes alone in the baby suggested the man. And that was he also in kilts, at the age of five, wearing long curls and holding a whip in his hand. It made Edna laugh, and she laughed, too, at the portrait in his first long trousers; while another interested her, taken when he left for college, looking thin, long-faced, with eyes full of fire, ambition and great intentions. But there was no recent picture, none which suggested the Robert who had gone away five days ago, leaving a void and wilderness behind him.

'Oh, Robert stopped having his pictures taken when he had to pay for them himself! He found wiser use for his money, he says,' explained Madame Lebrun. She had a letter from him, written before he left New Orleans. Edna wished to see the letter, and Madame Lebrun told her to look for it either on the table or the dresser, or perhaps it was on the mantelpiece

The letter was on the bookshelf. It possessed the greatest interest and attraction for Edna; the envelope, its size and shape, the post-mark, the handwriting. She examined every detail of the outside before opening it. There were only a few lines, setting forth that he would leave the city that afternoon, that he had packed his trunk in good shape, that he was well, and sent her his love and begged to be affectionately remembered to all. There was no special message to Edna except a postscript saying that if Mrs. Pontellier desired to finish the book which he had been reading to her, his mother would find it in his room, among other books there on the table. Edna experienced a pang of jealousy because he had written to his mother rather than to her.

Every one seemed to take for granted that she missed him. Even her husband, when he came down the Saturday following Robert's departure, expressed regret that he had gone.

'How do you get on without him, Edna?' he asked.

'It's very dull without him,' she admitted. Mr. Pontellier had seen Robert in the city, and Edna asked him a dozen questions or more. Where had they met? On Carondelet Street, in the morning. They had gone 'in' and had a drink and a cigar together. What had they talked about? Chiefly about his prospects in Mexico, which Mr. Pontellier thought were promising. How did he look? How did he seem – grave, or gay, or how? Quite cheerful, and wholly taken up with the idea of his trip, which Mr. Pontellier found altogether natural in a young fellow about to seek fortune and adventure in a strange, queer country.

Edna tapped her foot impatiently, and wondered why the children persisted in playing in the sun when they might be under the trees. She went down and led them out of the sun, scolding the quadroon for not being more attentive.

It did not strike her as in the least grotesque that she should be making of Robert the object of conversation and leading her husband to speak of him. The sentiment which she entertained for Robert in no way resembled that which she felt for her husband, or had ever felt, or ever expected to feel. She had all her life long been accustomed to harbor thoughts and emotions which never voiced themselves. They had never taken the form of struggles. They belonged to her and were her own, and she entertained the conviction that she had a right to them and that they concerned no one but herself. Edna had once told Madame Ratignolle that she would never sacrifice herself for her children, or for any one. Then had followed a rather heated argument; the two women did not appear to understand each other or to be talking the same language. Edna tried to appease her friend, to explain.

'I would give up the unessential; I would give my money, I would give my life for my children; but I wouldn't give myself. I can't make it more clear; it's only something which I am beginning to comprehend, which is revealing itself to me.'

'I don't know what you would call the essential, or what you mean by the unessential,' said Madame Ratignolle, cheerfully, 'but a woman who would give her life for her children could do no more than that – your Bible tells you so. I'm sure I couldn't do more than that.'

'Oh, yes you could!' laughed Edna.

She was not surprised at Mademoiselle Reisz's question the morning that lady, following her to the beach, tapped her on the shoulder and asked if she did not greatly miss her young friend.

'Oh, good morning, Mademoiselle; is it you? Why, of course I miss Robert. Are you going down to bathe?'

'Why should I go down to bathe at the very end of the season when I haven't been in the surf all summer,' replied the woman, disagreeably.

'I beg your pardon,' offered Edna, in some embarrassment, for she should have remembered that Mademoiselle Reisz's avoidance of the water had furnished a theme for much pleasantry. Some among them thought it was on account of her false hair, or the dread of getting the violets wet, while others attributed it to the natural aversion for water sometimes believed to accompany the artistic temperament. Mademoiselle offered Edna some chocolates in a paper bag, which she took from her pocket, by way of showing that she bore no ill feeling. She habitually ate chocolates for their sustaining quality; they contained much nutriment in small compass, she said. They saved her from starvation, as Madame Lebrun's table was utterly impossible, and no one save so impertinent a woman as Madame Lebrun could think of offering such food to people and requiring them to pay for it.

'She must feel very lonely without her son,' said Edna, desiring to change the subject.

'Her favorite son, too. It must have been quite hard to let him go.'

Mademoiselle laughed maliciously.

'Her favorite son! Oh, dear! Who could have been imposing such a tale upon you? Aline Lebrun lives for Victor, and for Victor alone. She has spoiled him into the worthless creature he is. She worships him and the ground he walks on. Robert is very well in a way, to give up all the money he can earn to the family, and keep the barest pittance for himself. Favorite son, indeed! I miss the poor fellow myself, my dear. I liked to see him and to hear him about the place – the only Lebrun who is worth a pinch of salt. He comes to see me often in the city. I like to play to him. That Victor! hanging would be too good for him. It's a wonder Robert hasn't beaten him to death long ago.'

'I thought he had great patience with his brother,' offered Edna, glad to be talking about Robert, no matter what was said.

'Oh! he thrashed him well enough a year or two ago,' said Mademoiselle. 'It was about a Spanish girl, whom Victor considered that he had some sort of claim upon. He met Robert one day talking to the girl, or walking with her, or bathing with her, or carrying her basket – I don't remember what – and he became so insulting and abusive that Robert gave him a thrashing on the spot that has kept him comparatively in order for a good while. It's about time he was getting another.'

'Was her name Mariequita?' asked Edna.

'Mariequita – yes, that was it; Mariequita. I had forgotten. Oh, she's a sly one, and a bad one, that Mariequita!'

Edna looked down at Mademoiselle Reisz and wondered how she could have listened to her venom so long. For some reason she felt depressed, almost unhappy. She had not intended to go into the water; but she donned her bathing suit, and left Mademoiselle alone, seated under the shade of the children's tent. The water was growing cooler as the season advanced. Edna plunged and swam about with an abandon that thrilled and invigorated her. She remained a long time in the water, half hoping that Mademoiselle Reisz would not wait for her.

But Mademoiselle waited. She was very amiable during the walk back, and raved much over Edna's appearance in her bathing suit. She talked about music. She hoped that Edna would go to see her in the city, and wrote her address with the stub of a pencil on a piece of card which she found in her pocket.

'When do you leave?' asked Edna.

'Next Monday; and you?'

'The following week,' answered Edna, adding, 'It has been a pleasant summer, hasn't it, Mademoiselle?'

'Well,' agreed Mademoiselle Reisz, with a shrug, 'rather pleasant, if it hadn't been for the mosquitoes and the Farival twins.'

Chapter Nineteen

It would be typical of leisure class society at the turn into the twentieth century that afternoon visits exchanged between women would reinforce the business relationships of their husbands. In addition, Edna's refusal to fulfil her obligations as a wife, represented by such gestures as the temporary discarding of her wedding ring and her abandonment of housekeeping are indicative of a profound sense of alienation from her role as conventional wife and mother. It is increasingly the case that Edna's most authentic experience is that spent in solitary pursuits, where she is able to indulge her fantasies and her memories but also to feel extremes of emotion which range between the completely bleak and the euphoric.

Edna could not help but think that it was very foolish, very childish, to have stamped upon her wedding ring and smashed the crystal vase upon the tiles. She was visited by no more outbursts, moving her to such futile expedients. She began to do as she liked and to feel as she liked.

She completely abandoned her Tuesdays at home, and did not return the visits of those who had called upon her. She made no ineffectual efforts to conduct her household *en bonne ménagère*,[1] going and coming as it suited her fancy, and, so far as she was able, lending herself to any passing caprice.

Mr. Pontellier had been a rather courteous husband so long as he met a certain tacit submissiveness in his wife. But her new and unexpected line of conduct completely bewildered him. It shocked him. Then her absolute disregard for her duties as a wife angered him. When Mr. Pontellier became rude, Edna grew insolent. She had resolved never to take another step backward.

'It seems to me the utmost folly for a woman at the head of a household, and the mother of children, to spend in an atelier[2] days which would be better employed contriving for the comfort of her family.'

'I feel like painting,' answered Edna. 'Perhaps I shan't always feel like it.'

'Then in God's name paint! but don't let the family go to the devil. There's Madame Ratignolle; because she keeps up her music, she doesn't let everything else go to chaos. And she's more of a musician than you are a painter.'

'She isn't a musician, and I'm not a painter. It isn't on account of painting that I let things go.'

'On account of what, then?'

'Oh! I don't know. Let me alone; you bother me.'

It sometimes entered Mr. Pontellier's mind to wonder if his wife were not growing a little unbalanced mentally. He could see plainly that she was not herself. That is, he could not see that she was becoming herself and daily casting aside that fictitious self which we assume like a garment with which to appear before the world.

Her husband let her alone as she requested, and went away to his office. Edna went up to her atelier – a bright room in the top of the house. She was working with great energy and interest, without accomplishing anything, however, which satisfied her even in the smallest degree. For a time she had the whole household enrolled in the service of art. The boys posed for her. They thought it amusing at first, but the occupation soon lost its attractiveness when they discovered that it was not a game arranged especially for their entertainment. The quadroon sat for hours before Edna's palette, patient as a savage, while the house-maid took charge of the children, and the drawing-room went undusted. But the

1   As a good housewife.
2   Studio.

house-maid, too, served her term as model when Edna perceived that the young woman's back and shoulders were molded on classic lines, and that her hair, loosened from its confining cap, became an inspiration. While Edna worked she sometimes sang low the little air, 'Ah! si tu savais!'[3] It moved her with recollections. She could hear again the ripple of the water, the flapping sail. She could see the glint of the moon upon the bay, and could feel the soft, gusty beating of the hot south wind. A subtle current of desire passed through her body, weakening her hold upon the brushes and making her eyes burn.

There were days when she was very happy without knowing why. She was happy to be alive and breathing, when her whole being seemed to be one with the sunlight, the color, the odors, the luxuriant warmth of some perfect Southern day. She liked then to wander alone into strange and unfamiliar places. She discovered many a sunny, sleepy corner, fashioned to dream in. And she found it good to dream and to be alone and unmolested.

There were days when she was unhappy, she did not know why – when it did not seem worth while to be glad or sorry, to be alive or dead; when life appeared to her like a grotesque pandemonium and humanity like worms struggling blindly toward inevitable annihilation. She could not work on such a day, nor weave fancies to stir her pulses and warm her blood.

Chapter Twenty-one

Edna's visit to Mademoiselle Reisz demonstrates her desire to bring about changes in the pattern of her existence. She is insistent that her time will be spent with people of her choice rather than dictated by custom and practice. The kind of verbal exchange she has with Mademoiselle Reisz is frank yet also coquettish. This is another instance of Edna gaining access to a letter from Robert written to a third person, and the tussle she has with Mademoiselle Reisz over the letter has very much the tone of a lovers' exchange. Just as her awakening to her own sexual potential comes partly through intimacy with Madame Ratignolle, so her arousal is sustained by engaging in the kind of passionate dialogue with Mademoiselle Reisz that propriety and distance prevent her from having with Robert.

It is also in this chapter that the dangers of Edna's decision to follow an individualistic path are given heightened expression. When Mademoiselle Reisz describes the artist as a 'brave soul. The soul that dares and defies' she is emphasising the difficulty of the choices which must be made if one is to separate oneself from the crowd. This is made literal in the place that Mademoiselle Reisz herself lives and in the arrangement of her life. Here she tries to make Edna aware of the consequences of her actions but Edna loses herself in the music and abandons herself again to tears.

3   Ah! If you only knew!

Some people contended that the reason Mademoiselle Reisz always chose apartments up under the roof was to discourage the approach of beggars, peddlars and callers. There were plenty of windows in her little front room. They were for the most part dingy, but as they were nearly always open it did not make so much difference. They often admitted into the room a good deal of smoke and soot; but at the same time all the light and air that there was came through them. From her windows could be seen the crescent of the river, the masts of ships and the big chimneys of the Mississippi steamers. A magnificent piano crowded the apartment. In the next room she slept and in the third and last she harbored a gasoline stove on which she cooked her meals when disinclined to descend to the neighboring restaurant. It was there also that she ate, keeping her belongings in a rare old buffet, dingy and battered from a hundred years of use.

When Edna knocked at Mademoiselle Reisz's front room door and entered, she discovered that person standing beside the window, engaged in mending or patching an old prunella gaiter.[1] The little musician laughed all over when she saw Edna. Her laugh consisted of a contortion of the face and all the muscles of the body. She seemed strikingly homely, standing there in the afternoon light. She still wore the shabby lace and the artificial bunch of violets on the side of her head.

'So you remembered me at last,' said Mademoiselle. 'I had said to myself, "Ah, bah! she will never come." '

'Did you want me to come?' asked Edna with a smile.

'I had not thought much about it,' answered Mademoiselle. The two had seated themselves on a little bumpy sofa which stood against the wall. 'I am glad, however, that you came. I have the water boiling back there, and was just about to make some coffee. You will drink a cup with me. And how is *la belle dame*? Always handsome! always healthy! always contented!' She took Edna's hand between her strong wiry fingers, holding it loosely without warmth, and executing a sort of double theme upon the back and palm.

'Yes,' she went on; 'I sometimes thought: "She will never come. She promised as those women in society always do, without meaning it. She will not come". For I really don't believe you like me, Mrs. Pontellier.'

'I don't know whether I like you or not,' replied Edna, gazing down at the little woman with a quizzical look.

The candor of Mrs. Pontellier's admission greatly pleased Mademoiselle Reisz. She expressed her gratification by repairing forthwith to the region of the gasoline stove and rewarding her guest with the promised cup of coffee. The coffee and the biscuit accompanying it proved very acceptable to Edna, who had declined refreshment at Madame Lebrun's and was now beginning to feel hungry. Mademoiselle set the tray which she brought in upon a small table near at hand, and seated herself once again on the lumpy sofa.

'I have had a letter from your friend,' she remarked, as she poured a little cream into Edna's cup and handed it to her.

'My friend?'

'Yes, your friend Robert. He wrote to me from the City of Mexico.'

---

1   An overshoe made of a strong heavy fabric.

'Wrote to *you?*' repeated Edna in amazement, stirring her coffee absently.

'Yes, to me. Why not? Don't stir all the warmth out of your coffee; drink it. Though the letter might as well have been sent to you; it was nothing but Mrs. Pontellier from beginning to end.'

'Let me see it,' requested the young woman, entreatingly.

'No; a letter concerns no one but the person who writes it and the one to whom it is written.'

'Haven't you just said it concerned me from beginning to end?'

'It was written about you, not to you. "Have you seen Mrs. Pontellier? How is she looking?" he asks. "As Mrs. Pontellier says," or "as Mrs. Pontellier once said." "If Mrs. Pontellier should call upon you, play for her that Impromptu of Chopin's, my favorite. I heard it here a day or two ago, but not as you play it. I should like to know how it affects her," and so on, as if he supposed we were constantly in each other's society.'

'Let me see the letter.'

'Oh, no.'

'Have you answered it?'

'No.'

'Let me see the letter.'

'No, and again, no.'

'Then play the Impromptu for me.'

'It is growing late; what time do you have to be home?'

'Time doesn't concern me. Your question seems a little rude. Play the Impromptu.'

'But you have told me nothing of yourself. What are you doing?'

'Painting!' laughed Edna. 'I am becoming an artist. Think of it!'

'Ah! an artist! You have pretensions, Madame.'

'Why pretensions? Do you think I could not become an artist?'

'I do not know you well enough to say. I do not know your talent or your temperament. To be an artist includes much; one must possess many gifts – absolute gifts – which have not been acquired by one's own effort. And, moreover, to succeed, the artist must possess the courageous soul.'

'What do you mean by, the courageous soul?'

'Courageous, *ma foi!*[2] The brave soul. The soul that dares and defies.'

'Show me the letter and play for me the Impromptu. You see that I have persistence. Does that quality count for anything in art?'

'It counts with a foolish old woman whom you have captivated,' replied Mademoiselle, with her wriggling laugh.

The letter was right there at hand in the drawer of the little table upon which Edna had just placed her coffee cup. Mademoiselle opened the drawer and drew forth the letter, the topmost one. She placed it in Edna's hands, and without further comment arose and went to the piano.

Mademoiselle played a soft interlude. It was an improvisation. She sat low at the instrument, and the lines of her body settled into ungraceful curves and

2   Indeed.

angles that gave it an appearance of deformity. Gradually and imperceptibly the interlude melted into the soft opening minor chords of the Chopin Impromptu.

Edna did not know when the Impromptu began or ended. She sat in the sofa corner reading Robert's letter by the fading light. Mademoiselle had glided from the Chopin into the quivering love-notes of Isolde's song, and back again to the Impromptu with its soulful and poignant longing.

The shadows deepened in the little room. The music grew strange and fantastic – turbulent, insistent, plaintive and soft with entreaty. The shadows grew deeper. The music filled the room. It floated out upon the night, over the housetops, the crescent of the river, losing itself in the silence of the upper air.

Edna was sobbing, just as she had wept one midnight at Grand Isle when strange, new voices awoke in her. She arose in some agitation to take her departure. 'May I come again, Mademoiselle?' she asked at the threshold.

'Come whenever you feel like it. Be careful; the stairs and landings are dark; don't stumble.'

Mademoiselle reentered and lit a candle. Robert's letter was on the floor. She stooped and picked it up. It was crumpled and damp with tears. Mademoiselle smoothed the letter out, restored it to the envelope, and replaced it in the table drawer.

Chapter Twenty-two

It is clear in this chapter that Léonce is bewildered by the changes in his wife and seeks, unsurprisingly, medical advice. Having already indulged her in what he sees as a peculiar desire to paint, he now looks for an alternative explanation for her conduct, and, in visiting the doctor, pathologises her behaviour. Doctor Mandelet's explanations are as much social as medical; he invokes the spectre of the bluestocking – 'pseudo-intellectual women' – as a source of social instability. The 1890s saw a massive expansion in the educational opportunities available to women and the fear that family and traditional values would be undermined was growing.

Chopin presents the Doctor as a generally sympathetic character, but even so he refers to women as a species – 'a very peculiar and delicate organism'. It is interesting that the most direct expression of Edna's iconoclastic views about marriage is made not by her but by Léonce in conversation with the Doctor. That 'a wedding is one of the most lamentable spectacles on earth' is an extremely radical statement which Chopin defuses by its being reported semi-ironically.

One morning on his way into town Mr. Pontellier stopped at the house of his old friend and family physician, Doctor Mandelet. The Doctor was a semi-retired physician, resting, as the saying is, upon, his laurels. He bore a reputation for wisdom rather than skill – leaving the active practice of medicine to his assistants and younger contemporaries – and was much sought for in matters of consultation. A few families, united to him by bonds of friendship, he still attended when they required the services of a physician. The Pontelliers were among these.

Mr. Pontellier found the Doctor reading at the open window of his study. His house stood rather far back from the street, in the center of a delightful garden, so that it was quiet and peaceful at the old gentleman's study window. He was a great reader. He stared up disapprovingly over his eye-glasses as Mr. Pontellier entered, wondering who had the temerity to disturb him at that hour of the morning.

'Ah, Pontellier! Not sick, I hope. Come and have a seat. What news do you bring this morning?' He was quite portly, with a profusion of gray hair, and small blue eyes which age had robbed of much of their brightness but none of their penetration.

'Oh! I'm never sick, Doctor. You know that I come of tough fiber – of that old Creole race of Pontelliers that dry up and finally blow away. I came to consult – no, not precisely to consult – to talk to you about Edna. I don't know what ails her.'

'Madame Pontellier not well?' marveled the Doctor. 'Why, I saw her – I think it was a week ago – walking along Canal Street,[1] the picture of health, it seemed to me.'

'Yes, yes; she seems quite well,' said Mr. Pontellier, leaning forward and whirling his stick between his two hands; 'but she doesn't act well. She's odd, she's not like herself. I can't make her out, and I thought perhaps you'd help me.'

'How does she act?' inquired the doctor.

'Well, it isn't easy to explain,' said Mr. Pontellier, throwing himself back in his chair. 'She lets the housekeeping go to the dickens.'

'Well, well; women are not all alike, my dear Pontellier. We've got to consider –'

'I know that; I told you I couldn't explain. Her whole attitude – toward me and everybody and everything – has changed. You know I have a quick temper, but I don't want to quarrel or be rude to a woman, especially my wife; yet I'm driven to it, and feel like ten thousand devils after I've made a fool of myself. She's making it devilishly uncomfortable for me,' he went on nervously. 'She's got some sort of notion in her head concerning the eternal rights of women; and – you understand – we meet in the morning at the breakfast table.'

The old gentleman lifted his shaggy eyebrows, protruded his thick nether lip, and tapped the arms of his chair with his cushioned fingertips.

'What have you been doing to her, Pontellier?'

'Doing! *Parbleu!*'

'Has she,' asked the Doctor, with a smile, 'has she been associating of late with a circle of pseudo-intellectual women – super-spiritual superior beings? My wife has been telling me about them.'

'That's the trouble,' broke in Mr. Pontellier, 'she hasn't been associating with

---

1   One of the main streets in New Orleans; Canal Street is positioned between the French and American quarters of the city.

any one. She has abandoned her Tuesdays at home, has thrown over all her acquaintances, and goes tramping about by herself, moping in the street-cars, getting in after dark. I tell you she's peculiar. I don't like it; I feel a little worried over it.'

This was a new aspect for the Doctor. 'Nothing hereditary?' he asked, seriously. 'Nothing peculiar about her family antecedents, is there?'

'Oh, no, indeed! She comes of sound old Presbyterian Kentucky stock. The old gentleman, her father, I have heard, used to atone for his weekday sins with his Sunday devotions. I know for a fact, that his race horses literally ran away with the prettiest bit of Kentucky farming land I ever laid eyes upon. Margaret – you know Margaret – she has all the Presbyterianism undiluted. And the youngest is something of a vixen. By the way, she gets married in a couple of weeks from now.'

'Send your wife up to the wedding,' exclaimed the Doctor, foreseeing a happy solution. 'Let her stay among her own people for a while; it will do her good.'

'That's what I want her to do. She won't go to the marriage. She says a wedding is one of the most lamentable spectacles on earth. Nice thing for a woman to say to her husband!' exclaimed Mr. Pontellier, fuming anew at the recollection.

'Pontellier,' said the Doctor, after a moment's reflection, 'let your wife alone for a while. Don't bother her, and don't let her bother you. Woman, my dear friend, is a very peculiar and delicate organism – a sensitive and highly organized woman, such as I know Mrs. Pontellier to be, is especially peculiar. It would require an inspired psychologist to deal successfully with them. And when ordinary fellows like you and me attempt to cope with their idiosyncrasies the result is bungling. Most women are moody and whimsical. This is some passing whim of your wife, due to some cause or causes which you and I needn't try to fathom. But it will pass happily over, especially if you let her alone. Send her around to see me.'

'Oh! I couldn't do that; there'd be no reason for it,' objected Mr. Pontellier.

'Then I'll go around and see her,' said the Doctor. 'I'll drop in to dinner some evening *en bon ami*.'[2]

'Do! by all means,' urged Mr. Pontellier. 'What evening will you come? Say Thursday. Will you come Thursday?' he asked, rising to take his leave.

'Very well; Thursday. My wife may possibly have some engagement for me Thursday. In case she has, I shall let you know. Otherwise, you may expect me.'

Mr. Pontellier turned before leaving to say: 'I am going to New York on business very soon. I have a big scheme on hand, and want to be on the field proper to pull the ropes and handle the ribbons. We'll let you in on the inside if you say so, Doctor,' he laughed.

'No, I thank you, my dear sir,' returned the Doctor. 'I leave such ventures to you younger men with the fever of life still in your blood.'

'What I wanted to say,' continued Mr. Pontellier, with his hand on the knob; 'I may have to be absent a good while. Would you advise me to take Edna along?'

'By all means, if she wishes to go. If not, leave her here. Don't contradict her. The mood will pass, I assure you. It may take a month, two, three months – possibly longer, but it will pass; have patience.'

---

2   As a good friend.

'Well, good-by, *à jeudi*,'[3] said Mr. Pontellier, as he let himself out.

The Doctor would have liked during the course of conversation to ask, 'Is there any man in the case?' but he knew his Creole too well to make such a blunder as that. He did not resume his book immediately, but sat for a while meditatively looking out into the garden.

Chapter Twenty-five

It is in this chapter that we are introduced to Alcée Arobin, whose amorality and glib charm make him a much more threatening version of the single man-about-town than Robert. Although going to the races is an acceptable pastime for the leisure class woman, Edna's decision to go alone with Arobin on her second visit signals her disregard for maintaining even the appearance of respectability. Chopin is succinct and sharp in her characterisation of Arobin; communicating in a few telling lines the essence of his nature as a man whose 'manner was so genuine that it often deceived even himself'. Edna's appetites, including a most unladylike rummage through the store cupboard for beer and cheese, are becoming more and more apparent as she recognises that she is drawn to Arobin; however, she registers these feelings in terms of the sexual betrayal of Robert rather than as the abandonment of wifely loyalty to her husband.

When the weather was dark and cloudy Edna could not work. She needed the sun to mellow and temper her mood to the sticking point. She had reached a stage when she seemed to be no longer feeling her way, working, when in the humor, with sureness and ease. And being devoid of ambition, and striving not toward accomplishment, she drew satisfaction from the work in itself.

On rainy or melancholy days Edna went out and sought the society of the friends she had made at Grand Isle. Or else she stayed indoors and nursed a mood with which she was becoming too familiar for her own comfort and peace of mind. It was not despair, but it seemed to her as if life were passing by, leaving its promise broken and unfulfilled. Yet there were other days when she listened, was led on and deceived by fresh promises which her youth held out to her.

She went again to the races, and again. Alcée Arobin and Mrs. Highcamp called for her one bright afternoon in Arobin's drag.[1] Mrs. Highcamp was a worldly but unaffected, intelligent, slim, tall blonde woman in the forties, with an indifferent manner and blue eyes that stared. She had a daughter who served her as a pretext for cultivating the society of young men of fashion. Alcée Arobin was one of them. He was a familiar figure at the race course, the opera, the fashion-

3   Until Thursday.
1   A sizeable four-horse coach which, typically, has seats inside and on top.

able clubs. There was a perpetual smile in his eyes, which seldom failed to awaken a corresponding cheerfulness in any one who looked into them and listened to his good-humored voice. His manner was quiet, and at times a little insolent. He possessed a good figure, a pleasing face, not overburdened with depth of thought or feeling; and his dress was that of the conventional man of fashion.

He admired Edna extravagantly, after meeting her at the races with her father. He had met her before on other occasions, but she had seemed to him unapproachable until that day. It was at his instigation that Mrs. Highcamp called to ask her to go with them to the Jockey Club[2] to witness the turf event of the season.

There were possibly a few track men out there who knew the race horse as well as Edna, but there was certainly none who knew it better. She sat between her two companions as one having authority to speak. She laughed at Arobin's pretensions, and deplored Mrs. Highcamp's ignorance. The race horse was a friend and intimate associate of her childhood. The atmosphere of the stables and the breath of the blue-grass paddock revived in her memory and lingered in her nostrils. She did not perceive that she was talking like her father as the sleek geldings ambled in review before them. She played for very high stakes, and fortune favored her. The fever of the game flamed in her cheeks and eyes, and it got into her blood and into her brain like an intoxicant. People turned their heads to look at her, and more than one lent an attentive ear to her utterances, hoping thereby to secure the elusive but ever-desired 'tip.' Arobin caught the contagion of excitement which drew him to Edna like a magnet. Mrs. Highcamp remained, as usual, unmoved, with her indifferent stare and uplifted eyebrows.

Edna stayed and dined with Mrs. Highcamp upon being urged to do so. Arobin also remained and sent away his drag.

The dinner was quiet and uninteresting, save for the cheerful efforts of Arobin to enliven things. Mrs. Highcamp deplored the absence of her daughter from the races, and tried to convey to her what she had missed by going to the 'Dante reading' instead of joining them. The girl held a geranium leaf up to her nose and said nothing, but looked knowing and noncommittal. Mr. Highcamp was a plain, bald-headed man, who only talked under compulsion. He was unresponsive. Mrs. Highcamp was full of delicate courtesy and consideration toward her husband. She addressed most of her conversation to him at table. They sat in the library after dinner and read the evening papers together under the droplight, while the younger people went into the drawing-room near by and talked. Miss Highcamp played some selections from Grieg upon the piano. She seemed to have apprehended all of the composer's coldness and none of his poetry. While Edna listened she could not help wondering if she had lost her taste for music.

When the time came for her to go home, Mr. Highcamp grunted a lame offer to escort her, looking down at his slippered feet with tactless concern. It was Arobin who took her home. The car ride was long, and it was late when they reached

---

2   An exclusive social club.

Esplanade Street. Arobin asked permission to enter for a second to light his cigarette – his match safe was empty. He filled his match safe, but did not light his cigarette until he left her, after she had expressed her willingness to go to the races with him again.

Edna was neither tired nor sleepy. She was hungry again, for the Highcamp dinner, though of excellent quality had lacked abundance. She rummaged in the larder and brought forth a slice of Gruyère and some crackers. She opened a bottle of beer which she found in the ice-box. Edna felt extremely restless and excited. She vacantly hummed a fantastic tune as she poked at the wood embers on the hearth and munched a cracker.

She wanted something to happen – something, anything; she did not know what. She regretted that she had not made Arobin stay a half hour to talk over the horses with her. She counted the money she had won. But there was nothing else to do, so she went to bed, and tossed there for hours in a sort of monotonous agitation. In the middle of the night she remembered that she had forgotten to write her regular letter to her husband; and she decided to do so next day and tell him about her afternoon at the Jockey Club. She lay wide awake composing a letter which was nothing like the one which she wrote next day. When the maid awoke her in the morning Edna was dreaming of Mr. Highcamp playing the piano at the entrance of a music store on Canal Street, while his wife was saying to Alcée Arobin, as they boarded an Esplanade Street car: 'What a pity that so much talent has been neglected! but I must go.'

When, a few days later, Alcée Arobin again called for Edna in his drag, Mrs. Highcamp was not with him. He said they would pick her up. But as that lady had not been apprised of his intention of picking her up, she was not at home. The daughter was just leaving the house to attend the meeting of a branch Folk Lore Society, and regretted that she could not accompany them. Arobin appeared nonplused, and asked Edna if there were any one else she cared to ask.

She did not deem it worth while to go in search of any of the fashionable acquaintances from whom she had withdrawn herself. She thought of Madame Ratignolle, but knew that her fair friend did not leave the house, except to take a languid walk around the block with her husband after nightfall. Mademoiselle Reisz would have laughed at such a request from Edna. Madame Lebrun might have enjoyed the outing, but for some reason Edna did not want her. So they went alone, she and Arobin.

The afternoon was intensely interesting to her. The excitement came back upon her like a remittent fever. Her talk grew familiar and confidential. It was no labor to become intimate with Arobin. His manner invited easy confidence. The preliminary stage of becoming acquainted was one which he always endeavored to ignore when a pretty and engaging woman was concerned.

He stayed and dined with Edna. He stayed and sat beside the wood fire. They laughed and talked; and before it was time to go he was telling her how different life might have been if he had known her years before. With ingenuous frankness he spoke of what a wicked, ill-disciplined boy he had been, and impulsively drew up his cuff to exhibit upon his wrist the scar from a saber cut which he had received in a duel outside of Paris when he was nineteen. She touched his hand as she scanned the red cicatrice on the inside of his white wrist. A quick impulse that was somewhat spasmodic impelled her fingers to close in a sort of clutch upon his hand. He felt the pressure of her pointed nails in the flesh of his palm.

She arose hastily and walked toward the mantel.

'The sight of a wound or scar always agitates and sickens me,' she said. 'I shouldn't have looked at it.'

'I beg your pardon,' he entreated, following her; 'it never occurred to me that it might be repulsive.'

He stood close to her, and the effrontery in his eyes repelled the old, vanishing self in her, yet drew all her awakening sensuousness. He saw enough in her face to impel him to take her hand and hold it while he said his lingering good night.

'Will you go to the races again?' he asked.

'No,' she said. 'I've had enough of the races. I don't want to lose all the money I've won, and I've got to work when the weather is bright, instead of –'

'Yes; work; to be sure. You promised to show me your work. What morning may I come up to your atelier? To-morrow?'

'No!'

'Day after?'

'No, no.'

'Oh, please don't refuse me! I know something of such things. I might help you with a stray suggestion or two.'

'No. Good night. Why don't you go after you have said good night? I don't like you,' she went on in a high, excited pitch, attempting to draw away her hand. She felt that her words lacked dignity and sincerity, and she knew that he felt it.

'I'm sorry you don't like me. I'm sorry I offended you. How have I offended you? What have I done? Can't you forgive me?' And he bent and pressed his lips upon her hand as if he wished never more to withdraw them.

'Mr. Arobin,' she complained, 'I'm greatly upset by the excitement of the afternoon; I'm not myself. My manner must have misled you in some way. I wish you to go, please.' She spoke in a monotonous, dull tone. He took his hat from the table, and stood with eyes turned from her, looking into the dying fire. For a moment or two he kept an impressive silence.

'Your manner has not misled me, Mrs. Pontellier,' he said finally. 'My own emotions have done that. I couldn't help it. When I'm near you, how could I help it? Don't think anything of it, don't bother, please. You see, I go when you command me. If you wish me to stay away, I shall do so. If you let me come back, I – oh! you will let me come back?'

He cast one appealing glance at her, to which she made no response. Alcée Arobin's manner was so genuine that it often deceived even himself.

Edna did not care or think whether it were genuine or not. When she was alone she looked mechanically at the back of her hand which he had kissed so warmly. Then she leaned her head down on the mantelpiece. She felt somewhat like a woman who in a moment of passion is betrayed into an act of infidelity, and realizes the significance of the act without being wholly awakened from its glamour. The thought was passing vaguely through her mind, 'What would he think?'

She did not mean her husband; she was thinking of Robert Lebrun. Her husband seemed to her now like a person whom she had married without love as an excuse.

She lit a candle and went up to her room. Alcée Arobin was absolutely nothing to her. Yet his presence, his manners, the warmth of his glances, and above all the touch of his lips upon her hand had acted like a narcotic upon her.

She slept a languorous sleep, interwoven with vanishing dreams.

Chapter Twenty-eight

This short chapter follows the first intimate encounter between Edna and Arobin and describes Edna's post-coital tristesse. As ever, she weeps, but this giving way to emotion is followed by a careful analysis of her own feelings in which, significantly, 'shame' and 'remorse' do not feature. As in Chapter Twenty-five she articulates the manner in which she betrays her husband and Robert as distinct; Léonce's 'reproach' is registered through the material fabric of their lives and Robert's through an abstract 'love'. This separation of material and spiritual acts provides the rationale for her decision, announced in Chapter Twenty-six, to move from the family home on Esplanade Street, to a smaller, self-funded house. As at other moments of significant change, Chopin here reaches for the sublime, as Edna's feelings enable her 'to look upon and comprehend the significance of life, that monster made up of beauty and brutality'.

Edna cried a little that night after Arobin left her. It was only one phase of the multitudinous emotions which had assailed her. There was with her an overwhelming feeling of irresponsibility. There was the shock of the unexpected and the unaccustomed. There was her husband's reproach looking at her from the external things around her which he had provided for her external existence. There was Robert's reproach making itself felt by a quicker, fiercer, more overpowering love, which had awakened within her toward him. Above all, there was understanding. She felt as if a mist had been lifted from her eyes, enabling her to look upon and comprehend the significance of life, that monster made up of beauty and brutality. But among the conflicting sensations which assailed her, there was neither shame nor remorse. There was a dull pang of regret because it was not the kiss of love which had inflamed her, because it was not love which had held this cup of life to her lips.

Chapter Thirty

The dinner party which Edna gives as she leaves the marital home signals a turning point in the narrative; as she moves into the 'pigeon house' so she visibly enacts the separation which she has already undergone emotionally. The evening constitutes a rite of passage in more ways than one; not only does it mark her house move, it also celebrates her birthday as she reaches the age of twenty-nine, a point in her life at which she might feel that she is saying goodbye to her youth.

Edna, the indifferent housewife, becomes here a hostess who pays minute attention to details of both décor and food. The table is dressed, as is Edna, in golden satin and lace, both she and the table sparkle with crystal and diamonds. As the evening goes on and some of the guests leave so the atmosphere becomes more heavily charged with a decadent air; this is heightened by the direct reference to the poetry of Swinburne, whose work was associated with sensual excess.

Though Edna had spoken of the dinner as a very grand affair, it was in truth a very small affair and very select, in so much as the guests invited were few and were selected with discrimination. She had counted upon an even dozen seating themselves at her round mahogany board, forgetting for the moment that Madame Ratignolle was to the last degree *souffrante*[1] and unpresentable, and not foreseeing that Madame Lebrun would send a thousand regrets at the last moment. So there were only ten, after all, which made a cozy, comfortable number.

There were Mr. and Mrs. Merriman, a pretty, vivacious little woman in the thirties; her husband, a jovial fellow, something of a shallow-pate, who laughed a good deal at other people's witticisms, and had thereby made himself extremely popular. Mrs. Highcamp had accompanied them. Of course, there was Alcée Arobin, and Mademoiselle Reisz had consented to come. Edna had sent her a fresh bunch of violets with black lace trimmings for her hair. Monsieur Ratignolle brought himself and his wife's excuses. Victor Lebrun, who happened to be in the city, bent upon relaxation, had accepted with alacrity. There was a Miss Mayblunt, no longer in her teens, who looked at the world through lorgnettes and with the keenest interest. It was thought and said that she was intellectual; it was suspected of her that she wrote under a *nom de guerre*.[2] She had come with a gentleman by the name of Gouvernail, connected with one of the daily papers, of whom nothing special could be said, except that he was observant and seemed quiet and inoffensive. Edna herself made the tenth, and at half-past eight they seated themselves at table, Arobin and Monsieur Ratignolle on either side of their hostess.

Mrs. Highcamp sat between Arobin and Victor Lebrun. Then came Mrs. Merriman, Mr. Gouvernail, Miss Mayblunt, Mr. Merriman, and Mademoiselle Reisz next to Monsieur Ratignolle.

There was something extremely gorgeous about the appearance of the table, an effect of splendor conveyed by a cover of pale yellow satin under strips of lace-work. There were wax candles in massive brass candelabra, burning softly under yellow silk shades; full, fragrant roses, yellow and red, abounded. There were

---

1   In pain, suffering.
2   Pseudonym.

silver and gold, as she had said there would be, and crystal which glittered like the gems which the women wore.

The ordinary stiff dining chairs had been discarded for the occasion and replaced by the most commodious and luxurious which could be collected throughout the house. Mademoiselle Reisz, being exceedingly diminutive, was elevated upon cushions, as small children are sometimes hoisted at table upon bulky volumes.

'Something new, Edna ?' exclaimed Miss Mayblunt, with lorgnette directed toward a magnificent cluster of diamonds that sparkled, that almost sputtered, in Edna's hair, just over the center of her forehead.

'Quite new, "brand" new, in fact, a present from my husband. It arrived this morning from New York. I may as well admit that this is my birthday, and that I am twenty-nine. In good time I expect you to drink my health. Meanwhile, I shall ask you to begin with this cocktail, composed – would you say "composed?" ' with an appeal to Miss Mayblunt – 'composed by my father in honor of Sister Janet's wedding.' Before each guest stood a tiny glass that looked and sparkled like a garnet gem. 'Then, all things considered,' spoke Arobin, 'it might not be amiss to start out by drinking the Colonel's health in the cocktail which he composed, on the birthday of the most charming of women – the daughter whom he invented.'

Mr. Merriman's laugh at this sally was such a genuine outburst and so contagious that it started the dinner with an agreeable swing that never slackened.

Miss Mayblunt begged to be allowed to keep her cocktail untouched before her, just to look at. The color was marvelous! She could compare it to nothing she had ever seen, and the garnet lights which it emitted were unspeakably rare. She pronounced the Colonel an artist, and stuck to it.

Monsieur Ratignolle was prepared to take things seriously: the *mets*, the *entre-mets*,[3] the service, the decorations, even the people. He looked up from his pompono[4] and inquired of Arobin if he were related to the gentleman of that name who formed one of the firm of Laitner and Arobin, lawyers. The young man admitted that Laitner was a warm personal friend, who permitted Arobin's name to decorate the firm's letterheads and to appear upon a shingle that graced Perdido Street.

'There are so many inquisitive people and institutions abounding,' said Arobin, 'that one is really forced as a matter of convenience these days to assume the virtue of an occupation if he has it not.'

Monsieur Ratignolle stared a little, and turned to ask Mademoiselle Reisz if she considered the symphony concerts up to the standard which had been set the previous winter. Mademoiselle Reisz answered Monsieur Ratignolle in French, which Edna thought a little rude, under the circumstances, but characteristic. Mademoiselle had only disagreeable things to say of the symphony concerts, and insulting remarks to make of all the musicians of New Orleans, singly and collectively. All her interest seemed to be centered upon the delicacies placed before her.

Mr. Merriman said that Mr. Arobin's remark about inquisitive people reminded him of a man from Waco the other day at the St. Charles Hotel – but as

3 Main course and side dishes.
4 Fish.

Mr. Merriman's stories were always lame and lacking point, his wife seldom permitted him to complete them. She interrupted him to ask if he remembered the name of the author whose book she had bought the week before to send to a friend in Geneva. She was talking 'books' with Mr. Gouvernail and trying to draw from him his opinion upon current literary topics. Her husband told the story of the Waco man privately to Miss Mayblunt, who pretended to be greatly amused and to think it extremely clever. Mrs. Highcamp hung with languid but unaffected interest upon the warm and impetuous volubility of her left-hand neighbor, Victor Lebrun. Her attention was never for a moment withdrawn from him after seating herself at table; and when he turned to Mrs. Merriman, who was prettier and more vivacious than Mrs. Highcamp, she waited with easy indifference for an opportunity to reclaim his attention. There was the occasional sound of music, of mandolins, sufficiently removed to be an agreeable accompaniment rather than an interruption to the conversation. Outside the soft, monotonous splash of a fountain could be heard, the sound penetrated into the room with the heavy odor of jessamine that came through the open windows. The golden shimmer of Edna's satin gown spread in rich folds on either side of her. There was a soft fall of lace encircling her shoulders. It was the color of her skin, without the glow, the myriad living tints that one may sometimes discover in vibrant flesh. There was something in her attitude, in her whole appearance when she leaned her head against the high-backed chair and spread her arms, which suggested the regal woman, the one who rules, who looks on, who stands alone.

But as she sat there amid her guests, she felt the old ennui overtaking her, the hopelessness which so often assailed her, which came upon her like an obsession, like something extraneous, independent of volition. It was something which announced itself; a chill breath that seemed to issue from some vast cavern wherein discords wailed. There came over her the acute longing which always summoned into her spiritual vision the presence of the beloved one, overpowering her at once with a sense of the unattainable.

The moments glided on, while a feeling of good fellowship passed around the circle like a mystic cord, holding and binding these people together with jest and laughter. Monsieur Ratignolle was the first to break the pleasant charm. At ten o'clock he excused himself. Madame Ratignolle was waiting for him at home. She was *bien souffrante*, and she was filled with vague dread, which only her husband's presence could allay.

Mademoiselle Reisz arose with Monsieur Ratignolle, who offered to escort her to the car. She had eaten well; she had tasted the good, rich wines, and they must have turned her head, for she bowed pleasantly to all as she withdrew from table. She kissed Edna upon the shoulder, and whispered: '*Bonne nuit, ma reine; soyez sage.*'[5] She had been a little bewildered upon rising, or rather, descending from her cushions, and Monsieur Ratignolle gallantly took her arm and led her away.

Mrs. Highcamp was weaving a garland of roses, yellow and red. When she had finished the garland, she laid it lightly upon Victor's black curls. He was reclining

---

5   Good night, my dear, be good.

far back in the luxurious chair, holding a glass of champagne to the light. As if a magician's wand had touched him, the garland of roses transformed him into a vision of Oriental beauty. His cheeks were the color of crushed grapes, and his dusky eyes glowed with a languishing fire.

'*Sapristi!*' exclaimed Arobin.

But Mrs. Highcamp had one more touch to add to the picture. She took from the back of her chair a white silken scarf, with which she had covered her shoulders in the early part of the evening. She draped it across the boy in graceful folds, and in a way to conceal his black, conventional evening dress. He did not seem to mind what she did to him, only smiled, showing a faint gleam of white teeth, while he continued to gaze with narrowing eyes at the light through his glass of champagne.

'Oh! to be able to paint in color rather than in words!' exclaimed Miss Mayblunt, losing herself in a rhapsodic dream as she looked at him.

> ' "There was a graven image of Desire
> Painted with red blood on a ground of gold" '[6]

murmured Gouvernail, under his breath.

The effect of the wine upon Victor was to change his accustomed volubility into silence. He seemed to have abandoned himself to a reverie, and to be seeing pleasing visions in the amber bead.

'Sing,' entreated Mrs. Highcamp. 'Won't you sing to us?'

'Let him alone,' said Arobin.

'He's posing,' offered Mr. Merriman; 'let him have it out.'

'I believe he's paralyzed,' laughed Mrs. Merriman. And leaning over the youth's chair, she took the glass from his hand and held it to his lips. He sipped the wine slowly, and when he had drained the glass she laid it upon the table and wiped his lips with her little filmy handkerchief.

'Yes, I'll sing for you,' he said, turning in his chair toward Mrs. Highcamp. He clasped his hands behind his head, and looking up at the ceiling began to hum a little, trying his voice like a musician tuning an instrument. Then, looking at Edna, he began to sing:

> 'Ah! si tu savais!'

'Stop!' she cried, 'don't sing that. I don't want you to sing it,' and she laid her glass so impetuously and blindly upon the table as to shatter it against a carafe. The wine spilled over Arobin's legs and some of it trickled down upon Mrs. Highcamp's black gauze gown. Victor had lost all idea of courtesy, or else he thought his hostess was not in earnest, for he laughed and went on:

> 'Ah! si tu savais
> Ce que tes yeux me disent'[7]–

---

6 From 'A Cameo' by A.C. Swinburne (1837–1909).
7 Ah! If you only knew!
   What your eyes are saying to me-

'Oh! you mustn't! you mustn't, exclaimed Edna, and pushing back her chair she got up, and going behind him placed her hand over his mouth. He kissed the soft palm that pressed upon his lips.

'No, no, I won't, Mrs. Pontellier. I didn't know you meant it,' looking up at her with caressing eyes. The touch of his lips was like a pleasing sting to her hand. She lifted the garland of roses from his head and flung it across the room.

'Come, Victor; you've posed long enough. Give Mrs. Highcamp her scarf.'

Mrs. Highcamp undraped the scarf from about him with her own hands. Miss Mayblunt and Mr. Gouvernail suddenly conceived the notion that it was time to say good night. And Mr. and Mrs. Merriman wondered how it could be so late. Before parting from Victor, Mrs. Highcamp invited him to call upon her daughter, who she knew would be charmed to meet him and talk French and sing French songs with him. Victor expressed his desire and intention to call upon Miss Highcamp at the first opportunity which presented itself. He asked if Arobin were going his way. Arobin was not.

The mandolin players had long since stolen away. A profound stillness had fallen upon the broad, beautiful street. The voices of Edna's disbanding guests jarred like a discordant note upon the quiet harmony of the night.

Chapter Thirty-six

Edna's disregard for propriety and convention is expressed in a number of familiar ways in this chapter. She speaks of her enthusiasm for walking, for food and for unfashionable places, revealing, as she does so, the constraints on women's lives. She is particularly impassioned on the subject of walking: 'I always feel so sorry for women who don't like to walk; they miss so much'; we already know that her solitary walks have provoked anxieties in both her husband and her doctor. Also notable in this chapter is her directness of expression; she is not prepared to waste time on pleasantries but says – and does – exactly what she feels. No longer the passive recipient of embraces from such as Arobin, she takes the initiative, giving Robert a 'soft, cool, delicate kiss'. However, despite having learned that sexual desire is not necessarily tied to love, and even with her bold assertions of independence – 'I give myself where I choose' – she is, ultimately, tied to a notion of enduring romantic love – 'We shall be everything to each other'.

There was a garden out in the suburbs, a small, leafy corner, with a few green tables under the orange trees. An old cat slept all day on the stone step in the sun, and an old *mulatresse*[1] slept her idle hours away in her chair at the open window, till some one happened to knock on one of the green tables. She had milk and

1   A woman of mixed race.

cream cheese to sell, and bread and butter. There was no one who could make such excellent coffee or fry a chicken so golden brown as she.

The place was too modest to attract the attention of people of fashion, and so quiet as to have escaped the notice of those in search of pleasure and dissipation. Edna had discovered it accidentally one day when the high-board gate stood ajar. She caught sight of a little green table, blotched with the checkered sunlight that filtered through the quivering leaves overhead. Within she had found the slumbering *mulatresse*, the drowsy cat, and a glass of milk which reminded her of the milk she had tasted in Iberville.

She often stopped there during her perambulations; sometimes taking a book with her, and sitting an hour or two under the trees when she found the place deserted. Once or twice she took a quiet dinner there alone, having instructed Celestine beforehand to prepare no dinner at home. It was the last place in the city where she would have expected to meet any one she knew.

Still she was not astonished when, as she was partaking of a modest dinner late in the afternoon, looking into an open book, stroking the cat, which had made friends with her – she was not greatly astonished to see Robert come in at the tall garden gate.

'I am destined to see you only by accident,' she said, shoving the cat off the chair beside her. He was surprised, ill at ease, almost embarrassed at meeting her thus so unexpectedly.

'Do you come here often?' he asked.

'I almost live here,' she said.

'I used to drop in very often for a cup of Catiche's good coffee. This is the first time since I came back.'

'She'll bring you a plate, and you will share my dinner. There's always enough for two – even three.'

Edna had intended to be indifferent and as reserved as he when she met him; she had reached the determination by a laborious train of reasoning, incident to one of her despondent moods. But her resolve melted when she saw him before her, seated there beside her in the little garden, as if a designing Providence had led him into her path.

'Why have you kept away from me, Robert?' she asked, closing the book that lay open upon the table.

'Why are you so personal, Mrs. Pontellier? Why do you force me to idiotic subterfuges?' he exclaimed with sudden warmth. 'I suppose there's no use telling you I've been very busy, or that I've been sick, or that I've been to see you and not found you at home. Please let me off with any one of these excuses.'

'You are the embodiment of selfishness,' she said. 'You save yourself something – I don't know what – but there is some selfish motive, and in sparing yourself you never consider for a moment what I think, or how I feel your neglect and indifference. I suppose this is what you would call unwomanly; but I have got into a habit of expressing myself. It doesn't matter to me, and you may think me unwomanly if you like.'

'No; I only think you cruel, as I said the other day. Maybe not intentionally cruel; but you seem to be forcing me into disclosures which can result in nothing;

as if you would have me bare a wound for the pleasure of looking at it, without the intention or power of healing it.'

'I'm spoiling your dinner, Robert; never mind what I say. You haven't eaten a morsel.'

'I only came in for a cup of coffee.' His sensitive face was all disfigured with excitement.

'Isn't this a delightful place?' she remarked. 'I am so glad it has never actually been discovered. It is so quiet, so sweet, here. Do you notice there is scarcely a sound to be heard? It's so out of the way; and a good walk from the car. However, I don't mind walking. I always feel so sorry for women who don't like to walk; they miss so much – so many rare little glimpses of life; and we women learn so little of life on the whole. Catiche's coffee is always hot. I don't know how she manages it, here in the open air. Celestine's coffee gets cold bringing it from the kitchen to the dining-room. Three lumps! How can you drink it so sweet? Take some of the cress with your chop; it's so biting and crisp. Then there's the advantage of being able to smoke with your coffee out here. Now, in the city – aren't you going to smoke?'

'After a while,' he said, laying a cigar on the table.

'Who gave it to you?' she laughed.

'I bought it. I suppose I'm getting reckless; I bought a whole box.'

She was determined not to be personal again and make him uncomfortable. The cat made friends with him, and climbed into his lap when he smoked his cigar. He stroked her silky fur, and talked a little about her. He looked at Edna's book, which he had read; and he told her the end, to save her the trouble of wading through it, he said.

Again he accompanied her back to her home; and it was after dusk when they reached the little 'pigeon-house.' She did not ask him to remain, which he was grateful for, as it permitted him to stay without the discomfort of blundering through an excuse which he had no intention of considering. He helped her to light the lamp; then she went into her room to take off her hat and to bathe her face and hands.

When she came back Robert was not examining the pictures and magazines as before; he sat off in the shadow, leaning his head back on the chair as if in a reverie. Edna lingered a moment beside the table, arranging the books there. Then she went across the room to where he sat. She bent over the arm of his chair and called his name.

'Robert,' she said, 'are you asleep?'

'No,' he answered, looking up at her.

She leaned over and kissed him – a soft, cool, delicate kiss, whose voluptuous sting penetrated his whole being – then she moved away from him. He followed, and took her in his arms, just holding her close to him. She put her hand up to his face and pressed his cheek against her own. The action was full of love and tenderness. He sought her lips again. Then he drew her down upon the sofa beside him and held her hand in both of his.

'Now you know,' he said, 'now you know what I have been fighting against since last summer at Grand Isle, what drove me away and drove me back again.'

'Why have you been fighting against it?' she asked. Her face glowed with soft lights.

'Why? Because you were not free; you were Léonce Pontellier's wife. I couldn't help loving you if you were ten times his wife, but so long as I went away from you and kept away I could help telling you so.'

She put her free hand up to his shoulder, and then against his cheek, rubbing it softly. He kissed her again. His face was warm and flushed.

'There in Mexico I was thinking of you all the time, and longing for you.'

'But not writing to me,' she interrupted.

'Something put into my head that you cared for me, and I lost my senses. I forgot everything but a wild dream of your some way becoming my wife.'

'Your wife!'

'Religion, loyalty, everything would give way if only you cared.'

'Then you must have forgotten that I was Léonce Pontellier's wife.'

'Oh! I was demented, dreaming of wild, impossible things, recalling men who had set their wives free, we have heard of such things.'

'Yes, we have heard of such things.'

'I came back full of vague, mad intentions. And when I got here –'

'When you got here you never came near me!' She was still caressing his cheek.

'I realized what a cur I was to dream of such a thing, even if you had been willing.'

She took his face between her hands and looked into it as if she would never withdraw her eyes more. She kissed him on the forehead, the eyes, the cheeks, and the lips.

'You have been a very, very foolish boy, wasting your time dreaming of impossible things when you speak of Mr. Pontellier setting me free! I am no longer one of Mr. Pontellier's possessions to dispose of or not. I give myself where I choose. If he were to say, "Here, Robert, take her and be happy, she is yours," I should laugh at you both.'

His face grew a little white. 'What do you mean?' he asked.

There was a knock at the door. Old Celestine came in to say that Madame Ratignolle's servant had come around the back way with a message that Madame had been taken sick and begged Mrs. Pontellier to go to her immediately.

'Yes, yes,' said Edna, rising; 'I promised. Tell her yes – to wait for me. I'll go back with her.'

'Let me walk over with you,' offered Robert.

'No,' she said; 'I will go with the servant.'

She went into her room to put on her hat, and when she came in again she sat once more upon the sofa beside him. He had not stirred. She put her arms about his neck.

'Good-by, my sweet Robert. Tell me good-by.' He kissed her with a degree of passion which had not before entered into his caress, and strained her to him.

'I love you,' she whispered, 'only you, no one but you. It was you who awoke me last summer out of a life-long, stupid dream. Oh! you have made me so unhappy with your indifference. Oh! I have suffered, suffered! Now you are here we shall love each other, my Robert. We shall be everything to each other. Nothing else in the world is of any consequence. I must go to my friend; but you will wait for me? No matter how late; you will wait for me, Robert?'

'Don't go; don't go! Oh! Edna, stay with me,' he pleaded 'Why should you go? Stay with me, stay with me.'

'I shall come back as soon as I can; I shall find you here.' She buried her face in his neck, and said good-by again. Her seductive voice, together with his great love for her, had enthralled his senses, had deprived him of every impulse but the longing to hold her and keep her.

Chapter Thirty-eight

Having just been present at the birth of Adèle's baby, Edna emerges from the Ratignolle house in a state of turmoil. Adèle's parting words to her: 'Think of the children, Edna,' are ringing in her ears as she dismisses Dr Mandelet's carriage, preferring to walk home alone. The Doctor, however, accompanies her and Edna's preoccupations are revealed when in response to his sympathetic allusion to the impact that the scene of childbirth may have had upon her, she refers to her own children. Whilst Edna and Dr Mandelet are talking, to a certain extent, at cross-purposes, his sensitivity to the rawness of her feelings allows her to voice some of her current confusions. Adèle's comments have forced Edna to think of her children in a new and pressing way as individuals for whom she has a real responsibility. Whilst Dr Mandelet talks in the abstract: 'Nature takes no account of moral consequences, of arbitrary conditions which we create, and which we feel obliged to maintain at any cost', Edna can only register what he says subjectively, saying, 'I don't want anything but my own way'.

As has been the pattern throughout the novel, Edna positions herself in an intermediate space, the porch, in order to think, to emote and to switch her thoughts back to her relationship with Robert. Such occupation of liminal space is used to allow Edna to free herself from the press of her domestic responsibilities and Chopin expresses the discarding of 'the tearing emotion of the last few hours' as the loosening of a constricting garment; a figurative representation of the physical act that Edna has so often performed at moments of personal crisis. The removal or easing of clothing, as well as having clear sexual overtones, carries the symbolic weight of many of the changes which Edna has undergone: learning to swim, awakening to a renewed sense of the beauty and power of her own body on *Chênière Caminada*, walking unaccompanied and untrammelled through the city streets, the abjuration of the formal gowns of the hostess and others. As Edna says: 'She could picture at that moment no greater bliss on earth than possession of the beloved one'; but this final romantic utterance is suffused with irony. Not only has the 'beloved one' fled, but she still, in spite of her own demands for freedom, can only articulate relationship as 'possession'.

Edna still felt dazed when she got outside in the open air. The Doctor's coupé had returned for him and stood before the *porte cochère*.[1] She did not wish to enter the coupé, and told Doctor Mandelet she would walk; she was not afraid, and would go alone. He directed his carriage to meet him at Mrs. Pontellier's, and he started to walk home with her.

Up – away up, over the narrow street between the tall houses, the stars were blazing. The air was mild and caressing, but cool with the breath of spring and the night. They walked slowly, the Doctor with a heavy, measured tread and his hands behind him; Edna, in an absent-minded way, as she had walked one night at Grand Isle, as if her thoughts had gone ahead of her and she was striving to overtake them.

'You shouldn't have been there, Mrs. Pontellier,' he said. 'That was no place for you. Adèle is full of whims at such times. There were a dozen women she might have had with her, unimpressionable women. I felt that it was cruel, cruel. You shouldn't have gone.'

'Oh, well!' she answered, indifferently. 'I don't know that it matters after all. One has to think of the children some time or other, the sooner the better.'

'When is Léonce coming back?'

'Quite soon. Some time in March.'

'And you are going abroad?'

'Perhaps – no, I am not going. I'm not going to be forced into doing things. I don't want to go abroad. I want to be let alone. Nobody has any right – except children, perhaps – and even then, it seems to me – or it did seem –'. She felt that her speech was voicing the incoherency of her thoughts, and stopped abruptly.

'The trouble is,' sighed the Doctor, grasping her meaning intuitively, 'that youth is given up to illusions. It seems to be a provision of Nature, a decoy to secure mothers for the race. And Nature takes no account of moral consequences, of arbitrary conditions which we create, and which we feel obliged to maintain at any cost.'

'Yes,' she said. 'The years that are gone seem like dreams – if one might go on sleeping and dreaming – but to wake up and find – oh! well! perhaps it is better to wake up after all, even to suffer, rather than to remain a dupe to illusions all one's life.'

'It seems to me, my dear child,' said the Doctor at parting, holding her hand, 'you seem to me to be in trouble. I am not going to ask for your confidence. I will only say that if ever you feel moved to give it to me, perhaps I might help you. I know I would understand, and I tell you there are not many who would – not many, my dear.'

'Some way I don't feel moved to speak of things that trouble me. Don't think I am ungrateful or that I don't appreciate your sympathy. There are periods of despondency and suffering which take possession of me. But I don't want any-thing but my own way. That is wanting a good deal, of course, when you have to trample upon the lives, the hearts, the prejudices of others – but no matter – still, I

1   Carriage entrance.

shouldn't want to trample upon the little lives. Oh! I don't know what I'm saying, Doctor. Good night. Don't blame me for anything.'

'Yes, I will blame you if you don't come and see me soon. We will talk of things you never have dreamt of talking about before. It will do us both good. I don't want you to blame yourself, whatever comes. Good night, my child.'

She let herself in at the gate, but instead of entering she sat upon the step of the porch. The night was quiet and soothing. All the tearing emotion of the last few hours seemed to fall away from her like a somber, uncomfortable garment, which she had but to loosen to be rid of. She went back to that hour before Adèle had sent for her; and her senses kindled afresh in thinking of Robert's words, the pressure of his arms, and the feeling of his lips upon her own. She could picture at that moment no greater bliss on earth than possession of the beloved one. His expression of love had already given him to her in part. When she thought that he was there at hand, waiting for her, she grew numb with the intoxication of expectancy. It was so late; he would be asleep perhaps. She would awaken him with a kiss. She hoped he would be asleep that she might arouse him with her caresses.

Still, she remembered Adèle's voice whispering, 'Think of the children; think of them.' She meant to think of them; that determination had driven into her soul like a death wound – but not to-night. To-morrow would be time to think of everything. Robert was not waiting for her in the little parlor. He was nowhere at hand. The house was empty. But he had scrawled on a piece of paper that lay in the lamplight: 'I love you. Good-by – because I love you.'

Edna grew faint when she read the words. She went and sat on the sofa. Then she stretched herself out there, never uttering a sound. She did not sleep. She did not go to bed. The lamp sputtered and went out. She was still awake in the morning, when Celestine unlocked the kitchen door and came in to light the fire.

Chapter Thirty-nine

In the final chapter of the novel Edna returns to Grand Isle, the scene of her initial awakening. To outward appearances she seems, to Victor and Mariequita, to be just another demanding and unexpected visitor, stipulating what she would like for dinner and obliging Victor to engage a more capable cook. However, as she walks down to the water, it becomes clear that she has passed a long dark night of the soul and has come to the realisation that there is no such thing as an existence without contingencies, that her feelings for Robert may undergo change but that she will always be judged by her performance as a wife and mother. This is expressed, typically, in heightened and dramatic language: 'The children appeared before her like antagonists who had overcome her, who had overpowered and sought to drag her into the soul's slavery for the rest of her days.' She walks towards the sea and as she goes, she banishes all thoughts of her responsibilities, surrendering to the promise of solitude, of autonomy, that immersion in the water seems to offer her wounded body and soul. Although the mantra, which enumerates the seductive power of the sea, is repeated from Chapter Six, Chopin differentiates between episodes by remarking that now, 'A bird with a broken wing was beating the air above, reeling, fluttering, circling disabled down, down to the water.' Having failed to 'soar above' (Chapter Twenty-seven) the constraints identified by Mademoiselle Reisz as likely to impede artistic or personal fulfilment, Edna is now, like the bird, 'broken'. However, the final loosening of her clothing, which leaves her totally naked, is her ultimate act of defiance and statement of individuality; she revels in the 'delicious' sensation of her exposure to the elements. Her life, as we have come to understand it, passes before her eyes, as she swims out into the open sea. Chopin's last words take us back to Edna's account of her adolescence; she experiences the past through the sensations of smell, hearing and sight whilst the sea holds her body 'in its soft close embrace'.

Victor, with hammer and nails and scraps of scantling, was patching a corner of one of the galleries. Mariequita sat near by, dangling her legs, watching him work, and handing him nails from the tool-box. The sun was beating down upon them. The girl had covered her head with her apron folded into a square pad. They had been talking for an hour or more. She was never tired of hearing Victor describe the dinner at Mrs. Pontellier's. He exaggerated every detail, making it appear a veritable Lucillean feast.[1]

The flowers were in tubs, he said. The champagne was quaffed from huge golden goblets. Venus rising from the foam could have presented no more entrancing a spectacle than Mrs. Pontellier, blazing with beauty and diamonds at the head of the board, while the other women were all of them youthful houris,[2] possessed of incomparable charms.

She got it into her head that Victor was in love with Mrs. Pontellier, and he gave her evasive answers, framed so as to confirm her belief. She grew sullen and cried a little, threatening to go off and leave him to his fine ladies. There were a dozen men crazy about her at the *Chênière*, and since it was the fashion to be in love with married people, why, she could run away any time she liked to New Orleans with Célina's husband.

Célina's husband was a fool, a coward, and a pig, and to prove it to her, Victor intended to hammer his head into a jelly the next time he encountered him. This assurance was very consoling to Mariequita. She dried her eyes, and grew cheerful at the prospect.

They were still talking of the dinner and the allurements of city life when Mrs. Pontellier herself slipped around the corner of the house. The two youngsters stayed dumb with amazement before what they considered to be an apparition. But it was really she in flesh and blood, looking tired and a little travel-stained.

1   After the 1st century Roman General, Lucullus, renowned for his opulent banquets.
2   Beautiful virgins of the Koranic paradise.

'I walked up from the wharf' she said, 'and heard the hammering. I sup-posed it was you, mending the porch. It's a good thing. I was always tripping over those loose planks last summer. How dreary and deserted everything looks!'

It took Victor some little time to comprehend that she had come in Beaudelet's lugger, that she had come alone, and for no purpose but to rest.

'There's nothing fixed up yet, you see. I'll give you my room; it's the only place.'

'Any corner will do,' she assured him.

'And if you can stand Philomel's cooking,' he went on, 'though I might try to get her mother while you are here. Do you think she would come?' turning to Mariequita. Mariequita thought that perhaps Philomel's mother might come for a few days, and money enough.

Beholding Mrs. Pontellier make her appearance, the girl had at once suspected a lovers' rendezvous. But Victor's astonishment was so genuine, and Mrs. Pontellier's indifference so apparent, that the disturbing notion did not lodge long in her brain. She contemplated with the greatest interest this woman who gave the most sumptuous dinners in America, and who had all the men in New Orleans at her feet.

'What time will you have dinner?' asked Edna. 'I'm very hungry; but don't get anything extra.'

'I'll have it ready in little or no time,' he said, hustling and packing away his tools. 'You may go to my room to brush up and rest yourself. Mariequita will show you.'

'Thank you,' said Edna. 'But, do you know, I have a notion to go down to the beach and take a good wash and even a little swim, before dinner?'

'The water is too cold!' they both exclaimed. 'Don't think of it.'

'Well, I might go down and try – dip my toes in. Why, it seems to me the sun is hot enough to have warmed the very depths of the ocean. Could you get me a couple of towels? I'd better go right away, so as to be back in time. It would be a little too chilly if I waited till this afternoon.'

Mariequita ran over to Victor's room, and returned with some towels, which she gave to Edna.

'I hope you have fish for dinner,' said Edna, as she started to walk away; 'but don't do anything extra if you haven't.'

'Run and find Philomel's mother,' Victor instructed the girl. 'I'll go to the kit-chen and see what I can do. By Gimminy! Women have no consideration! She might have sent me word.'

Edna walked on down to the beach rather mechanically, not noticing anything special except that the sun was hot. She was not dwelling upon any particular train of thought. She had done all the thinking which was necessary after Robert went away, when she lay awake upon the sofa till morning.

She had said over and over to herself: 'To-day it is Arobin; to-morrow it will be some one else. It makes no difference to me, it doesn't matter about Léonce Pontellier – but Raoul and Etienne!' She understood now clearly what she had meant long ago when she said to Adèle Ratignolle that she would give up the unessential, but she would never sacrifice herself for her children.

Despondency had come upon her there in the wakeful night, and had never lifted. There was no one thing in the world that she desired. There was no human being whom she wanted near her except Robert; and she even realized that the day would come when he, too, and the thought of him would melt out of her existence, leaving her alone. The children appeared before her like antagonists who had overcome her, who had overpowered and sought to drag her into the soul's slavery for the rest of her days. But she knew a way to elude them. She was not thinking of these things when she walked down to the beach.

The water of the Gulf stretched out before her, gleaming with the million lights of the sun. The voice of the sea is seductive, never ceasing, whispering, clamoring, murmuring, inviting the soul to wander in abysses of solitude. All along the white beach, up and down, there was no living thing in sight. A bird with a broken wing was beating the air above, reeling, fluttering, circling disabled down, down to the water. Edna had found her old bathing suit still hanging, faded, upon its accustomed peg. She put it on, leaving her clothing in the bath-house. But when she was there beside the sea, absolutely alone, she cast the unpleasant, pricking garments from her, and for the first time in her life she stood naked in the open air, at the mercy of the sun, the breeze that beat upon her, and the waves that invited her.

How strange and awful it seemed to stand naked under the sky! how delicious! She felt like some new-born creature, opening its eyes in a familiar world that it had never known.

The foamy wavelets curled up to her white feet, and coiled like serpents about her ankles. She walked out. The water was chill, but she walked on. The water was deep, but she lifted her white body and reached out with a long, sweeping stroke. The touch of the sea is sensuous, enfolding the body in its soft, close embrace.

She went on and on. She remembered the night she swam far out, and recalled the terror that seized her at the fear of being unable to regain the shore. She did not look back now, but went on and on, thinking of the blue-grass meadow that she had traversed when a little child, believing that it had no beginning and no end. Her arms and legs were growing tired.

She thought of Léonce and the children. They were a part of her life. But they need not have thought that they could possess her, body and soul. How Mademoiselle Reisz would have laughed, perhaps sneered, if she knew! 'And you call yourself an artist! What pretensions, Madame! The artist must possess the courageous soul that dares and defies.'

Exhaustion was pressing upon and overpowering her.

'Good-by – because, I love you.' He did not know; he did not understand. He would never understand. Perhaps Doctor Mandelet would have understood if she had seen him – but it was too late; the shore was far behind her, and her strength was gone. She looked into the distance, and the old terror flamed up for an instant, then sank again. Edna heard her father's voice and her sister Margaret's. She heard the barking of an old dog that was chained to the sycamore tree. The spurs of the cavalry officer clanged as he walked across the porch. There was the hum of bees, and the musky odor of pinks filled the air.

4

Further Reading

Further Reading

Recommended Editions

Kate Chopin, *The Awakening*, A Norton Critical Edition, ed. by Margo Culley, New York: Norton, 1976, 1994.
   The Norton edition provides a comprehensive and well-documented context for *The Awakening*.

Kate Chopin, *The Awakening*, London: The Women's Press, 1978, 2002.
   For this edition Helen Taylor provides a helpful and informative introduction.

Kate Chopin, *The Awakening*, ed. by Nancy Walker, Boston: Bedford St Martin, 1993, 2000.
   This edition contains a good collection of critical material.

Kate Chopin, *The Awakening and Other Stories*, ed. by Pamela Knights, Oxford: Oxford University Press, 2000.
   Knights places *The Awakening* alongside a selection of Chopin's other fiction and provides an introduction and notes to the text.

Further Reading

Biography

Rankin, Daniel S., *Kate Chopin and her Creole Stories*, Philadelphia: University of Pennsylvania Press, 1932.
Seyersted, Per, *Kate Chopin: A Critical Biography*, Baton Rouge: Louisiana State University Press, 1969.
Toth, Emily, *Kate Chopin: A Life of the Author of The Awakening*, London: Random Century, 1990.

General

Ammons, Elizabeth, *Conflicting Stories: American Women Writers at the Turn into the Twentieth Century*, Oxford: Oxford University Press, 1991.

Arnavon, Cyrille, *Edna*, Paris, 1953.

Beer, Janet, *Kate Chopin, Edith Wharton and Charlotte Perkins Gilman: Studies in Short Fiction*, Basingstoke: Macmillan, 1997.

—— '*Sister Carrie* and *The Awakening*: The Clothed, the Unclothed, and the Woman Undone', Karen L. Kilcup, ed., *Soft Canons: American Women Writers and Masculine Tradition*, Iowa City: University of Iowa Press, 1999.

Bender, Bert, 'The Teeth of Desire: *The Awakening* and *The Descent of Man*', *American Literature* No. 3, Sept. 1991, pp. 459–73.

Berthoff, Warner, *The Ferment of Realism: American Literature, 1884–1919*, Cambridge: Cambridge University Press, 1965.

Birnbaum, Michelle A., 'Alien Hands: Kate Chopin and the Colonization of Race', *American Literature*, Vol. 66, No. 2, June 1994, pp. 301–23.

Boren, Lynda S. and Sara deSaussure Davis, eds, *Kate Chopin Reconsidered: Beyond the Bayou*, Baton Rouge: Louisiana State University Press, 1992.

Fox-Genovese, Elizabeth, '*The Awakening* in the Context of the Experience, Culture, and Values of Southern Women', Bernard Koloski, ed., *Approaches to Teaching Chopin's The Awakening*, New York: MLA, 1988, pp. 34–9.

Gilbert, Sandra, 'The Second Coming of Aphrodite: Kate Chopin's Fantasy of Desire', *Kenyon Review*, 5, Summer 1983, pp. 42–66.

Hochman, Barbara, '*The Awakening* and *The House of Mirth*: Plotting Experience and Experiencing Plot', Donald Pizer, ed., *The Cambridge Companion to American Realism and Naturalism: Howells to London*, Cambridge: Cambridge University Press, 1995.

Koloski, Bernard, ed., *Approaches to Teaching Chopin's The Awakening*, New York: MLA, 1988.

Martin, Wendy, ed., *New Essays on The Awakening*, Cambridge: Cambridge University Press, 1988.

Moers, Ellen, *Literary Women*, New York: Doubleday, 1977.

Rosowski, Susan J., 'The Novel of Awakening', *Genre* 12, 1979, pp. 313–32.

Seyersted, Per, *The Complete Works of Kate Chopin*, Baton Rouge: Louisiana State University Press, 1969.

Seyersted, Per and Emily Toth, eds, *A Kate Chopin Miscellany*, Natchitoches: Northwestern State University Press, 1979.

——, *Kate Chopin's Private Papers*, Bloomington: Indiana University Press, 1998.

Showalter, Elaine, *Sister's Choice: Tradition and Change in American Women's Writing*, Oxford: Oxford University Press, 1991.

Taylor, Helen, *Gender, Race and Region in the Writings of Grace King, Ruth McEnery Stuart, and Kate Chopin*, Baton Rouge: Louisiana State University Press, 1989.

—— 'Walking Through New Orleans: Kate Chopin and the Female Flâneur', *Symbiosis*, Vol. 1, No. 1, April 1997, pp. 69–85.

Walker, Nancy, 'The Historical and Cultural Setting', Bernard Koloski, ed., *Approaches to Teaching Chopin's The Awakening*, New York: MLA, 1988, pp. 67–72.

—— *Kate Chopin: A Literary Life*, Basingstoke: Palgrave, 2001.

Wilson, Edmund, *Patriotic Gore: Studies in the Literature of the American Civil War*, New York: Norton, 1962.

Wolff, Cynthia Griffin, 'Thanatos and Eros: Kate Chopin's *The Awakening*', *American Quarterly*, 25, October 1973, pp. 449–71.

—— 'Un-utterable Longing: The Discourse of Feminine Sexuality in *The Awakening*', *Studies in American Fiction*, Vol. 24, No. 1, 1996, pp. 3–22.

Ziff, Larzer, *The American 1890s: Life and Times of a Lost Generation*, New York: Viking, 1966.

Index

Note: page numbers in bold indicate quoted material.